Discourse of Twitter and Social Media

BLOOMSBURY DISCOURSE SERIES

Series Editor:
Professor Ken Hyland

Discourse is one of the most significant concepts of contemporary thinking in the humanities and social sciences as it concerns the ways language mediates and shapes our interactions with each other and with the social, political and cultural formations of our society. The Bloomsbury Discourse Series aims to capture the fast-developing interest in discourse to provide students, new and experienced teachers and researchers in applied linguistics, ELT and English language with an essential bookshelf. Each book deals with a core topic in discourse studies to give an in-depth, structured and readable introduction to an aspect of the way language in used in real life.

Other titles in the series:

The Discourse of Text Messaging, Caroline Tagg
Historical Discourse: The Language of Time, Cause and Evaluation, Caroline Coffin
Metadiscourse: Exploring Interaction in Writing, Ken Hyland
Professional Discourse, Britt-Louise Gunnarsson
Using Corpora in Discourse Analysis, Paul Baker
Workplace Discourse, Almut Koester

BLOOMSBURY DISCOURSE

Discourse of Twitter and Social Media

MICHELE ZAPPAVIGNA

Bloomsbury Academic India
An imprint of Bloomsbury Publishing Plc

BLOOMSBURY
NEW DELHI • LONDON • OXFORD • NEW YORK • SYDNEY

First published in India 2018
First published 2012 Published in paperback 2013
Reprinted by Bloomsbury Academic 2015

Bloomsbury Academic India
An imprint of Bloomsbury Publishing Plc
BLOOMSBURY, Bloomsbury Academic India and the Diana logo are trademarks of Bloomsbury Publishing Plc

This edition published with permission from Bloomsbury Publishing Plc,
50 Bedford Square, London, WC1B3DP, UK

British Library Cataloguing-in-Publication Data
A catalogue record for this book is available from the British Library.

Library of Congress Cataloging-in-Publication Data
Zappavigna, Michele.
The discourse of Twitter and social media/Michele Zappavigna.
p. cm. – (Continuum discourse) Includes bibliographical references and index.
ISBN 978-1-4411-4186-6 – ISBN 978-1-4411-2303-9 (pdf)
1. Sociolinguistics. 2. Social media. 3. Twitter (Firm) 4. Digital media.
5. Technological innovations–Social aspects. 6. Discourse analysis–Social aspects.
I. Title.
P107.Z36 2012 306.44–dc23
2011051176

ISBN 978 93 88002 26 4
10 9 8 7 6 5 4 3 2 1
For sale in the Indian subcontinent only

Bloomsbury Publishing India Pvt. Ltd
Second Floor, Building No. 4
DDA Complex LSC, Pocket C – 6 & 7
Vasant Kunj, New Delhi 110070
www.bloomsbury.com

Series: Bloomsbury Discourse

Typeset by Newgen Imaging Systems Pvt Ltd, Chennai, India
Printed at Manipal Technologies Limited, Manipal

For my mother, Jill, and my grandmother, Elma, who babysat tirelessly so that I could complete this work during my maternity leave

CONTENTS

ACKNOWLEDGEMENTS

I would like to thank Chris Cléirigh, Jim Martin and Sumin Zhao for their comments and editing, and Mark Assad for his wonderful technical support.

CONVENTIONS USED IN THIS BOOK

Systems of appraisal are shown in SMALL CAPS so as to differentiate them from their plain English equivalents. Codings of appraisal systems use the following conventions: AFFECT in **bold**, JUDGEMENT in **<u>bold underline</u>** and APPRECIATION in ***<u>bold italics</u>***. Linguistic features to be highlighted in general examples are shown in **bold**. All usernames in tweets, aside from those of celebrities and institutions, have been anonymised with the convention @user.

PREFACE

The history of linguistics is punctuated by sea changes of culture afforded by new technologies of communication – first writing, then audio recording and most recently Web 1.0 and Web 2.0. The invention of writing enabled the emergence of linguistics as a discipline and certainly encouraged the shift from a more rhetorical orientation to language focusing on speaking to a more logical orientation taking writing as a norm. It then took a couple of millennia before audio recording enabled linguists to effectively tackle spoken language again, as they set to work on phonetics and phonology and on dialectal and registerial variation with renewed vigour. Throughout the twentieth century, however, collecting and transcribing audio records remained costly, with advancing computer technology facilitating storage and retrieval but not offering a great deal of help with data gathering or analysis. Then comes Web 1.0, making huge quantities of essentially monologic data available for the first time, and then Web 2.0 and the launch of social networking. How has this positioned linguistics for the next decade and beyond?

In this volume Michele Zappavigna lays the foundation for a forthcoming generation of work in internet linguistics, drawing on her training in social semiotics, linguistics and information technology. This necessarily involves discussion of how to gather data from Web 2.0, how to use corpus linguistics to process it, how to use functional linguistics to interpret it and how to use social semiotics to make sense of what is going on. The most dramatic turn here, as far as linguistics is concerned, is her interpersonal focus on ambient sociality. This she explores in terms of the way in which tweeters affiliate through searchable talk, demonstrating for the first time in a large scale study how communities constitute themselves through shared values – where it's not just interaction that matters but shared meaning and where what is being shared is feelings about ideas (not just the ideas themselves). This axiological orientation, based as it is on appraisal theory and quantitative analysis, goes a long way to balancing the ideational bias which has for so long delimited linguistics as a theory of writing and holds great promise for the evolution of a more social sensitive and socially responsible discipline in the years to come.

This turn is not of course without its challenges. The sheer scale of the enterprise makes it hard to see the forest for the trees, making the development of novel two- and three-dimensional animated visualisations a priority. Alongside this are the trials of streaming data, as a microblog unfolds, as a blogger develops and as Web 2.0 evolves; the contingencies of time matter and cannot be theorized away. Finally, and perhaps most challengingly, Web. 2.0 is more than words, and ever more so; this demands not just a linguistics of words but a semiotics of multimodality, with all the implications for data gathering, analysis, interpretation and theorizing such entails. To her credit, Zappavigna dodges none of these issues and, with respect to the first two, shows us the way forward. We'll be hearing a lot more from her along these lines.

As communication changes, so must its theorists. I for one welcome our new social semiotic overlords! :P

J. R. Martin

CHAPTER ONE

Introduction

The social web and searchable talk

mum broke the blender. #fail

my prayers and thoughts are for those in #Christchurch #eqnz YOU GUYS WILL PULL THROUGH!!!!

The above microposts[1] were published online with a microblogging service; that is, an online platform for posting small messages to the internet in chronological sequence. The first post describes a mundane event in daily life. The hashtag #Fail aligns this personal expression with other potential instances of quotidian failure sharing the same tag. Hashtags are an emergent convention for labelling the topic of a micropost and a form of metadata incorporated into posts. The second post is a more public declaration of support for victims of an earthquake in the New Zealand city of Christchurch. It is similar to many other microposts produced during natural disasters and crises throughout the world. Like the first post, the hashtags #Christchurch and #eqnz, in this instance, seek parallel voices. The two posts differ greatly in the kind of connection they construe with a putative audience. Yet both actively invite connection with that audience by incorporating a hashtag to label the meanings they express. This kind of discourse tagging is the beginning of *searchable talk*, a change in social relations whereby we mark our discourse so that it can be found by others, in effect so that we can bond around particular values (Zappavigna 2011b).

Here we have the potential for users to commune within the aggregated gaze made possible with digital media, which I shall call ambient affiliation in this book. In other words, virtual groupings afforded by features of electronic text, such as metadata, create alignments between people who have not necessarily directly interacted online. Indeed these users may never be able to grasp the extent of the emergent complexity in which they are involved due to the fast paced, organic quality of the connections generated. The social relationships made possible will emerge over time, generated and influenced by unfolding linguistic patterns.

The social web, or Web 2.0, are popularized terms used to signal a shift toward the internet as an interpersonal resource rather than solely an informational network. In other words, the social web is about using the internet to enact relationships rather than simply share information, although the two functions are clearly interconnected. Table 1.1 gives an overview of the ways in which the social web is said to differ from the first incarnation of the internet. At its centre is 'user-generated content'; that is, self-publication by users[2] of multimedia content such as blogs (websites displaying entries in reverse chronological order), vlogs (video blogs such as those posted regularly by millions of users on YouTube) and microblogs (streams of small character-constrained posts). This book will deal primarily with microblogging, sometimes seen as a cousin of more lengthy blogging, although likely quite a different meaning-making resource entirely.

The advent of social media, technology that aims to support ambient interpersonal connection, has placed new and interesting semiotic pressure on language. This book is concerned with the interpersonal dimension of making meaning using this new media. Social media is an umbrella term generally applied to web-based services that facilitate some form of social interaction or 'networking'. This includes websites where the design-principle behind the service is explicitly about allowing users to create and develop online relationships with 'friends' or 'followers'. The term also encompasses platforms where the focus is on generating and sharing content, but in a mode that allows comment and, potentially, collaboration.

Table 1.1 A general comparison between Web 1.0 and Web 2.0, taken from (Hsu and Park, p. 2)

	Web 1.0	Web 2.0
Mode of usage	Read	Write and contribute
Unit of content	Page	Record
State	Static	Dynamic
How content is viewed	Web browser	Browsers, RSS (Really Simple Syndication) readers, mobile devices, etc.
Creation of content	By website authors	By everyone
Domain of	Web designers and geeks	A new culture of public research?

Because of the rapid development of social media technologies and their constant change, they can be somewhat of a 'moving target' for scholars (Hogan and Quan-Haase 2010).

While I will comment on social media in general, my analysis will focus on patterns of meaning in microblogging. The method adopted in this book for exploring this patterning combines quantitative analysis of a large 100 million word corpus of microposts, HERMES, with a qualitative social semiotic approach to discourse analysis. These posts were taken from the microblogging service Twitter. Developed in 2006, Twitter allows users to post messages of 140 characters or less to the general internet or to a set of users who subscribe to a user's message 'stream',[3] known collectively as followers. These microposts are referred to as tweets and are presented to the user in reverse chronological order as an unfolding stream of content. This content is public and searchable unless the user actively makes his or her account private. Tweets may be accessed, sent and received via a variety of methods such as the web, email, SMS (Short Message Service) and third-party clients, often running on mobile devices. A tweet may also incorporate links to micromedia, small-scale multimedia and shortened aliases of longer hyperlinks (tiny URLs) intended to conserve characters within the constrained textual environment. In addition, Twitter collects supplementary metadata about a tweet, such as the time it was generated, the ID of the user to which the tweet was directed (if applicable) and information about the user's account, including the number of followers and the number of tweets the user has posted.

An example of a tweet is the following, which, as we will see in the third chapter, contains one of the most common patterns in microblogging, namely, a user thanking a follower for promoting him or her in the community:

> @User1 thanks for the #FF

This post thanks User1 for the mention as part of Follow Friday, a collective practice where users are encouraged to endorse noteworthy tweeters. Tweets also contain metadata for managing interaction with others, for instance, @ indicating address (or reference) and # labelling topic. I will explore these features in more detail later in this book. While most of the metadata collected by Twitter is not presented directly to the general user, a notable exception is hashtags. These tags, a kind of in-text tagging visible within the body of a tweet, arose out of community use and were later incorporated into Twitter's search interface.

From a simplified technical perspective, Twitter consists of a farm of large databases that store the tweets that users have posted. The volume of this database of natural language is extremely large, with many millions of tweets being posted each day. Since its inception, Twitter has seen an extremely large increase in its user base. Prior to 2008–09 the service was mainly used within the technology scene in the United States, after which it became more mainstream, with users posting status updates on everything from the most innocuous details of their personal lives to serious political opinion and reporting (Marwick 2010). Twitter's technical architecture has had to cope with a very high volume of traffic:

> Folks were tweeting 5,000 times a day in 2007. By 2008, that number was 300,000, and by 2009 it had grown to 2.5 million per day. Tweets grew 1,400% last year to 35 million per day. Today, we are seeing 50 million tweets per day – that's an average of 600 tweets per second. (Weil 2010)

From the viewpoint of users, Twitter consists of an interface that allows people to post new tweets, configure various settings, such as privacy, manage their list of followers and search historical tweets. Users may also interact with the service via a third-party application that presents the feeds of microposts in different ways, in some cases in novel visual forms. The extremely large volume of naturally occurring language is of great interest, as data, to linguists.

An important property of the social web is how it responds to time. Social media content is most often chronologically displayed. Indeed, many commentators describe the emergence of a 'real-time web'[4]; that is, a paradigm whereby web content is streamed to users via syndication. Tools, such as a feed reader, are used to aggregate many web feeds into a single view, meaning that users do not have to visit sources individually for current information. This type of convergent, real-time web experience combines with the social web to produce a semiotic world in which users have almost immediate access to what is being said in their social networks at any given moment. Users are able to subscribe to feeds of their associates' status updates and multimedia content (e.g. photos and video). Often these updates are shared via a mobile device at the time an event occurs or an observation is made.

An example of the real-time web in action might be the reactions to a major public event, such as the 2008 US presidential election (see Chapter 9), that are shared via microblogging. Even local, less significant events, such as weather, can trigger communal response. For instance, during a recent hailstorm in Sydney, a proliferation of comments about hail and photographs of hail rapidly appeared in my online social network via status updating on Facebook and Twitter. Many other kinds of events generate widespread social media response, including natural disasters, such as the 2008 Sichuan earthquakes (Li and Rao 2010), and celebrity deaths, a notable example being the collective outpouring of grief seen on Twitter after the death of Michael Jackson in 2009 (Sanderson and Hope Cheong 2010).

An important function of social media is sharing experience of the everyday within this real-time paradigm. In microblogging this often involves bonding around collective complaint about life's little daily irritations (see Chapter 8). While social media can be used 'like Momus windows of Greek mythology, revealing one's innermost thoughts for all to see' (van Manen 2010), most users are conscious of not overexposing their followers to banalities, a practice known as over-sharing, or 'attention whoring' (Marwick 2010).

Perhaps the most commonly used form of social media is the social networking service (SNS). This technology, used by millions of people worldwide, generates a very large volume of multimedia text. At the time of writing in 2010, Facebook had over 500 million users, each with an average of 130 Facebook 'friends' (Facebook 2010), and Twitter users were generating 65 million Tweets a day (Schonfeld 2010). SNSs are services with which users create an online profile about themselves with the goal of connecting with other people and being 'findable'. Boyd and Heer (2006) suggest the role of online social network profiles in identity performance as an 'ongoing conversation in multiple modalities'. Indeed, interactions via social media are usually likened to some form conversation. Depending on the kind of relationship being construed, the 'dialogue' may be fairly limited, often involving two main avenues: making initial contact with a user and then maintaining occasional contact at important dates, such as birthdays (2010).

Most SNSs have in common a number of basic functions: profile creation, the ability to generate a list of affiliated users, privacy customization, and a mechanism for viewing the activities of affiliated users. These affiliated users are often referred to as 'friends' (e.g. Facebook friends) or 'followers' (e.g. Twitter followers). Boyd (2010, p. 39) categorizes SNSs as a genre of 'networked publics' involving an 'imagined collective' arising from particular permutations of users, their practices and the affordances of technology. Four affordances Boyd suggests are of particular significance:

- persistence (capture and archiving of content);
- replicability (duplication of content);
- scalability (broad visibility of content);
- searchability (access to content via search).

As we will see in the next chapter, these properties, particularly persistence and searchability, mean that SNSs afford an opportunity to collect and analyse many different aspects of online discourse. The large volume of data made publically available by these services offers a fascinating window on social life, though it also raises a range of ethical concerns about how this data is used (Parrish 2010).

Interpersonal search

Through the social web, talk is 'searchable' in a way and to an extent that has never been seen in history. The advent of social media means that the function of online talk has become increasingly focused on negotiating and maintaining relationships. From a semiotic perspective the searchability affords new forms of sociality. We can now search to see what people are saying about something at a given moment, not just to find information. This makes possible what I will refer to as *interpersonal search*; that is, the ability to use technology to find people so that you can bond around shared values (or clash over discordant ones!). The searchability is particularly useful for linguists collecting particular kinds of discourse, for example, online chatter about a particular topic or language occurring in a particular geographical region. The conversation-like interactions possible with social media can be tracked in ways not readily achievable with face-to-face interaction in the real world, where it would be invasive to monitor a person's private interactions.

In popular terms, it is becoming increasingly useful to search the 'hive mind': the stream of online conversation occurring across semiotic modes (e.g. blogs, online chat and social networking sites). The kind of real-time discourse search that Twitter affords has been described as a rival to a Google search, with commentators claiming that searching Twitter may soon be one of the most effective ways to gather useful information (Rocketboom 2009). Microblogging streams offer a way of finding out about dominant trends in what people are saying. For instance, consider the following anecdote by Boyd (2009), who applies an ethnographic perspective to her social media research:

> I have a funny habit. Every day, I login to search Twitter and search for common words. Admittedly, I primarily search in English because my language skills in other languages are poor. But sometimes, I entertain myself by looking in other languages just for fun. I search for words like 'the' or, better yet, 'teh' just to see what people will write. I look for common names or random words.
>
> Why on earth do I do this? I do this in order to habitually look at worlds that are different than my own. As a researcher and a scholar, this is an essential technique. I am familiar with Twitter and Facebook and MySpace as a participant, but to observe, I need to move beyond my narrow frame. Thank goodness for search and browse. I look into the lives of people in order to get a sense of the different cultural practices that are emerging. But you can also look into what people are doing.

This notion of interpersonal search is a linguistic perspective on the concept of social search used within information science. The term 'social search' refers to a mode of searching that leverages a user's social networks, for example, by asking a question on a social networking site. This mode of search is deemed complementary to an informational search with a search engine. Evans and Chi (2008) provide the following definition:

> 'Social search' is an umbrella term used to describe search acts that make use of social interactions with others. These interactions may be explicit or implicit, co-located or remote, synchronous or asynchronous. (Evans and Chi 2008, p. 485)

Meredith Ringel and colleagues surveyed users of social networking services, such as Twitter and Facebook, about the nature and motivation of the questions they asked using these media. Recommendation and opinion questions were the most frequent; a recommendation question was defined as asking 'for a rating of a specific item' and an opinion question as 'open-ended request for suggestions' (2010, p. 1742). The most common motivation expressed by respondents for engaging in this form of social search was a higher perceived level of trust in their friends to provide replies to questions deemed too subjective to be effectively answered by a search engine. Indeed, one study found differences in the kinds of queries issued to the Twitter search engine compared with those issued to a web search engine and that 'Twitter results included more social content and events, while Web results contained more facts and navigation' (Teevan et al. 2011, p. 44). These studies suggest that interpersonal meaning is at the heart of social search. Social bonds have becoming increasingly important in the way information is located and consumed with the internet. The significance of interpersonal search forms part of an explanation for the proliferation of social recommendation sites, social bookmarking, crowdsourcing[5] and related practices that make use of the social opinions extractable from online networks.

Approaches to online social networks

Social media affords a lens on types of social interaction previously not easily viewed. The streams of online social contact produced by users leave permanent traces that can be captured and modelled by researchers trying to understand the properties of the social networks arising with these social media feeds. Emerging areas of interest range across a large number of disciplines: marketing and opinion mining, information systems, computational linguistics and psychology. An example of the last is a study of the relationship of personality to social media which found extroversion to be positively associated with social media use and emotional stability to be negatively associated (Correa et al. 2010). The scope of networking practices seen with social media is immense. This book deals primarily with microblogging networks, which, due to the particularities of the channels within which they are formed and evolve, may be distinct from practices developing in other kinds of social media. As a consequence this section will primarily review research into social networks formed in microblogging.

Most studies of social media communities, particularly computationally oriented studies of microblogging communities, use some derivative of social network analysis (SNA) (Wasserman and Faust 1994). SNA typically models and visualizes links between users based on a range of criteria such as frequency of contact and topic of message. It generally focuses on the topology, structure and evolution of these networks (Lin et al. 2009; Ahn et al. 2007; Wilson and Nicholas 2008; Holme et al. 2004). For example, Kumar and colleagues (2010, p. 612) note the prevalence of star structures in online social networks, where this structure represents 'a single charismatic individual (in the online sense) linked to a varying number of other users who have very few other connections'. According to the study these networks are made up of 'singletons' (non-participatory users), star-structured 'isolated communities', and 'a giant' component (a core region of the network unaffected by removal of star networks). Some studies look at how one variable (for instance, restricting the number of a user's friends) affects the topological properties of a network (Ghosh et al. 2010).

Computationally, interest generally lies in trying to understand the properties of online social networks. In general this kind of work uses techniques from computational linguistics to answer questions such as 'Given a social network and known preferences or behaviors of individuals in the network, how can we employ the connectivity to determine the preferences or behaviors of others in the network?' (Tang et al. 2010, p. 1). For example, we might build models using supervised[6] machine learning to predict which users will post tweets containing which URLs (Galuba et al. 2010). Alternatively the modelling may use unsupervised machine learning. For example, topic models can be used in predicting network structure. One study suggested that topic models can outperform some supervised alternatives derived from traditional social network analysis for determining network structure (Puniyani et al. 2010, p. 19). Another approach would be to track a particular social variable with no a priori definition of the social network's shape.

Alongside considering the shape of a social network is interest in how information travels through the network. The concept of 'influence' (Weng et al. 2010; Cha et al. 2010) refers to which users have the most impact on 'information diffusion', where diffusion is defined as the patterns by which information spreads 'virally' through a network (Liere 2010). Work has also been undertaken on the authority of a microblogger's posts by considering the link structure of explicit connections made between users and also by supplementing this link structure by factoring in messages that are rebroadcast by other users (Yamaguchi et al. 2010).

These notions of influence and authority give rise to theorizing how communal attention operates in social media. In terms of users' interaction with content, microblogging seems to involve a kind of 'information snacking' (Brooks and Churchill, p. 4), where users pay attention to content that interests them at the time they happen to be accessing the service, dropping in and out of the discourse over time. Users, however, are still able to leverage this form of sporadic attention for their own social purposes. Marwick (2010, p. 230) suggests that the particular type of attention that social media encourages commodifies online persona, with many users aiming to achieve a form of 'micro-celebrity'. In other words they adopt 'a mindset and set of practices in which one's online contacts are constructed as an audience or fan base, popularity is maintained through ongoing fan management, and self-presentation is carefully assembled to be consumed by others'. Users' streams of updates become a means for establishing their 'brand' and social status, measurable by the level of attention the brand attracts, as manifest in the number of followers the user accumulates.

Attention is also significant when thinking about social media in terms of its relationship to existing news media. For example, while microblogging has a broader, more varied body of content producers, 'attention remains highly concentrated, where roughly 0.05% of the population accounts for almost half of all attention' (Wu et al. 2011). Wu and colleagues also note that networks of elite users have a highly homophilous structure in terms of attention, 'with celebrities following celebrities, media following media, and bloggers following bloggers'.

Practical applications of research into online social networks include 'opinion mining' in marketing, which is concerned with determining consumer opinion about brands (Jansen et al. 2009). Another less dominant area is the development of health-related services. Examples include the detection of influenza outbreaks with analysis of large quantities of microblogging posts (Culotta 2010) or monitoring of public concern about health issues, such as the H1N1 outbreak in 2009 (Chew and Eysenbach 2010). The principal area of application aimed at capitalizing financially on social media is viral, 'word-of-mouth' marketing. Viral marketing relies on brand awareness generated by content, often a video or image, that spreads rapidly throughout a social media network.

Language and affiliation in social media

Since forming and maintaining social bonds is one of the main functions of language, it seems reasonable to conclude that linguistic analysis may offer a useful lens on how networks of interpersonal relationships are formed and maintained. A linguistic perspective on virtual community aims to describe explicitly how people use language to construe social bonds by creating interpersonal meaning. Historically, interpersonal meaning has been marginalized as an area of inquiry in linguistics (Poynton 1990). The reasons are both practical and political. Interpersonal meaning is difficult to study because it is prosodic in nature – in other words, it is not reducible to constituent parts (Martin 1996; Halliday 1979). Since a constituent structure is a prerequisite for annotation and statistical analysis, prosodic meanings may evade quantification. In addition Poynton (1990, p. 8) suggests that 'because of the hegemony of Chomskian linguistics from the 1960s, . . . when linguists wanted to get back to the social (as increasingly they have from the 1970s), there is a built-in hierarchy which gives priority to the cognitive and individual over the interpersonal and social'.

While studies of online discourse from a linguistic perspective are relatively established (Crystal 2006; Baron 2008; Herring 1996), whether analysis of linguistic function and structure can serve as evidence for defining online communities is an emergent area of inquiry. Approaches to affiliation within sociolinguistics and discourse analysis have used concepts such as speech communities (Labov 1972; Bolinger 1975), discourse communities (Swales 1990; Nystrand 1982) and communities of practice (Wenger 1998; Meyerhoff 2008) to explore linguistic patterning and social structure. These concepts have resounded with the interest of CMC (Computer-mediated Communication) studies in online community formation (for an overview, see Androutsopoulos [2006], who has summarized some of the main tendencies in CMC in this respect).

Using linguistics as a lens on community means that we are using semiotic evidence to group instances of meaning-making, rather than simply using contextual speaker variables, such as age or geography. Evidence of this kind is important to ensuring that the classification is more than a folk categorization. As Herring (2004) notes, much research into CMC tends towards generalization rather than applying a particular strategy for empirically analysing the evidence about the online behaviour studied:

> Internet research often suffers from a premature impulse to label online phenomena in broad terms, e.g., all groups of people interacting online are 'communities';[1] the language of the Internet is a single style or 'genre'[2]. Notions such as 'community' and 'genre' are familiar and evocative, yet notoriously slippery, and unhelpful (or worse) if applied indiscriminately. An important challenge facing Internet researchers is thus how to identify and describe online phenomena in culturally meaningful terms, while at the same time grounding their distinctions in empirically observable behavior. (Herring 2004, p. 338)

The basic notion of online community was popularized in Rheingold's work on 'virtual community', where he suggests that virtual communities 'emerge from the Net when enough people carry on . . . public discussions long enough, with sufficient human feeling, to form webs of personal relationships in cyberspace' (1993, p. 5). Since the emergence of this definition, often criticized for its vagueness, there has been a debate surrounding which criteria establish the bounds of an online community and the structure of such community and how communities are built or emerge (see, for example, Wellman 2001; Hagel and Armstrong 1997; Jones 1997; Burnett 2000; Herring 1996, 2004, 2008). No stable definition of online community has prevailed. The metadata collected by most SNSs may assist with these problems and be used in quantitative studies of SNS usage, as well as to complement discourse analysis.

Some language-based research into social media communities has been begun by computational linguists in the area of sentiment analysis – and natural language processing more generally. This work attempts to automate the detection of language patterns for categorizing groups of users into social networks (Haythornthwaite and Gruzd 2007; Gruzd 2009). Nguyen and colleagues (2010, p. 23) propose 'grouping patterns of communities purely from their sentiment'. This study used both mood tags, a form of metadata applied to blog posts by their authors, and 'emotion-bearing words' (Nguyen et al. 2010, p. 26), extracted from the content of posts, to classify sentiment. Chapter 4, on appraisal in microblogging, explores how a rich linguistic model of evaluative language can assist in understanding how sentiment is construed in social media. Following on from this, in Chapter 5, I provide a model of a type of ambient affiliation seen around evaluative targets marked by Twitter hashtags.

A social semiotic perspective

The perspective on ambient bonding applied in this book relies upon a social semiotic approach to language as it is used in its functional contexts (Halliday 1978). The discourse analysis undertaken is informed by systemic functional linguistics (SFL). SFL acknowledges that language is itself 'full of resources for negotiating community – both across metafunctions (ideational resources such as technical and specialized lexis, interpersonal resources such as naming and vocatives) and across strata (accents in phonology, grammatical variation and discourse semantic style)' (Martin 2010, p. 24). The theory refers to the domain of meaning making associated with forging social bonds as interpersonal meaning (for a more detailed overview of SFL, see the next chapter). It is interpersonal meaning that builds and sustains online social networks. The language used in social media, particularly microblogging, is under significant interpersonal pressure. On the one hand, it is deployed in a modality where interpersonal meanings that might otherwise be expressed paralinguistically must be expressed via other means.[7] On the other hand, it is bound by the need for linguistic economies arising from the character constraints imposed on microposts. Page (2011) has noted how the resources used to signal interpersonal bonding in social media vary according to the nature of the web genre in question.

In adopting a social semiotic approach, I look both qualitatively and quantitatively at the ways interpersonal meaning co-patterns with ideational meaning in texts. The theoretical basis of this approach is the concept of 'coupling' introduced by Martin (2000a) and taken up by Zhao (2010, 2011) and Zappavigna and colleagues (2008) for looking at textual relations:

> **Coupling** concerns the temporal relation of '*with*': variable *x* comes with variable *y*. To put it another way, it is the relation formed between two semiotic elements at one given point in time within the logogenetic timeframe. Coupling can be formed between metafunctional variables (e.g. ideational and interpersonal), between different semiotic resources (e.g. image and verbiage) and across strata (e.g. semantics and phonology). (Zhao 2011, p. 144)

This perspective is adopted in tandem with concepts drawn from corpus linguistics of collocation and clustering (in particular n-grams; that is, word-level sequences) as a means for exploring syntagmatic relationships in texts.

Coupling is also central to the view of community and affiliation proposed in this book. Zhao (2011) argues that cultures incline toward stable coupling patterns when viewed from the perspective of a particular time frame (e.g. a historical perspective) and that a set of stable coupling patterns can theoretically be described, noting that coupling is a process and that cultures change over time. This modelling perspective is akin to Bakhtin's (1986) work on speech genres as stable patterns of utterance. To this perspective I add the notion developed within complexity theory that cultures are complex adaptive systems[8] and that, as self-organizing ecosocial systems, they look different depending upon the timescale from which they are viewed (Lemke 2000). Adopting these two perspectives, we can theorize that the overlapping bounds of communities of microbloggers will incline towards stable coupling patterns. These coupling patterns will have high dimensionality, and therefore the social semiotician has two options: using some form of expert knowledge of the culture to isolate particular couplings to use as markers for particular communities, or adopting a text of visualization strategy that can reveal patterns which manual analysis and the human gaze of the analyst cannot perceive directly (Zappavigna 2011a).

In this book I focus on couplings of ideational and interpersonal meanings in memes, slang, humour and political discourse in microblogging in order to explore how these textual relations realize social relations, particularly the shift toward searchable talk as a bonding strategy. In so doing, I draw on an additional, complementary perspective that also uses the concept of coupling as its basis: Knight's (2010 a,b,c) model of offline affiliation. This theory, developed through analysis of conversational humour, describes 'communal identity' as discursively negotiated in text (Knight 2010c, p. 43). It applies Martin and White's (2005) framework of evaluative language to understand how communities form as people rally around, defer or reject different values construed in language (Knight 2008). According to Knight, social bonds are negotiated via couplings of ideational and interpersonal meaning in discourse. She comments on these couplings as follows:

> Specifically, couplings realize bonds of value with experience linguistically, as bonds are on a higher order of abstraction in the socio-cultural context. We discursively negotiate our communal identities through bonds that we can share, and these bonds make up the value sets of our communities and culture, but they are not stable and fixed. (Knight 2010c, p. 43)

This book will employ coupling theory to think about processes of affiliation with searchable talk as ongoing negotiation of couplings in text. From a theoretical perspective focusing on textual patterns to explore community is in line with the principle of 'emergence' from systems theory, namely, that complex patterns arise from interactions of simple elements (such as coupling) (Lewes 1875). The aim is to avoid imposing a predetermined structure or hierarchy of organization on the patterns that become visible.

Due to the online channel of microblogging, different practices of negotiation are in play to those seen in face-to-face casual conversation of the kind Knight explores. For example, users may be 'familiar strangers' who share common interests and attributes but do not necessarily know each other (Agarwal et al. 2009), and they may not even engage in direct exchanges. Instead users may be involved in communal performances, such as hashtagging, mentioned earlier in this chapter. For instance, applying Knight's perspective to the tweet introduced at the beginning of this book illuminates the hashtag as the ideational target of the values expressed. In other words, expressing support for the victims of the Christchurch earthquake involves a coupling of positive attitude with the ideational topic realized in the hashtag (i.e. eqnz). Chapter 5 will show how these type of tags are used to label the ideational meanings which users axiologize around, so forming ambient communities of value.

The structure of this book

The chapter which follows will explain why linguists should be interested in social media such as microblogging services as natural language corpora. It details HERMES, a 100 million word Twitter corpus that forms the major dataset used in the book and explains the methodology used: a corpus-based discourse analysis that makes use of both quantitative corpus analysis and close discourse analysis informed by SFL. The chapter provides an overview of the major issues facing researchers when using and managing internet language data.

Chapter 2 gives an overview of the essential features of microblogging and an introduction to the dominant kinds of research in this area. The chapter also begins to explore some of the dominant linguistic patterns in HERMES. Following on from this, Chapter 3 looks in detail at the kinds of evaluative language used in microblogging. Evaluative patterns in HERMES are explored by drawing upon appraisal theory (Martin and White 2005) and corpus-based theories of stance and emotion (Bednarek 2006). The aim is to show that people use Twitter and other microblogging services to share their experiences and enact relationships rather than to simply narrate the mundane details of their activities, as has been claimed in the popular press.

The middle chapters of the book deal with a number of specialized corpora of microposts employed in following case studies:

- Ambient affiliation – An examination of hashtags (e.g. #Obama) used to mark the topic of tweets in a process of 'ambient affiliation', whereby people sharing associated values bond around these user-defined topics.
- Social media memes – An investigation of the function of phrasal template memes used for affiliation (e.g. im in ur [noun] [present infinitive verb] ur [noun]).
- Social media slang – An exploration of how slang (e.g. noob) functions in social media to invoke solidarity.
- Social media humour and fail – A study of how the fail meme (e.g. epic fail, full of fail, bucket of fail.) is used for bonding via internet humour.
- Political discourse – A study of evaluative language in microposts related to politics (e.g. a corpus of tweets containing the name Obama, collected in the 24 hours following the 2008 US presidential election).

The theme tying these studies together is 'ambient affiliation': how social bonds are realized in language, in particular, the emerging searchable talk of microblogging.

CHAPTER TWO

Social media as corpora

Working with internet corpora

Research into new media and the internet from a communication perspective is a diverse area that began to emerge around 1996 (Tomasello et al. 2009). Generally the field is referred to with the umbrella term computer-mediated communication (CMC), encompassing a wide range of perspectives on language across a number of disciplines, from information systems to linguistics. Studies of web-based discourse are a subdiscipline of CMC. Depending on the theoretical orientation adopted, these studies may employ close analysis of small volumes of text or wider analysis using corpora consisting of texts derived from internet media. Some studies are interested in particular features of language as manifest within web-based communication, while others explore more generally the patterning of web-based genres. Most often, these researchers will build their own corpora since CMC is under-represented in most available corpora. However, very large web-based billion-word corpora are beginning to emerge, such as the 25 billion word USENET corpus (2005–09) (Shaoul and Westbury 2011), a corpus consisting of public USENET[1] postings collected between October 2005 and January 2010, and the Birmingham blog corpus (http://wse1.webcorp.org.uk/blogs/), consisting of approximately 629 million words of blog texts extracted from the web.

The notion that the web itself can be used as a corpus holds much appeal due to the large volume of data available and the relative ease of collection compared with, for example, recording spoken discourse. Web-based data has proven to be of use to linguists working in many areas, such as 'lexicography, syntax, semantics and translation' (Volk 2002). A fundamental premise of corpus linguistics, equally applicable to web-based data as to more traditional data sources, is that corpora should be built according to carefully constructed selection criteria. These criteria define the type and scope of data to be included in the corpus, and it is this careful consideration that makes a true corpus different to a text archive. The World Wide Web consists of hypertext documents that are linked together in various ways, and, in this sense, it can be thought of as a large collection of texts. It is a multimodal assortment since web documents may comprise a range of multimedia, including text, image and video. Unprocessed, the web is, however, not a corpus in the traditional sense, as it has not been built following selection criteria but instead has evolved as people have added, modified and deleted documents. Nevertheless, there is a body of research interested in finding ways to process web data so that it may be made useful to corpus linguists and more closely approximate the rigours of traditional corpora (Baroni and Bernardini 2006; Kilgarriff and Grefenstette 2003; Hundt et al. 2007; Bernardini et al. 2006).

Like traditional corpora, web corpora are bound by issues of representativeness, balance and comparability (Leech 2007). Hoffman (2007, p. 69) notes that 'fundamentals of corpus linguistic methodology such as the concept of corpus representativeness, the replicability of linguistic findings or the use of normalized frequency counts cannot be easily applied to internet-based data'. Representativeness is a concept used in statistics to refer to the extent to which a sample reflects the patterns in a larger population. Linguists face the problem that since language is such a complex social phenomenon, specifying its scope is inherently fraught. Balance refers to the issue that a corpus should contain an equi-distributed sample of the range of possible genres, were it possible to catalogue genres with any kind of exhaustive way. Comparability refers to the potential to compare different corpora by holding steady all parameters used for its construction except the one to be studied. Determining how these issues of representativeness, balance, and comparability may be addressed in light of the features of networked, electronic texts is a non-trivial problem. Add the dimension of time, very important to many kinds of electronic texts, such as social media streams, and corpus construction becomes even more complex.

Internet data can be highly 'noisy' in the sense that methods for automating text collection will retrieve results that were not intended by the linguist. In particular, most web documents will contain formatting and metadata that need some kind of processing before the main text can be included in a plain text file corpus or in a relational database that also stores metadata about the texts. Fletcher (2004) offers a number of strategies for corpus linguists trying to prepare web documents for inclusion in corpora, including techniques for noise reduction that identify and filter out duplicate documents, find highly repetitive documents, and separate connected prose from fragmentary texts.

Time is of particular significance to online texts, particularly social media texts. Social media corpora are inevitably time-bound datasets, often shifting, networked assemblages of streaming data. Streaming data, as we will see with the HERMES corpus introduced in this chapter, is data that is produced as a sequence. A common example is the data feeds produced by blogs and consumed by audiences via feed readers. 'Information streams' (Chen et al. 2010) are important in social media due to the important role of time, given the potential for both immediate information and asynchronous retrieval. Streaming data produced with social media include unfolding status updates, such as microblog feeds or sequential blog posts, and feeds of images and video.

Bernardini and colleagues (2006, p. 10) suggest four senses in which the web can be conceived as a corpus, summarized as follows:

1. The Web as a corpus surrogate – the researcher employs a standard commercial search engine to address a linguistic query such as a translation task.
2. The Web as a corpus shop – the researcher builds a specialized corpus by using a search engine to locate texts that conform to some criteria. This procedure may be partially automated.
3. The Web as corpus proper – the researcher employs some form of web sampling to create a traditional corpus with which to explore the general nature of web-based language.
4. The mega-corpus/mini-web – the researcher creates an extremely large corpus with web-derived texts that are annotated and support sophisticated querying. This corpus is able to address both the interests of researchers using the web to explore systems of language and those investigating language to explore the social function of the web itself.

A number of corpus-query tools have been developed for exploring the web as a corpus. For example WebCorp Linguist's search engine (WebCorpLSE) (www.webcorp.org.uk/), which is crawling the web to create a 10-billion-word text corpus independent of commercial search engines (Renouf 2003). Sharoff (2006) explores using search engine queries to create corpora, adopting the perspective of (2) according to the framework of Ludeling and colleagues (2007, p. 20). Indeed, linguists fantasize about a search engine that could filter internet data based on linguistic selection criteria and eliminate noise from the retrieved results:

> While there is no major theoretical / algorithmic roadblock to the realization of a linguist's search engine, its implementation requires major computational resources and very serious, coordinated, high-efficiency programming – a far cry from the 'do it yourself with a Perl script on whatever computer is available' approach typical of corpus linguistics. (Ludeling et al. 2007, p. 20)

Work in this area is extremely exciting and will provide resources important to understanding the very significant role that the internet plays in social life. I will now explore some of the practical and often mundane issues that face researchers working with a particular kind of web-based data – social media data – specifically, corpora consisting of microposts scraped from social media-streaming data feeds.

Microposts as corpora

Microblogging data is episodic in nature, with posts added to a user's stream over time, often at frequent intervals. Marwick (2010, p. 16) refers to the near synchronous character of social media updating as 'lifestreaming', that is, an 'ongoing sharing of personal information to a networked audience'. In this way the data is temporally bound, and the period in time over which a corpus of microposts is collected has a significant impact on the properties of the corpus and the ways in which it can be used. Contextual phenomena such as high profile events, crises, seasons and holidays all have an impact on the kind of online talk occurring via this media. While contextual variables (such as time of updating) intervene in all corpora, the impact appears to be particularly concentrated in micropost corpora, particularly on simple measures, such as word-frequency lists. For example, Valentine's Day fell within the corpus collection period for HERMES, resulting in a high number of Valentine's Day-related lexis and language patterns. The 2010 Vancouver Winter Olympics was also held within the time interval of corpus construction, increasing the ranking of sport-related language in the word-frequency list. This influence might be reduced by collecting a corpus over a longer period of time or sampling at specific time intervals, creating a form of diachronic corpus. In essence, microblogging produces 'time-sensitive text' (Cataldi et al. 2010, p. 2). Visualization of feeds shows that lexis varies depending on time of day (Clark 2009). The effect is detectable because of the nature of the streaming data and would likely occur in any linguistic dataset sampled continuously.

The variation of language over time is itself of intrinsic interest and the objective of studies that work with traditional diachronic corpora.[2] Within the domain of social media research, time is of particular interest to researchers studying patterns of trending topics (Cataldi et al. 2010). Trending topics are a list of the latest keywords occurring with high frequency in current posts, displayed under the search box. These trends are not long-term patterns; instead trending topics emphasize immediacy. Twitter defines trending topics as follows:

> Twitter's Trending Topics algorithm identifies topics that are immediately popular, rather than topics that have been popular for a while or on a daily basis, to help people discover the 'most breaking' news stories from across the world. We think that trending topics which capture the hottest emerging trends and topics of discussion on Twitter are the most interesting. (Twitter 2001)

In this way trending topics emphasize immediacy rather than long-term trends. The archetypal example of a topic which frequently trends is tweets related to the Canadian teenage pop idol Justin Bieber,[3] whose continued presence as a trending topic has precipitated both amusement and disdain among the population of users. Entertainment and sport are the two most common domains for trending topics (Cheong 2010).[4]

The volume of data can quickly become large when collecting streams of microposts. This is particularly the case if we want to track relations based on metadata alongside the content of the posts. For example, one study claimed to analyse the entire Twittersphere at the time, resulting in a collection of '41.7 million user profiles, 1.47 billion social relations, 4, 262 trending topics, and 106 million tweets' (Kwak et al. 2010, p. 600). This magnitude of data permits quantitative claims about the properties of social media networks to be made, such as the finding that topology analysis of the follower/following relationship shows 'a non-power-law follower distribution, a short effective diameter, and low reciprocity, which all mark a deviation from known characteristics of human social networks' (Kwak et al. 2010, p. 600).

Studies attempting to automate analysis and classification of microposts have identified a number of features that make this type of corpora difficult to work with. For example (Laboreiro et al. 2010, pp. 81–2) note the following features:

- Omitted characters and white space, ignored casing rules, and non-standard abbreviation due to the highly condensed orthography required for text economy.
- Frequent oral markers and non-standard or omitted punctuation due to the conversational nature of the posts.
- Spelling errors since posts are generated using mobile devices on-the-fly.

These types of textual features mean that it is not possible to use tools such as off-the-shelf POS (Part of Speech) taggers on micropost corpora without significant training of the tagger.

The specific challenges faced when building the HERMES corpus were both technical and theoretical, spanning the following areas:

- Non-standard orthography
- XML and escaped characters
- Emoticons and hashtags
- Abridged posts
- The status of automated and 're-broadcast' material

I will explain each of these issues in the sections that follow.

Non-standard orthography

Microposts typically contain non-standard orthography. In general 'tools for corpus search and annotation, developed with standard orthography and "traditional" text genres in mind, need to be adapted to the peculiarities of CMC discourse genres' (Beißwenger and Storrer 2008, p. 303), and this is particularly true for microblogging. Linguists can learn from the body of work in computational linguistics, where many of these types of text-processing problems are encountered, when trying to automate various kinds of linguistic analyses. For example, Puniyani and colleagues (2010, p. 19) note that 'Twitter contains highly non-standard orthography that poses challenges for early-stage text processing'. The two examples the authors provide, punctuation for tokenization (punctuation marking a break between words) and punctuation inside a token (punctuation within a word, e.g. ! to represent i), were also issues for HERMES due to the presence in the Twitter stream of posts such as the following:

> @user: Never had anyone but my hand make me a quiche for breakfast. Sadly I have to agree with u too!Lol.They don't make em like that

> @user LOL !D RATHA NOT TRY. D!S 1 G!RL SAYD ! GOT DA MOUF DA BE GREAT @ !T. DAS ENUF FA ME LOL

XML and escaped characters

The corpus linguist trying to work with tweets that have been scraped[5] from an internet feed may encounter the trivial but real problem of escaped special characters[6] if the input text has not been 'unescaped' properly. XML files have characters that have special meanings, for instance < > are used to demark an XML tag and separate the content from the mark-up. If one of these characters occurs in the raw text of a tweet, it must be 'escaped' by being represented by another set of characters. This in turn may cause issues if the escaped-character sequences are not converted back to their original form when generating, for example, word lists in concordance software, since concordance software may handle special characters in ways that can produce unexpected results.

Although HERMES itself is an English-language corpus, many tweets are in languages other than English, and this carries with it all the problems of internationalization of text. The main problem is that many text editors and text-processing software are limited to working with English text. This means that when you encounter text in other languages, the software will produce unpredictable characters such as question marks, boxes and other symbols in place of the correct characters. A related problem is the intentional use of specific symbols in text by users. A common feature of microblog texts is the use of symbols in posts, for example, the love-heart dingbat symbol ♥.

Emoticons and hashtags

As Chapter 4 explores, emoticons are an extremely common feature of microblogging. Emoticons can pose a significant concordancing problem. Depending on the configuration of the concordance software used, some of the characters used in emoticons are not considered valid letters for that system and so will be filtered out of the concordance. They may also be interpreted as marking word breaks. In addition some characters may have other special meanings to the system. For instance, Wordsmith Tools (hereafter Wordsmith) (Scott 2008), the concordance system used for analyses of HERMES, uses the hash character # to represent, as a group, all numbers that occur in the corpus. This is to avoid the situation where the word frequency list is polluted by numbers that interfere with interpretation of lexis. In addition, Wordsmith does not treat the hash character itself as a valid letter and responds as if it were punctuation.

Abridged posts

Twitter users may avoid the constraint of limiting their update to 140 characters by using a web service to extend their message (such as longertweets.com). These services allow the user to present an abridged version of the tweet in their stream, usually with a link to the full 140+ character post. The result is that some tweets appear in an abridged form in the corpus. Alternatively, the tweet may contain punctuation indicating that it continues in a subsequent tweet in the stream. The abridging can cause various kinds of problems for concordancing; for example, the following tweet appeared in HERMES in the concordance lines for 'twit':

> RT @User: Farmville players outnumber real farmers in the US by a ratio of 60 to 1. --> More info: Farmville is bigger than Twit. . . .

The final word was most likely Twitter in the extended version of the post. Depending on the strategy used to extend the tweet, the elaborating tweet may not be captured when the corpus is constructed. However, these types of tweets are relatively uncommon and may be filtered out of the corpus if the analyst can identify regular syntactic patterns with which they can be identified and removed.

The status of automated and rebroadcast material

Any corpus scraped from Twitter will contain spam tweets; that is, automated tweets by non-humans. They will also contain rebroadcast material in the form of retweeted tweets reposted by a user other than the original author (Grier et al. 2010). The status of these tweets in a corpus is an important theoretical question. Depending on the intended use of the corpus, a researcher may consider some or all of these tweets as noise and decide to

- filter out all instances of repetition;
- filter out any tweets that seem to be spam;
- filter out retweeted tweets;
- filter out any automated, non-human tweets.

The decisions that are made in this respect will clearly have an impact upon any corpus statistics that are generated.

For the work conducted with HERMES, I made the decision to keep all of this material, viewing it as part of the systems of discourse that characterize the Twitter stream. Instead, at the stage of analysis, I filtered out non-human spam and different forms of repetition, depending on the kind of analysis I was undertaking. Some web services will produce an automated tweet indicating that a user has performed an action with their service, such as 'favouriting' a YouTube video. For example the consistent syntax suggests that the following tweets have been automatically generated in this way:

> I favorited a YouTube video – Mala – In Luv http://youtu.be/8ArEnBMYL_I?a
>
> I favorited a YouTube video – DITC – Day One Instrumental http://youtu.be/-ZeUmoeRDVo?a
>
> I favorited a YouTube video – Aidan Davis: Low – Britain's Got Talent 2009 – The Final http://youtu.be/Wzv_4E_4OIs?a

This pattern may be regular enough that 'favorited a YouTube video' appears as a highly frequent 4-gram when running an n-gram analysis on the corpus. I discarded these kinds of results at the analysis stage. In addition, I made the decision to preserve retweets since they give important insight into what is considered significant enough to republish within Twitter communities. While I am mainly concerned with how users affiliate in microblogging in the present study, I am still interested in how much of this kind of automated discourse contributes to the unfolding of the Twitter stream.

The HERMES corpus

HERMES was briefly introduced in the previous chapter and is the main corpus used throughout this book. The corpus contains over 100 million words[7] and close to 7 million tweets. It was collected using the Twitter streaming application programming interface (API). The API is the language that software tools use to communicate with Twitter's back-end database. Since the API is public, developers can use it to write custom applications that interface with Twitter's data feeds. For example, Twittervision (Twittervision.com) is a web mash-up[8] that combines Twitter feeds with Google Maps to create a display of tweets unfolding in real time on a map. The API was used to construct HERMES, the large-scale corpus used throughout this book.

The API allows developers to collect a subset of tweets from the public Twitter feed – in other words, all tweets from accounts that are set to allow public access. The tweets are made available via what is termed the 'garden hose stream', which is in turn randomly sampled from the larger 'firehose stream' of all public tweets with a sampling algorithm generated by Twitter. The Twitter API documentation describes the algorithm as follows:

> The sampling algorithm, in conjunction with the statusID assignment algorithm, will tend to produce a random selection. A proportion of all statuses are selected, and the public statuses within that proportion are delivered. Therefore, as the rate of non-public statuses varies, the proportion of sampled statuses to total statuses will also vary. Additionally, the sampled rates exhibit the same strong diurnal and weekly patterns as the overall status creation rate. (Twitter 2010)

Due to this randomization, much of the sequential nature of the streaming data is lost, and hence some other corpus collection strategy is required for exploring sequences of exchanges between users.

Examples of the body text of a tweet include the following instances:

> In the train on the way to see JLS! EEEEEEEEK!
>
> @User1 I aim to please . . .
>
> Haircuttttttt thennnn GTL'n ittttt!!! Lolllll

The multimodal representation of a tweet (layout, colour etc.) is dependent on the mode of access to the service. If accessing the tweet via the official Twitter web interface, the body text is accompanied by an icon chosen by the user, a username, the content of the tweet, the time the tweet was posted and the medium used to post the tweet (e.g. third party software such as Tweetdeck running on an iPhone). Metadata about a tweet can at present[9] be retrieved using the Twitter API. Linguists can make use of the API to build corpora that contain different kinds of metadata retrieved from Twitter. This metadata may provide some simple contextual variables that offer complementary information in addition to considering the content of a micropost. For the purposes of working with HERMES in a standard concordancing application, this information was stripped out of the JSON files (the data encoding format used by the Twitter API) extracted from Twitter when the corpus was built.

Since Twitter is an international service, tweets may be posted in a range of languages. For the purposes of this study we are interested in English language tweets. In order to ensure that HERMES contained only English tweets, posts with non-English characters were removed from the corpus, and then a statistical language model written in pearl (Simões 2010) was used to further filter out non-English tweets.

The general method used to build the corpus may be summarized by the following high-level steps:

1. Download all the unfiltered tweets from Twitter across a particular time-window or until a certain quantity is captured (keeping in mind that, in step 4, non-English tweets will be removed, reducing the overall number of tweets).
2. Separate the content of the tweets from other metadata, depending on how they will be imported/processed by the particular concordance software to be used with the corpus.
3. Convert any entity sequences, such as escaped characters, into their native form.
4. Filter the text so that it contains only English tweets (or tweets from the particular language of interest). This step is not an exact science as current language filtering technologies are not 100 per cent accurate.[10]

There are many reference texts that cover general techniques for scraping streaming data and other forms of data from the internet, including *Text Processing in Python* (Mertz 2003) and *Mining the Social Web* (Russell 2011). These may be of use to analysts with more specific requirements. An in-depth tutorial on scraping data with the Twitter API is not provided here since the way Twitter allows developers to access its data and the extent of the granted access is changing as Twitter determines ways to generate income from the data. Hence, any proposed method is likely to quickly become obsolete.

A functional, corpus-based approach to analysing online talk

The methodology used in this book for analysing microposts is a form of corpus-based discourse analysis applying SFL (systemic functional linguistics). SFL posits language as a meaning-making resource. It is a theory tailored to answering questions about how meanings operate within the particular contexts in which they are made and is in this sense 'functional'. Eggins (1994, p. 23) suggests that SFL is distinct among linguistic theories as 'it seeks to develop both a theory about social process AND an analytical methodology which permits the detailed and systematic description of language patterns'. SFL is aligned with the functional tradition in linguistics manifest in the Prague school (Jakobson 1971) and arose out of the linguistic school known as Firthian systemics (Firth 1957).

As a method for managing the multiple dimensions of language use, SFL stratifies language into phonology (systems of sounds/writing), lexicogrammar (systems of wording), discourse semantics (systems of meaning), and context (genre and register). The strata are related to each other in terms of emergent complexity: as patterns of patterns (Lemke 1984). For example, discourse semantics is a higher order patterning of lexicogrammatical patterns that are, in turn, patterns of phonological patterns. According to the theory, language enacts three simultaneous functions, referred to as metafunctions: an ideational function of enacting experience, an interpersonal function of negotiating relationships, and a textual function of organizing information (Halliday and Matthiessen 2004). A linguist using this theory will attempt to consider these three functions when analysing any instance of linguistic meaning.

SFL draws its ideas about context from the work of the anthropologist Malinowski, who introduced the notion of an ethnographic theory of language. Malinowski argued that 'the real linguistic fact is the full utterance within its context of situation' (Malinowski 1935, p. 11). By context, Malinowski means phenomena that the anthropologist must describe in order to understand, for example, the meaning of a word in a different culture. Translation of a word that has no equivalent in the language of the anthropologist is made possible by description of its context. SFL appropriates two broad types of context from Malinowski: the context of culture and the context of situation. The context of culture is a semiotic system, a system of meaning configuring and configured by language. When using language, people make choices from the options that the culture makes available to them. They make these choices within a particular circumstance, the 'context of situation'. For example, an IT help desk employee answering a user's question makes choices about how to address that user that are influenced by the culture of the institution. They also make choices that depend on the particular type of answer they will provide (answering a telephone-based help desk question, answering an email etc.), that is, the context of situation.

Matthiessen (1995, p. 36) suggests that context is 'functionally diversified' as combinations of field, tenor and mode. 'Field' is akin to the popular notion of 'topic', answering the question 'what is happening or what is the text about?' while 'tenor' considers the social relationship of the participants, where the relationship is defined in terms of the roles that the participants occupy and the patterns that constitute their interaction. The final component in this functional combination is mode. 'Mode' refers to the medium facilitating the communication and the rhetorical function of that communication. Martin (2004, p. 56) adds another level of context to the model, which he refers to as genre and which 'is concerned with systems of social processes, where the principles for relating social processes to each other have to do with texture, that is, the ways in which field, mode and tenor variables are phased together in a text'. In exploring ambient affiliation, this book is largely concerned with tenor relationships and how they are reconfigured by the particular permutation of mode generated by the microblogging channel.

The kind of discourse analysis undertaken in the chapters that follow employs the functional orientation to meaning just described. It uses evidence from corpora to guide the analyst to important sites of meaning-making likely to illuminate the social patterns that characterize microblogging. In addition, it uses close analysis of the meanings made in these instances to inform which quantitative investigations are then pursued. In this way I adopt a two-pronged approach to corpus-based discourse analysis of the kind advocated by Baker (2006). When looking at general patterns, the corpus HERMES is used. However, the chapters focusing on specific linguistic systems, such as social media slang, supplement this general analysis with examination of patterns in smaller specialized corpora. In this way, I also adopt a three-pronged approach similar to that of Bednarek (2009), combining consideration of a large reference corpus, smaller corpora and close-discourse analysis.

CHAPTER THREE

The language of microblogging

Alongside comment on the discourses of social media in general, my more particular focus throughout this book will be on the language used in microblogging. Microblogging is a form of length-delimited (hence 'micro') communication using a social networking service. These services allow short posts to be published online and users to subscribe to feeds of other users' updates. The services are syndicated and may be accessed via an official website or third-party applications, often running on mobile devices such as smartphones. The first part of this chapter gives an overview of microblogging as a semiotic activity. The second section begins an analysis of the main linguistic patterns in the HERMES corpus.

Because of the character limitations imposed on microposts, they are interesting data to observe how meaning can be made in constrained environments. The brevity encouraged by the medium affords frequent and continuous updating, and consequently, jokes abound about the egocentricity of telling the world the minutiae of personal experiences that constitute your everyday life. Generally, however, microblogging has been positively portrayed in the press (Arceneaux and Schmitz Weiss 2010) and is a social phenomenon experiencing rapid increase.

Unlike other social networking services, microblogging services generally allow asymmetrical relationships between accounts. While Facebook requires that both parties explicitly consent to becoming 'friends' via an explicit link, microblogging services generally allow the user to subscribe to another user's feed of microposts without any binding expectation of reciprocation. In the case of Twitter this subscription practice is referred to as 'following', and a user who has subscribed to your tweets is termed a follower. I may choose to follow an individual who posts content that I find interesting without a social bond being inferred. By way of contrast, declining a Facebook friend request is viewed as an act of social rejection and in 'choosing who to include as Friends, participants more frequently consider the implications of excluding or explicitly rejecting a person as opposed to the benefits of including them'. (Boyd 2010, p. 44).

A micropost may have a wide range of social functions realized by different microgenres, though it is not yet clear whether the linguistic patterning seen is best described through the lens of genre. In SFL, genres have generally been explored using more extended texts (Martin and Rose 2008). It is yet to be understood whether or how the intersection of different textual timelines that constitute a user's stream of posts can be modelled in terms of genre theory. However, Myers (2010) uses genre to explore blogging which may be argued to be an antecedent to microblogging. As I will note later, some kind of visualization support is likely required to perceive the patterning and better ways of approaching texts as processes rather than static products (Zhao 2010). As Russell (2011, p. 10) suggests, 'Because the social web is first and foremost about the linkages between people in the real world, one highly convenient format for storing social web data is the graph'.

Users may confess their personal thoughts and feelings with emotional language (see Chapter 4), complain about their everyday existence (see Chapter 8), contribute to a micro-meme (see Chapter 6), engage in humour (see Chapter 8) or express political opinion (see Chapter 9). In all these cases the act of microblogging has enough semiotic pull that the user has stopped whatever he or she may have been doing to post a thought. This will have been undertaken with varying degrees of deliberation, depending on the context. In some cases, 'Similar to fashion, there is a self-consciousness and self-reflection when deciding what to share' (Subramanian and March 2010), and in others the post may be hurried, embedded in ongoing activity while out and about with a mobile device.

The phatic dimension of microblogging

Some studies claim that microblogging has a phatic function. Malinowski introduced the notion of 'phatic communion' as a way of describing communication in the service of establishing or solidifying bonds of companionship rather than serving 'any purpose of communicating ideas' (2004, p. 250). This notion may be extrapolated to relationships formed via social media as part of an overall 'phatic media culture', where 'content is not king, but "keeping in touch" is' (Miller 2008, p. 395):

> More important than anything said, it is the connection to the other that becomes significant, and the exchange of words becomes superfluous. Thus the text message, the short call, the brief email, the short blog update or comment, becomes part of a mediated phatic sociability

> necessary to maintain a connected presence in an ever expanding social network. (Miller 2008, p. 395)

If conceived in this way, microblogging functions as what Makice (2009) describes, using a computer metaphor, 'linguistic ping'.[1] Just as a computer on a network can be pinged, we may think of microbloggers declaring to their ambient audience, 'I'm still here!'. This kind of phatic function is complementary to the more ideational description of Web 2.0 as driven by user-generated content. The extent of this function across microblogging platforms is likely to vary since, for example, status updating on Facebook within a semi-private network of peers encourages different forms of expression to the more public networking seen with Twitter (Page 2011).

It is unlikely that this phatic dimension with all its interpersonal potential was anticipated in the original design of Twitter (with its origins in a concept for status updating via SMS). The first paragraph of the service's self-description on Twitter's About page, privileges the ideational function of communication, referring to itself as an information network:

> Twitter is a real-time information network that connects you to the latest information about what you find interesting. Simply find the public streams you find most compelling and follow the conversations. (Twitter 2010)

The social importance of information sharing influences the content of tweets, and, as we will see in this chapter, the marker identifying a hyperlink is the fifth most common lexical item in HERMES, showing the extent to which users share web links with each other. Nevertheless, there is much accompanying evidence that interpersonal meanings are also critical, and in any case, the ways in which information is shared is always subject to tenor variables, such as power relations.

The distinction between an ideational focus on information and an interpersonal emphasis on social connection should not be conceived in binary terms since language makes multiple kinds of meaning simultaneously. As mentioned earlier, Halliday and Matthiessen (2004) refer to this concurrent meaning potential, as metafunctions: an ideational function of enacting experience, an interpersonal function of negotiating relationships and a textual function of organizing information. Thus, a tweet may have both an information-sharing and a bonding function, as the following example illustrates:

> http://www.loftcube.net/ Why do we all live in these big homes . . . how cool is this!!

Here a hyperlink to an architectural website is offered to the putative audience alongside evaluation of its content, drawing upon both ideational and interpersonal resources for making these meanings.

As with social media research in general, work on microblogging is generally interdisciplinary or cross-disciplinary, spanning areas as diverse as library science (Murphy 2008; DeVoe 2009; Cuddy 2009; Aharony 2010; Hricko 2010; Kushin and Yamamoto 2010), language learning (Borau et al. 2009) and spam detection (Moh and Murmann 2010) to name but a few. There has been a tendency in the research to taxonomize the functions of microposts based on user intention. Java, Song and colleagues (2007) suggest that 'daily chatter', 'conversations', 'sharing information/URLs' and 'reporting news' are the most common reasons people use Twitter. They identify three main kinds of users in terms of this classification: 'information sources', 'friends', and 'information seekers'. Naaman, Boase and colleagues (2010) extend this work, arguing, via content analysis, that users can be categorized into 'meformers', largely concerned with self, and 'informers', interested in sharing information. Many similar content-oriented studies of microblogging categorize posts or types of users by topic, for example, by most frequent topic (Ramage et al. 2010). Complementary to this content-based perspective is a more functional orientation considering how microposts make meaning and requiring detailed linguistics analyses. This kind of functional orientation informs the chapters which follow.

Microblogging as conversation

Descriptions of microblogging usually imply that it is a form of conversation involving some kind of 'conversational exchange' (Honeycutt and Herring 2009). It is variously described as 'lightweight chat' (Kate et al. 2010, p. 242), as 'prompting opportunistic conversations' (Zhao and Rosson 2009, p. 251), as 'a specific social dialect, in which individual users are clearly singled out and engaged in a conversation' (Grosseck and Holotescu 2009) and as constituted by 'dialogue acts' (Ritter et al. 2010, p. 172). Yardi and Boyd (2010) suggest that the conversational exposure afforded by Twitter may have an edifying impact on the general population of users:

> Twitter affords different kinds of social participation. In the same way a reader has to skim the front page of a physical newspaper to get to the comic section, most Twitter users will be exposed to varied slices of news. Thus, many people may be witnessing diverse conversations and also participating in topics they otherwise may not have. (p. 325)

Indeed, Twitter's About page invites users to 'follow the conversations' to locate information of interest to them (Twitter 2010). Businesses are advised to 'be where the conversations are' (Bradley 2010). This commercialization of conversation sees microblogging interaction used to develop personal branding (Marwick 2010), to publicize professional blogs, to generate word-of-mouth interest in a product and to generally create buzz around something for profit.

Most studies do not offer a theoretical basis for the description of microblogging as a form of conversation, though they often invoke a sociological definition. This disciplinary orientation is different to that which would be adopted by a linguist:

> Sociologists ask 'How do we do conversation?', and recognize that conversation tells us something about social life. Linguists, on the other hand, ask 'How is language structured to *enable* us to do conversation?', and recognize that conversation tells us something about the nature of language as a *resource* for doing social life. (Eggins and Slade 1997, p. 7)

The kinds of structural configurations possible with microblogging are mediated by the nature of the channel, and this is also true of face-to-face conversation. However, as I am working with a randomized corpus of tweets, it is not possible to retrieve extended sequences of exchanges between users; so I will make little comment on conversational structure, aside from the few general observations made here.

Most definitions of conversation presuppose some version of 'turn taking'. This is a concept for theorizing how exchanges are managed in interactions, usually attributed to Sacks et al. (1974). Sacks argued, 'For socially organized activities, the presence of "turns" suggests an economy, with turns for something being valued – and with means for allocating them, which affect their relative distribution, as in economies' (Sacks et al. 1974, p. 696). The field of conversation analysis takes the notion of an adjacency pair as the fundamental unit of conversation. Other perspectives, such as that of Martin (2000b) and Eggins and Slade (1997), employ a more elaborated framework that considers how exchanges work within the genres in which people are called to operate. This perspective also demonstrates the value of accounting for the role that the prosodic patterning, particularly of evaluative language, plays in negotiating meaning (Martin 2000b).

There are a number of significant problems in directly applying the idea of turn-taking to microblogging. I have already mentioned that microblogging services generally allow asymmetrical relationships, where reciprocation of a follower is not obligatory, nor is non-reciprocation interpreted as rejection. Similarly, there is little social expectation that users reply to a given micropost, and even where a direct address is made to a particular user, the obligation to reply is relatively weak. Oulasvirta, Lehtonen et al. (2010, p. 244) refer to this as a kind of 'dilution of conversational obligations'. In addition, as mentioned in the previous chapter, a different kind of attention seems to be at work, with microblogging involving a kind of 'information snacking', where users are not obligated to complete a conversational exchange. In this way, given the asynchronous nature of Twitter CMC, 'Twitter usage is akin to a radio-like information source, turned on or dialled into as needed to pragmatically address "in the moment" curiosity or information needs' (Brooks and Churchill, p. 4).

Another issue is that since posts are persistent, available for viewing and reply long after they were originally produced, users will drop in and out of an exchange, and exchanges will overlap. Fast-paced multicast (many-to-many broadcast) problematize the concept of an adjacency pair so fundamental to traditional conversation analysis. This property of CMC has long been recognized in studies of email and Listservs (Harrison 1998). Boyd (2010, p. 47) notes with concern the potential for conversation to be 'consumed outside of its original context' given the persistence afforded by social networking technologies.

The back channel as shadowing conversation

Microblogging can be used as a form of 'back-channel communication' (McNely 2009; Sarita 2006). The back channel is supplementary media running in parallel to some main form of communication. As such, it forms a kind of 'intangible, clandestine community' (Sarita 2006, p. 852) and allows novel forms of ancillary participation in events. Back channelling may act as a kind of 'conversational shadow' to live media events, such as the 2008 US presidential election (Shamma et al. 2010), as we will see in Chapter 9. Other contexts in which back channelling may occur include collaborative learning environments (Yardi 2006), education (Ebner et al. 2010), conferences (McCarthy and Boyd 2005; Reinhardt et al. 2009; Grosseck and Holotescu 2010), question-and-answer sessions (Harry et al. 2009) and other kinds of large events, such as fashion trade shows (Bisker et al. 2008). In addition, the back channel has been incorporated into mainstream television, with feeds of tweets sometimes appearing in news broadcasts or during programmes involving audience commentary, such as chat shows. Anstead and O'Loughlin (2010) term the emergence of viewers who engage with new media as they respond to broadcasts 'the rise of the Viewertariat – a section of the audience that, aided by emerging technologies such as Twitter, comments on events on the screen, responds and gives meaning to the broadcast in real time'.

Atkinson (2010, pp. 58–9) suggests a number of functions for the back channel: reporting information by posting informational highlights, enhancing information by adding additional material and commenting on information by offering an opinion. In addition, he suggests that the back channel offers new ways in which conference participants may engage with each other: monitoring what others are saying (reading posts), amplifying what others are saying (retweeting a post), helping others (e.g. posting a message to assist with a technical problem) and arranging face-to-face meetings (pp. 60–1). Indeed, academic and technology conferences will often adopt a designated hashtag that conference participants may follow. For example, #ISWS2009 was used at the 8th International Semantic Web Conference (Letierce et al. 2010). Other examples are #Online09 at the Online Information 2009 Conference (Ebner et al. 2010).

Some conferences will also implement a live feed running in the background of a conference presentation (Ebner 2009). While a feed may support a presentation with additional useful material, it can lead to distraction from the main content, as occurred with Dana Boyd's presentation at Web 2.0 Expo 2009. In this case the back channel disrupted the speaker because the live feed was not visible to her, and she was unable to contextualize audience response. As she later explained on her blog,

> I walked off stage and immediately went to Brady and asked what on earth was happening. And he gave me a brief rundown. The Twitter stream was initially upset that I was talking too fast. My first response to this was: OMG, seriously? That was it? Cuz that's not how I read the situation on stage. So rather than getting through to me that I should slow down, I was hearing the audience as saying that I sucked. And responding the exact opposite way the audience wanted me to. This pushed the audience to actually start critiquing me in the way that I was imagining it was. And as Brady went on, he said that it started to get really rude so they pulled it to figure out what to do. But this distracted the audience and explains one set of outbursts that I didn't understand from the stage. And then they put it back up and people immediately started swearing. More outbursts and laughter. The Twitter stream had become the center of attention, not the speaker. Not me. (Boyd 2009)

This incident is an example of how important interpersonal meaning is to microblogging and the consequences that arise when the technology is deployed as if it had only an ideational function. The back channel here took on more than a supplementary function of elaborating information given in the presentation and interfered with the interpersonal dynamics of the academic conference presentation genre itself.

Microblogging and heteroglossia

While first-generation microblogging services have not been designed to directly support conversation, perhaps with the exception of Jaiku's message-threading capabilities, there is a social need among users to engage with the other voices that they encounter despite the speed at which microblogging streams unfold in time. Indeed, as we have seen in the previous section, the phenomenon of back channelling is in general a collaborative endeavour. Hence, in the case of Twitter, we see creative use of punctuation to address other users and to tag common topics. Consider, for example, the following tweet:

> **RT** @user: #wordsthatcanstartawar mariah carey thinks she's still 20

This text references other voices through various types of grammatical resources, such as projection via a mental process (Mariah carey thinks). These resources, as we will see in Chapter 4, form part of the ENGAGEMENT, a discourse semantic system for adopting a stance in relation to other potential positions (Martin and White 2005). Alongside making use of these resources, the text deploys two typographic conventions, shown in bold, that leverage the affordances of electronic text and that have emerged through grass-roots use. These conventions centre around three linguistic markers:

- addressing and referencing other users with @;
- republishing other tweets with RT;
- labelling topics with #.

Address and @mentions

The first convention marks address with the @ character when a user wishes to explicitly direct a micropost at another user. In these instances @ will be deployed as a deictic marker, as in the following example:

> **@User** Thanks for the #FF

Used in this way, the @ character indicates that the user name[2] which it precedes is directly addressed in the tweet. As such, it functions to mark a vocative, often occupying initial position in a clause, though it also can occur in medial or final position. When not in initial position, @+user name is more likely to indicate a reference to a user rather than to explicitly inscribe an address. For example:

> Talking to **@User1** about how I've known her for over 11 years! I am getting old, but like Dorian Gray, she remains young.

This tweet is not directly addressing User1 and instead indirectly refers to this user with what is termed a 'mention'.

Mentioning a user with the @ character in this way is a kind of amplified reference and potential tool for self-promotion since, depending on privacy settings and the evolving functionality of Twitter,[3] other users who follow this user may view the mention. The @mention is also amplified in the sense that the @ character is searchable. Mentions can be aggregated, and other users can search for particular instances. It is possible to retrieve all instances of @mentions to a given user (within a particular time window) with the Twitter search interface or using metadata and the Twitter API.

Considering @ more generally in electronic discourse, Honeycutt and Herring (2009, p. 4) provide an overview of the various uses of the character (examples added):

1 Addressivity – e.g. @user I really like you.
2 Reference – e.g. I really enjoyed @user's talk today.
3 Emoticons – e.g. @_@
4 Email – user@email.com
5 Locational 'at' – Eating pizza @ Mimmo's
6 Non-locational 'at' – I'm doing two things @ the same time.
7 Other – This is so @#%*ing stupid!

Taking into account current Twitter usage, the @ character seems to have undergone an evolution toward being an increasingly interpersonal resource. This follows a general trend in the evolution of punctuation identified by Knox (2009), namely. an evolution from textual functions toward a more interpersonal functions.

Retweeting

Another way of bringing external voices into a tweet is to republish another user's tweet within your own tweet. This is known as retweeting and is usually marked by the initialism RT to indicate that the body of the tweet is quoted text. In other words, RT marks grammatical projection, economically standing for 'User X has posted the following'. In most instances RT will be followed by the @ character to attribute the retweeted text to its original author. The following tweet uses this structure to indicate that @User2 is the source:

> RT @User2: Perhaps having people grow gardens shows them that it's a little harder to grow food than they think. #agcast

Thus retweeting 'allows members to relay or forward a tweet through their network' (Nagarajan et al. 2010, p. 295), marking the quoted text as notable and effectively recommending it to their followers.

Retweeting can significantly amplify the reach of a tweet, particularly when a user with a large body of followers, such as a celebrity, chooses to retweet something. Beyond rebroadcasting, retweeting 'contributes to a conversational ecology in which conversations are composed of a public interplay of voices that give rise to an emotional sense of shared conversational context' (Boyd et al. 2010, p. 1). The convention marks a tweet as worth the attention within this conversational context. As we will see in Chapter 4, the emergent convention allows the retweeter to display a stance toward the retweeted text and project it as inherently valuable to the community. This kind of evaluative appendage has also been noted by Page (2011), who, approaching media from the perspective of narrative, has suggested the role of retweeting in new 'co-tellership practices' and noted the tendency of celebrities to append evaluative assessment to their retweets as a means of aligning with their audience.

Hashtagging

Lastly, hashtags, explored in detail in Chapter 5, are a convention for marking an annotation of the topic of a tweet. As the name implies, a hashtag involves a hash (otherwise known as a pound) symbol marking the label appended to the tweet, for example #linguistics. Where there is more than one word assigned, it will usually be represented without spaces (e.g. #Iheartlinguistcs). Hashtag are a form of conversational tagging (Huang et al. 2010). The hashtag is a form of metadata that emerged through community use on Twitter. Its use may derive from internet relay chat (IRC) conventions for naming channels (#channelname), where a channel is the essential mechanism that people use to communicate with each other during an IRC session. As used on Twitter, the # character is used to mark a label that the user has assigned to a tweet. For example, #python in the following indicates that the tweet is about the programming language Python:

> Oh well at least the next Chapter should be fun 'Objects and Object Orientation' :) #python

The label means that that other users interested in Python can find the tweet even though this lexical item does not occur in the body of the tweet. They may do this by searching for the tag via the search interface that Twitter provides, or, if they are likely to have an ongoing interest in the tag, they may elect to subscribe to a feed of tweets containing this tag: a process known as following the tag.

The kind of collaborative tagging evolving with community use in social media is often referred to as a practice of folksonomy (Vander Wal 2007), or social tagging. This community-based metadata is very different to the top-down hierarchical approaches developed by subject classification in libraries. Whereas document classification involves experts, social tagging engages communities of general users. For example, it is used heavily on photo-sharing sites, such as Flickr, where it functions as a cooperative form of verbal indexing involving a bottom-up approach to the kind of classification previously achieved by reference librarians. Indeed hashtags have been likened to the concept 'better known to librarians as a subject heading' (Ovadia 2009, p. 203). The tags assigned provide 'access to the reader's view of aboutness in a way which was previously possible only on a small scale through elicitation experiments' (Kehoe and Gee 2011). A popular social-tagging site at the time of writing was Delicious, a service that encourages users to assign tags in the form of social 'bookmarks' describing the content of their favourite websites so that they can share these resources publically. Consensus and divergence in vocabulary choice for tags have been one of the main areas of research from an information science perspective. Some studies, for example, Schifanella and colleagues (2010, p. 279), look at consensus in terms of the patterning of the social network itself. This study looked at lexical and topical alignment in social networks and found that there was a local alignment in tag vocabularies among users even where the social-tagging system (e.g. Flickr) did not have a globally shared vocabulary.

Microblogging and communities of value

Microblogging, and social media in general, affords new insight into aspects of everyday life that have hitherto not been readily made public. Personal expression of routine experiences has never been subject to real-time mass dissemination in the way that we are currently witnessing. Microblogging services provide a forum where these routine experiences may be almost instantaneously broadcast, whether to share a positive moment or to satisfy the very human need to complain (see, for example, the type of minor, commonplace misfortunes posted with the fail meme in Chapter 8). Microposts frequently provide an opportunity for bonding around the quotidian, affording the private realm of daily experience a public audience.

The increasing pervasiveness of this form of personal disclosure arises from the history of online journaling and blogs, where authors often use their own lives as the focus of their material. The microblogger is engaging in a practice that 'centers on making the ordinary visible to others' (Oulasvirta et al. 2010, p. 238). A social need to remain in the collective consciousness of the social stream as it unfolds in time seems to motivate this kind of disclosure:

> What needs to be explained is somebody's willingness to stop the current activity, take out the phone, and expend effort to actively create such a 'peephole' for others. The key is to understand that a microblogger 'exists' through a staccato of one-liners, organized in reverse chronological

> order such that the most recent one fixes others' interpretation of his or her most current doings. (Oulasvirta et al. 2010, p. 248)

In this way microblogging can be seen as an ongoing performance of identity. Perhaps another significant explanatory factor is the human desire for affiliation: we exist within communities of other voices with which we wish to connect. The stances we adopt and observations and evaluations we share all exist relative to the meaning-making of the other members of our social network and to all other potential networks of meaning. In other words, we perform our online identities in order to connect with others.

The range of potential bonds that may be offered in a micropost is vast. A common bond around which users may affiliate is appreciation of a microcelebrity (Marwick 2010), a form of celebrity, distinct from traditional celebrity, that arises out of connection with an ambient audience via a kind of 'amping up' of popularity using social media (Senft 2008, p. 25). An example is the popular blogger Dooce, whose internet fame began when she was fired for writing about her colleagues on her blog. Alongside her blog content, this user produces additional content about her life and family via Twitter, where she commands an audience of followers of over 1.5 million.

Traditional celebrities also populate Twitter, attracting communities of fans who engage in public performances of affiliation (Marwick and Boyd 2011).The most frequently parodied community developing around one of these celebrities is that which concentrates around the singer Justin Beiber, who at the beginning of 2011 had a follower base of more than 7.5 million users, exceeding that of the US president at the time. These users are often mocked as 'beliebers', a reference to their apparent emotional fanaticism and manifest in expressions of Bieber-targetted affect (e.g. user names such as UserLuvBieber). Such a large user base means that Beiber frequently precipitates trending topics. For example, the following tweet by Beiber rapidly elevated the phrase Latin girls to a trending topic on 27 February 2011:

> shoutout to all of Latin America . . . i got love for all my Latin Girls

As one user quipped:

> Beliebers run Twitter. Hater or not. You have at least 1 belieber following you.

This user humorously comments on the way Justin Beiber fandom polarizes opinion on Twitter, with public appreciation of celebrities creating both an in-group rallying around positive values targeted at the public figure and an out-group who mock those values. For example, the following tweet is an example of the discourse of the latter:

> Attention all **#Beiber** fans! I am not a fan, in fact I hate the spastic! Don't follow me thinking I am, I'm not! I repeat, I am not!!

As I will elaborate in Chapter 5, hashtags play a role in coordinating such mass expression of value by focusing it around a particular ideational target (e.g. #Beiber). In other words, hashtags align users into 'overlapping communities of attitudinal rapport' (Martin 2004, p. 323).

Time and microblogging

Time is an important variable in microblogging. As part of the real-time web, microposts tend to disseminate material at the time it was generated and '[t]he stories told in Twitter prioritize the present moment (as signaled through the use of temporal adverbs like today, tonight and tomorrow)' (Page 2011, p. 161). Two different types of time are in play in microblogging: the unfolding of meaning in a text, that is, 'text time', and the 'real time' associated with the unfolding stream of posts. Meaning unfolds in a text 'dynamically as currents flowing through a stratified semiotic system' (Halliday 1991, p. 40). Halliday (Halliday and Martin 1993) described three kinds of semiotic change, or semogenesis: logogenesis, the unfolding of text, phylogenesis, the evolution of culture, and ontogenesis, the development of the meaning-making potential of a human over time. Once contiguity relations are added to a model of language such as SFL that primarily considers paradigmatic relations, the linguist is 'taking on a dynamic commitment' (Halliday 1991, p. 40). As such they are involved in modelling semiotic change.

Alongside logogenetic text time, there is the common time in which tweets unfold in the Twitter stream. This is captured as temporal metadata by Twitter and also displayed to users as a time stamp via the Twitter-web interface. Updates to the Twitter stream are almost instantaneous from a mobile device, meaning that this text time bears a close relationship to the lived experience of time by users. To adequately account for both kinds of time, discourse analysts require support in order to make plain the complex patterns generated as language patterns in microposts that emerge over time. This support should assist them in understanding how the linguistic features they are interested in increase or diminish in frequency and change over time. A likely technology for achieving this is text visualization (Zappavigna 2011a). The patterns may be within single user's Twitter stream, across groups of users or across the entire microblogging feed.

Twitter metadata allows exploration of collocation in the traditional corpus linguistics sense of the term to be extended diachronically. It affords a

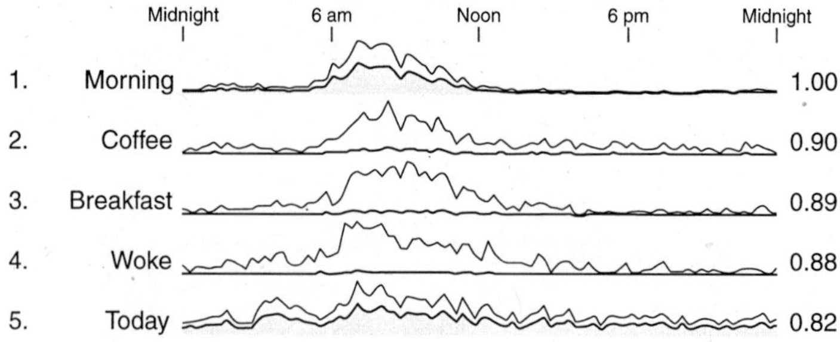

Figure 3.1 Words having a positive time correlation with "morning" (Clark 2009)

view of how particular couplings of meaning shift and change, enabling us to consider relationships between linguistic features in time series. For example, Figure 3.1 shows words that have a positive time correlation with a time series of word counts for 'morning' in the Twitter stream. The collocation of 'coffee' and 'morning' was a pattern present in HERMES, for example:

> @User That is hilarious! I needed a good laugh with my **morning coffee**! thx. ;)
>
> wow, a **coffee** in the **morning** is the best thing ever !!!
>
> partaking in my **morning coffee** and dose of Sportscenter. then spending the rest of the morning writing w/ @User. afternoon plans?
>
> @User I need **coffee** in the **mornings**! It's my picker upper!!

These tweets offer coffee appreciation as a potential rallying point for users who are concurrently engaging in practices of complaining about being up too early in the morning or of having to go to work. Figure 3.1 allows us to see the time dependency of the association between morning and coffee and the fact that, unsurprisingly, the relationship between these two words peaks in the early part of the day (which will clearly be different depending on the geographical location of the microbloggers).

In this book I use the text visualization software Twitter StreamGraph (Clark 2009) to show snapshots of lexis unfolding over short time periods in the Twitter stream. Streamgraphs are an example of a text visualization technique that does not efface logogenesis, the unfolding of text over time (Zappavigna et al. 2011). The visualization 'shows the usage over time for the words most highly associated with the search word' (Clark 2009). While an area graph usually shows a single data series, streamgraphs are a form of stacked area graph that represent multiple data series by stacking one on top of the other and presenting the series as unfolding 'streams'. Smooth curves are generated for these streams by interpolating between points to produce a flowing river of data. In a stacked area graph the height of the curve at a given point represents the total frequency of all features at that point, and thus each data series should be read as starting at zero rather than at the accumulative height.

This streamgraph technique is most useful to a linguist interested in the general trend of a data series or, in other words, the qualitative ebb and flow of features over the time series. It is also a useful technique for appreciating the relationships between the data series as they unfold by the overall impression of the relative amount of colour. The technique has been used to visualize box office revenues changing over time (Byron and Wattenberg 2008), changes in music-listening habits (Byron 2008), shifts in lexical themes in corpora with time (Havre et al. 2002) and changes in word association in Twitter status messages (Clark 2009).

In the case of microblogging texts and, in particular, Twitter, StreamGraphs allow multiple lexical items in tweets to be depicted as coloured streams flowing with the time series on a single graph. For example, Figure 3.2 shows a Twitter StreamGraph[4] for the lexical item 'coffee'. To generate the StreamGraph in Figure 3.2, the user has entered the search term 'coffee'. The coloured streams displayed represent lexis that collocates with coffee in the twitter stream over an interval of time (17:50 to 18:29) close to the time at which the query was made. The stream representation allows us to see how the frequency of a lexical item varies over time at the same time as other co-occurring items. For example, the stream selected in red is the word 'morning', and we can see its association with the search term coffee and with other words such as Starbucks, drink, and cup. The local

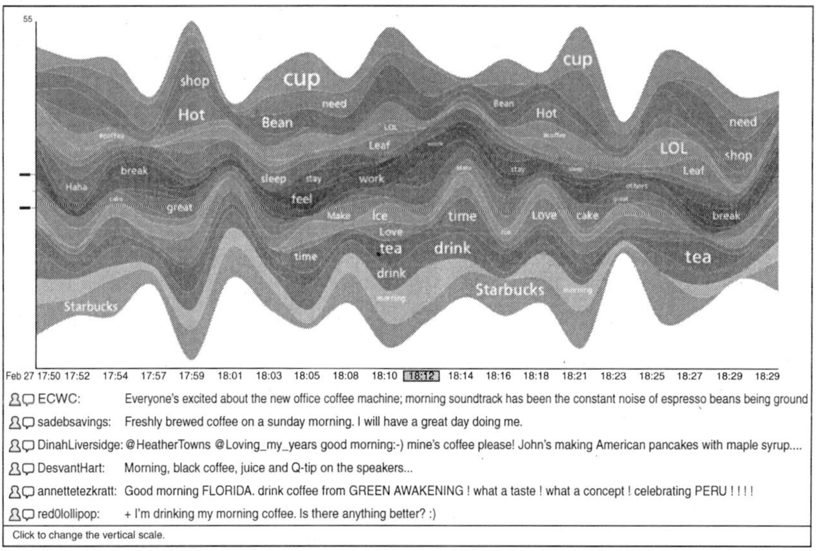

Figure 3.2 Twitter StreamGraph for 'coffee' (Clark 2009)

association of these terms is apparent within a single tweet; for example, the following tweet was part of the dataset used to generate the graph (a sample of which is shown under the graph in the figure):

+ I'm drinking my morning coffee. Is there anything better? :)

The streamgraph representation provides us with a view of more global patterns of collocational flow over time. While current automatic text-processing techniques mean that we are largely restricted to considering lexis rather than more complex discourse semantic features, the visualization offers some initial guidance to the discourse analyst attempting to understand the unfolding complexity of streams of microposts.

Linguistic patterns in the HERMES

In order to understand the linguistic tendencies seen in microblogging, I will look at some of the most common patterns in the HERMES. We will begin with a top-down approach by inspecting a word-frequency list. Following this broad view I will consider some frequent n-grams that reveal common syntagmatic patterns in the corpus. N-grams are used within corpus linguistics to look at clusters of words in texts of different lengths (e.g. a 3-gram is a 3-word cluster, where n is equal to 3). The general principle is that previous $n-1$ words in a sequence can be used to predict the next word as part of models trained on very large corpora. These techniques are not employed as an end in themselves but instead to guide close discourse analysis of specific instances of texts.

Table 3.1 shows the 20 most common words in the corpus as a ranked frequency list. Three items which would not be expected to occur in a frequency list for a traditional, non-CMC corpus have been highlighted in grey in the table. These are

- @ – The 'at' character is usually used to address as tweet to another user.
- *HTTP* – The characters HTTP (Hyper Text Transfer Protocol[5]) appear at the beginning of weblinks in HERMES followed by a colon which the Wordsmith system has interpreted as a word break. Nevertheless, HTTP acts as a marker indicating that the full sequence included a weblink and, as such, is useful in counting the number of weblinks that occurred in the HERMES.
- # – The hash character is used to mark a hashtag, typically to indicate the topic of a tweet.
- *RT* – Two characters that refer to a 'retweet', the act of republishing another tweet within your own tweet.

Table 3.1 The 20 most frequent words in the Twitter corpus

N	Word	Frequency	%
1	***@word***	**4,037,829**	**4.04**
2	THE	3,358,659	3.15
3	TO	2,379,223	2.23
4	I	2,236,470	2.10
5	A	1,674,654	1.57
6	**HTTP**	**1,631,187**	**1.53**
7	AND	1,545,943	1.45
8	OF	1,217,398	1.14
9	***#word***	**1,253,853**	**1.25**
10	YOU	1,194,631	1.12
11	IS	1,120,058	1.05
12	IN	1,118,227	1.05
13	**RT**	**990,287**	**0.93**
14	ON	906,996	0.85
15	FOR	891,100	0.84
16	THAT	871,925	0.82
17	MY	858,657	0.81
18	IT	853,209	0.80
19	THIS	678,193	0.64
20	ME	676,702	0.63

All of these items are examples of resources for bringing voices from other texts into a tweet (theorized as associated with the ENGAGEMENT system, explained in Chapter 4). It is interesting that these three items in this frequency list that are dependent on the mode of communication (i.e. the microblogging service) are items that work in the service of interactivity. This interpersonal orientation is an important pattern that will be illuminated further in this chapter as we look at common n-grams that characterize HERMES.

Word lists as stand-alone entities are of limited utility and are more useful when compared with lists derived from other corpora, particularly reference corpora. However, determining an appropriate reference corpus for use with HERMES is a problematic task given that it is larger than most available traditional corpora. In addition, we are dealing with a corpus of 'international' English, and many traditional corpora focus on a single kind of English, for example, the British national corpus. Further, building corpora of computer-mediated communication is an emergent area, and so appropriately balanced corpora are difficult to access. A candidate reference corpus was the 25-billion-word USENET corpus (Shaoul and Westbury 2011); however, the large size of this corpus was beyond the computing power of this project and would have required a cluster of computers to generate analyses such as n-grams.

Table 3.2 Comparing the 20 most frequent words in the Corpus of Contemporary American English (COCA) with those in HERMES

COCA			HERMES		
N	Word	Frequency	N	Word	Frequency
1	THE	22,038,615	1	@word	**4,037,829**
2	BE	12,545,825	2	THE	3,358,659
3	AND	10,741,073	3	TO	2,379,223
4	OF	10,343,885	4	I	2,236,470
5	A	10,144,200	**5**	A	1,674,654
6	IN	6,996,437	6	**HTTP**	**1,631,187**
7	TO	6,332,195	7	AND	1,545,943
8	HAVE	4,303,955	8	OF	1,217,398
9	TO	3,856,916	**9**	***#word***	**1,253,853**
10	IT	3,872,477	10	YOU	1,194,631
11	**I**	**3,978,265**	**11**	IS	1,120,058
12	THAT	3,430,996	12	IN	1,118,227
13	FOR	3,281,454	13	**RT**	**990,287**
14	YOU	3,081,151	14	ON	906,996
15	HE	2,909,254	15	FOR	891,100
16	WITH	2,683,014	16	THAT	871,925
17	ON	2,485,306	17	MY	858,657
18	DO	2,573,587	18	IT	853,209
19	SAY	1,915,138	19	THIS	678,193
20	THIS	1,885,366	20	ME	676,702

We might compare the HERMES frequency list with frequency lists from the 410-million-word Corpus of Contemporary American English (COCA). American English is frequent in HERMES since the majority of Twitter users reside in the United States. A significant limitation of the comparison is that COCA does not include a CMC in its constituent registers (spoken, fiction, magazine, newspaper, academic). Table 3.2 shows the 20 most frequent words in COCA alongside those in HERMES.

The most common item in HERMES, @ symbol, was most often used as part of an @mention. Its frequency indicates the prominence of dialogic interaction in the corpus, a point also recognized by Honeycutt and Herring (2009), who note the conversationality of Twitter stemming from the addressivity afforded by @. In addition, at first glance, Twitter discourse appears more focused on the self, given the higher ranking in HERMES of *I* (4 in HERMES; 11 in COCA), *me* (20 in HERMES; 62 in COCA), and *my* (17 in HERMES; 44 in COCA). However, we should also note the higher ranking in HERMES of *you* (10 in HERMES; 14 in COCA), suggesting Twitter's dialogic function where people use the service to interact and converse (the variant *u* was not tracked in this count but would likely increase the ranking). The dominance of the interpersonal will also be seen in the most common n-grams in the corpus explored in the next section.

Syntagmatic patterns in HERMES

While a word list offers an interesting starting point for discourse analysis, its utility is limited since meanings are made logogentically as texts unfold via complex, multidimensional syntagmatic and paradigmatic patterns. I will now consider some of the most frequent syntagmatic patterns in HERMES. The technique used throughout this book for inspecting these patterns is n-gram analysis (otherwise known as cluster analysis), where n is the number of items in the cluster. N-grams were computed automatically using the software application Wordsmith. Table 3.3 shows the 20 most frequent 3-grams in HERMES. The most common 3-gram, 'Thanks for the', will be considered in detail in this chapter, while some of the other clusters in this table will be explored in relation to evaluative language in the next chapter.

However, in keeping with a systemic functional approach to language, I will also assume a paradigmatic perspective on the corpus by using concordance lines. Bednarek (2010, p. 239) suggests that concordance lines offer the potential for such a dual lens along paradigmatic and syntagmatic axes. For example, following her logic, we can inspect 'thanks for the' (the most common 3-gram in the corpus) along both axes. Along the syntagmatic axis, we can see the collocates of this structure (marked by the border around the first entry in the concordance lines in Figure 3.3).

Table 3.3 The 20 most common 3-grams[6] in HERMES

N	Word	Frequency	%
1	THANKS FOR THE	26,498	0.02
2	I HAVE TO	21,230	0.02
3	I HAVE A	20,919	0.02
4	I WANT TO	18,835	0.02
5	GOING TO BE	18,480	0.02
6	I NEED TO	18,443	0.02
7	ONE OF THE	18,158	0.02
8	WE ARE THE	18,026	0.02
9	I'M GOING TO	17,516	0.02
10	TO GO TO	17,096	0.02
11	A LOT OF	16,904	0.02
12	ARE THE WORLD	16,071	0.02
13	TRY IT HTTP	14,999	0.01
14	I THINK I	14,947	0.01
15	IS GOING TO	13,713	0.01
16	I LOVE YOU	13,415	0.01
17	OF THE DAY	12,892	0.01
18	TO BE A	12,765	0.01
19	LOOKING FORWARD TO	12,755	0.01
20	CHECK IT OUT	12,615	0.01

@User	**Thanks for the**	ff babe x
@User Hi -	**thanks for the**	RT. Much appreciated :)
@User	**thanks for the**	follow hun
	Thanks for the	RTs @User @User2 @User3 @User4 Happy #FF!
@User	**thanks for the**	Tip. i guess i expect that software with millions of users to work properly :)
	thanks for	Support, love ya @User @User2 :)

Figure 3.3 The dual affordance of concordance lines

Along the paradigmatic axis we can see that ff could be substituted by RT, tip and support, affording a perspective on the choice of collocates. This paradigmatic gaze is shown in grey in the figure. These two kinds of approaches to patterning are employed in the next section, which explores this 3-gram in more detail.

The most frequent 3-gram in HERMES: 'Thanks for the'

Inspecting common clusters in HERMES provides the first significant clue pointing to the importance of interpersonal meaning in microblogging. The most common 3-gram, 'Thanks for the', is a pattern indicating interpersonal reciprocity. The pattern is an example of Twitter users directing a message of thanks to other users and was most usually accompanied by the @ character, rendering it a direct address. It occurred in the following tweet, for example, where an author thanked another user for retweeting one of his or her microposts:

> @user **Thanks for the** RT. Hope you are having a wonderful week.

The most frequent target of thanks was a Follow Friday (FF) mention, for example:

> @User Thanks for the FF :)

'FF', refers to Follow Friday, a Twitter meme[7] with the function of 'promoting other people on Twitter – anyone you think your followers should also be following for any reason' (Horovitch 2009). The concept centres upon users mentioning in a tweet people worthy of such subscription each Friday. For example (positive evaluation in bold):

> #followfriday @User – always **inspiring** art and a **nice** guy!

This tweet invites the audience to follow @User, deploying the hashtag #followfriday to indicate allegiance with the meme. Users tracking this hashtag will automatically see this tweet, or, alternatively, a user can search by using the hashtag as a query.

Being the most frequent 3-gram in HERMES and inherently dialogic in this way, the cluster strongly suggests that microblogging is more than simply posting about the day's activities. The pattern provides some initial evidence that an important facet of microblogging is reciprocation of social bonds. Users are typically thanking each other for providing some form of interpersonal recognition or support. Processes of thanking also have a

Table 3.4 Examples of the most frequent occupants of R1 for the 3-gram 'thanks for the'

N	R1	Example
1	FF	@User Thanks for the ff babe x
2	RT	@User Hi – thanks for the RT. Much appreciated :)
3	follow	@User thanks for the follow hun
4	RTs	Thanks for the RTs @User @User2 @User3 @User4 Happy #FF!
5	tip	@User thanks for the tip. i guess i expect that software with millions of users to work properly :)
6	support	Thanks for the support, love ya @User @User2 :)

politeness function (Brown and Levinson 1978). Table 3.4 shows examples of the most common items that occupied R1, the position directly to the right of the cluster, giving an indication of the targets of the thanks. The first four of these items in R1 (FF, RT, follow and RTs) refer to social practices that have emerged on Twitter for recognizing other users.

The second most common item in R1 was RT. As explained earlier, this typographic convention indicates that the post involves a retweet, republication of another tweet within your own, as in the following example:

> #followfriday **RT @User2**: want to get my followers up to 30.000, it's been stuck at 28,794 for too bloody long, converts come forward!

User2's original post has been republished in this tweet along with the Follow Friday hashtag to indicate that the person posting this tweet endorses the appeal for a wider body of followers made by the original poster. This is an example where the @ symbol is functioning as an attribution marker, working in tandem with the RT to specify the original authorship of the tweets. The pattern 'thanks for the RT' involves users expressing appreciation for this rebroadcast:

> @User Hi – thanks for the RT. Much appreciated :)

As this example suggests the thanks is usually accompanied by positive evaluative language. Examples 5 and 6 in Table 3.4 are typical of a second function of 'thanks for the', namely, expressing gratitude for some service rendered. Lexis that occupied this R1 slot also included *hugs*, *concern*, *time*, *offer to help*, and *feedback*, *input*, *link*, *heads up*, *article*. The former group are examples of emotional support and counsel, while the latter group tend toward an offer of information (although this category is fuzzy and blurs into 'advice').

Thus the two main functions of 'thanks for the' appear to be offering appreciation for public acknowledgement received and showing gratitude for counsel. The target of the thanks being social processes rather than goods accords with the highly interpersonal nature of Twitter and the value placed on social relations. Looking at the frequent collocates of 'thanks for the' in COCA, this latter kind of gratitude for some kind of material object (e.g. thanks for the book) is much more frequent in HERMES. Tweets are highly dialogic and part of a heteroglossic (Bakhtin 2008) Twitter stream in which an important social process is showing reciprocity by public thanking of other users. These users are clearly doing more than broadcasting the personal, self-indulgent or mundane details of their daily routine. They are producing more than a kind of monoglossic, self-indulgent stream of consciousness that is oblivious to other texts. This is not to say, however, that microposts are not highly self-promoting (Page 2011). The act of thanking someone for a RT or FF is a means of demonstrating a high perceived status in the community and displaying one's place within the social network.

CHAPTER FOUR

Evaluation in microblogging

In this chapter I will argue that microblogging is rarely about presenting bald facts or narrating activity. While it can be an immediate way to deliver information to an audience, this is not undertaken in an interpersonal void. We use social media in the service of sharing values as a way of communicating our experience of the world and bonding with others. Microblogging services, such as Twitter, are often parodied as the domain of the self-obsessed or compulsive, the kind of user who would post 'I had toast for breakfast', 'Just finished breakfast', and 'About to leave for work'. While amusing, this kind of characterization does not reflect the complex ways in which microblogging is integrating itself into social life and its rapid growth as a technology for sharing social bonds. Some commentators, however, have begun to appreciate the importance of interpersonal meaning, observing that valued (and thus highly retweeted) tweets 'tend to make an observation, take a stance, or crack a joke – none of which fall under the umbrella of using Twitter to tell the world what you're doing' (McCracken 2009).

Many studies outside linguistics have considered evaluation in social media. Within linguistics there is a significant body of research that considers evaluation from the perspective of corpus linguistics (Hunston 2011; Bednarek 2008; Morley and Partington 2009). However, to date, the field that has most thoroughly explored microblogging as a resource for understanding emotional language is sentiment analysis, a subdomain of computational linguistics. This area, sometimes also referred to as opinion mining, aims to automatically[1] detect emotional language in text, for example, in film reviews (Whitelaw et al. 2005). These studies often use data sets derived from social media in the form of public reaction to major events, such as the Olympics (Gruzd et al. 2011). Bollen and colleagues (2009) 'regard an individual tweet as a temporally authentic microscopic instantiation of public mood state', suggesting that modelling this kind of data can reveal collective emotive trends (Bollen et al. 2009). Applications of sentiment detection using social media include prediction of the stock market based on 'Twitter mood' (Bollen et al. 2011). Interestingly, one study found 'strong evidence that important events in Twitter are associated with increases in average negative sentiment strength' (Thelwall et al. 2011). However, we should use caution drawing conclusions about meaning from automated analysis of evaluative language given that the subjectivity of categorizing evaluative language poses difficulties for a human linguist, let alone a machine!

I will begin this chapter by explaining appraisal theory (Martin and White 2005), a theory of evaluative language developed with SFL. Examples of evaluative language in HERMES will be used to illustrate the different regions of meaning that the theory traverses. As a first step into considering the role of evaluation in microblogging, I will also explain some of the main patterns in HERMES for each system of appraisal. Following this, the focus will be the interplay of emotional language and emoticons, textual representations associated with expressing attitude. The approach taken combines evidence from corpus patterns and close discourse analysis.

Introducing Appraisal theory

Evaluation is a domain of interpersonal meaning where language is used to express attitudes and to adopt stances about other texts. Appraisal theory argues that the emotional reaction to the world through infant protolanguage develops as we are socialized into a culture and into institutions (Martin and White 2005, p. 45). Feeling becomes institutionalized as ethics and morality, forming the JUDGEMENT system with which we construe rules and regulations regarding behaviour (top example, Figure 4.1). Feeling is also institutionalized as aesthetics and value, forming the APPRECIATION system with which we generate assessments based on our reactions to phenomena (bottom example, Figure 4.1). The sections which follow explain each of the discourse semantic systems involved in making these meanings.

A system network for Appraisal

Before considering the systems of evaluation defined by appraisal theory, it is necessary to explain what 'system' means within the theory and the particular modelling strategy that is uses to represent systems, namely the system network. SFL systematizes meaning as choice. This systemic orientation arose out of the Firthian tradition in linguistics (Firth 1957). Firth asserted that a distinction needed to be made between structure

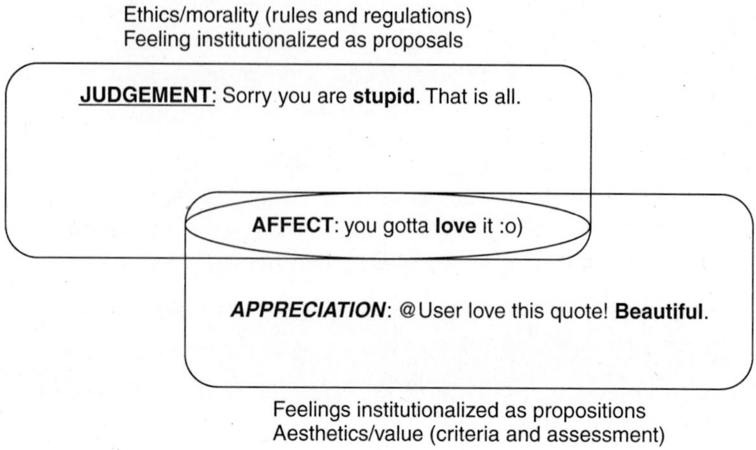

Figure 4.1 The institutionalization of AFFECT (adapted from Martin and White 2005, p. 45)

and system, that is, between syntagmatic and paradigmatic relations in language. Firth's ideas about how the notion of a system might be used to model language were taken up in Halliday's development of system networks. System networks are networks of interrelated options that are organized paradigmatically, in terms of 'what could go instead of what', rather than syntagmatically in terms of structure (Halliday and Matthiessen 2004, p. 22). They are an alternative to modelling language as a catalogue of structures.

System networks are aligned with thinking quantitatively about the patterning in a text or corpus. Within a single text or a corpus of texts some patterns are more likely than others since the 'grammar of language is not only the grammar of what is possible but also a grammar of what is probable' (Nesbitt and Plum 1988, p. 9). Within SFL, work on probabilistic profiling of grammar was begun by Halliday in a quantitative study that argued that the selection of features in a system is either equi-probable or skewed (Halliday 1991). According to Halliday, modelling tendency with the theoretical construct known as probability 'is just the technicalizing of "modality" from everyday grammar' and our ability to comment on such tendency 'is what makes it possible for natural language to function as metalanguage' (Halliday and Webster 2005, p. 238). In this tradition, Matthiessen (2006) has argued that 'systemic profiles' produced using analyses of corpora offer a way of representing the patterning of particular texts, text types and the overall systemic potential of language. These profiles are counts of selections from linguistic systems that can be made along the cline of instantiation.[2]

This type of work is taken up in some sections of computational linguistics.[3] For example, there has been work in the area of text

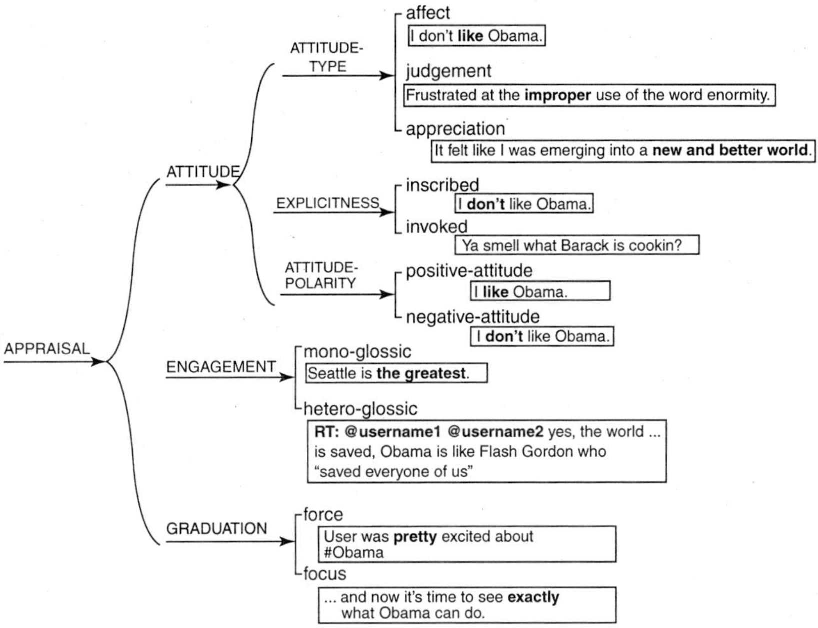

Figure 4.2 The appraisal system (Martin and White 2005)

categorization using systemic features to automatically group texts into registers or other categorization schemes. Machine learning on 'functional lexical features' has been used for stylistic text classification to differentiate texts in terms of, for example, the kind of appraisal language that they employ (Argamon et al. 2007). Systemic features, that is, lexical items that are the most delicate manifestation of particular system networks, have been used in tasks such as financial scam classification, where they have been employed to separate documents into registers based on variance in levels of interpersonal distance in texts (Whitelaw et al. 2006).

Figure 4.2 provides examples of each region of appraisal displayed on a system network as theorized by Martin and White (2005). The network adopts the convention whereby capitalized labels above the arrows indicate different systems of meaning, and the lowercase labels at the end of each path mark features within systems. A square bracket represents a choice between two options in a system (an 'or' relation), while a brace represents simultaneous choices (an 'and' relation). For example, the ATTITUDE system involves three more delicate systems from which a choice can be made:

- AFFECT – expressing emotion
- JUDGEMENT – assessing behaviour
- APPRECIATION – estimating value

The examples in the boxes, tweets from the Obama Win corpus (Chapter 9), illustrate each type of attitudinal appraisal. This network may be further specified to greater levels of delicacy depending on the kind of analysis in which it is being used.

Depending on the target and source of the evaluation, lexis such as 'good' can work with any of the ATTITUDE systems. Consider the difference between JUDGEMENT in the following tweet:

> Thank god is the weekend, time off for **good** behaviour

and affect:

> I feel really **good**, finally reached the 1,000 followers who wanted both!!

or appreciation:

> Got to have some best friend time tonight, pack a few boxes and drink some **good** wine. Going to bed content.

While microbloggers may expend a great deal of semiotic energy complaining about life, microblogging is also a resource of expressing aesthetic pleasure. The third most frequent 5-gram in HERMES was 'going to be a good' (582 instances), where 'good' almost always functioned as APPRECIATION:

> On my way into town to meet the girls :D **going to be a good** day!

In the cluster 'going to be a good day', 'day' is the target of the POSITIVE APPRECIATION. Some frequent targets of good that occupied R1 position are shown in Table 4.1. As this table suggests, the targets of APPRECIATION are usually things rather than people (which as we will see are typically JUDGED rather than APPRECIATED).

The AFFECT system

AFFECT is the region of meaning concerned with 'registering positive and negative feelings: do we feel happy or sad, confident or anxious, interested or bored?' (Martin and White 2005, p. 42). It is not uncommon for users to devote an entire micropost to detailing their current sentiment, offering up this expression as a potential bond that they contribute to the ecosystem of ambient emoters. Table 4.2 gives examples of the types of AFFECT Martin and White specify, with illustrative tweets from HERMES distinguished

Table 4.1 The most common R1[4] collocates for 'going to be a good'

N	R1	Example
1	DAY	Already feeling like it's going to be a good day! :)
2	NIGHT	Hair..nails..make up . . . tonight is going to be a good night =)
3	ONE	@user Not sure if that was your own quote but it was a good one. Thanks keeping it real man
4	WEEKEND	@user Hope you feel better soon and have a good weekend if your not on xx
5	YEAR	Got my licence back, yee yee!!! And my tags. this is gonna be a good year
6	WEEK	@user hello sweetness, how are you? Did u have a good week?
7	TIME	I am finding that now is a good time for sleeping . . .
8	MOVIE	The kid in the striped pajamas is a depressing but hella good movie.
9	FRIDAY	@user good night I promise i will talk tomorrow have a good Friday
10	SHOW	The deep end is a pretty good show

Table 4.2 Types of affect, adapted from Martin and White (2005, p. 51)

Affect	Positive	Negative
Dis/inclination	@User seriously – I *long* to come back and lounge poolside for five or six days . . .	@User I'm *wary* to say. Don't want you laughing at me.
Un/happiness	@user and I *adore* you.	Can't shake this *melancholy*. Early back to work from the doctor's office. I hope work feels good.
In/security	@User has emily been getting more *confident* with her skating?	@User I have not thought much about anteaters before, and I am now truly *freaked out*.
Dis/satisfaction	@User Congrats Darius! So *chuffed* you made the final! Good luck for next week!	fckn sick of takin these nasty ass pills! ughhhh :(

by polarity (examples marked in bold). Users are most commonly reporting on their own affectual state with 'I' being the most frequent collocate of AFFECT such as 'love*' in HERMES.

Indeed 'love' is the most common instance of AFFECT in HERMES. I LOVE YOU was the sixteenth most frequent 3-gram in the corpus and the only INSCRIBED AFFECT in the top 20 3-grams. This pattern was frequently followed by the heart emoticon <3 and coupled with a direct @ address as shown in the following tweet, where the user addressed is the trigger for the POSITIVE AFFECT.

Going to bed. Goodnight dear @User **! I love you <3**

Further examples are given in the ensuing concordance lines shown below:

@User whooo! have a great show everyone:) kelly	**i love you**	!!!:D
@User	**I love you**	lotss and lotsss like jelly tots!! ;-) xxxxxxxxxx
@User	**I love you**	so much girly!! Your the best and everything will be okay! Your awesome B!
@User HEHEHEHEHHE!	**I love you**	too and think 'bout you all the time. I can't wait to see you again! x Night.
@User thankyou for following me :D	**i love you!**	Xx

Other common 3-grams involving love are shown in Table 4.3. A very frequent target of the second most common 3-gram listed, I LOVE THE, was the domain of music. This pattern was associated with the most frequent hashtag in HERMES, *#nowplaying* used to bond around values of music appreciation (see Chapter 5). Similarly, I LOVE THAT was usually used to share a common positive assessment by referencing something in another tweet:

@User I love that show!

The HERMES corpus collection period coincided with Valentine's Day and thus may have resulted in an over-representation of tweets either directly about romance or playing on a romantic theme. These were sometimes

Table 4.3 The top ten 3-grams for 'love*' in HERMES

N	Cluster	Freq.	Example
1	I LOVE YOU	14,102	@User thanks sweetie for #FF i love you too :)
2	I LOVE THE	9,786	Is it weird that I love the smell of #windex
3	I LOVE THAT	6,553	@User wow, I LOVE that movie!
4	I LOVE IT	6,134	SOOOOON as UberTwitter stops acting up I will show yall how crazy this snow is lol I LOVE IT
5	I LOVE THIS	5,991	#nowplaying We gotta liiiiiiiiiiiiiiive like we're dying *.* oh gosh, i love this song!
6	LOVE LOVE LOVE	5,366	@User Omg – the acoustic in that song makes me weeeeeak! I love love love it too!

labelled with #vday to indicate that they were about Valentine's Day and, as we will see in the following chapter, to invite other users to bond around this topic:

> Happy Valentine's Day everyone! I love all of my followers! #love #vday http://myloc.me/3OhnQ

As the examples I have selected to exemplify AFFECT have suggested, this system is most often used in the tweets as a resource for sharing observations about common feelings as well as expressing personal sentiment.

The APPRECIATION system

This system is a discourse semantic resource for expressing attitudes about objects, states and processes. Martin and White (2005, p. 56) define APPRECIATION as those resources by which the value of things are construed: 'our "reactions" to things (do they catch our attention; do they please us?), their "composition" (balance and complexity), and their "value" (how innovative, authentic, timely etc.)' (Martin and White 2005, p. 56). For example, the evaluative word *beautiful* in Figure 4.1 is an example of APPRECIATION because it makes an aesthetic assessment. Table 4.4 provides examples from HERMES of each type of APPRECIATION.

Table 4.4 Type of appreciation, adapted from Martin and White (2005, p. 56)

	Positive	Negative
Reaction: impact 'did it grab me?'	Biathlon event in Vancouver is fascinating. We're talking cross-country skiing and rifle shooting here.	@User lmao thats how dull my life is ;) LOL.
Reaction: quality 'did I like it?'	@User any reasons why? i would of thought it would be quite appealing	His ear is really ugly and gross.
Composition: balance 'did it hang together?'	@ROtotheD a powder u mix with milk or juice 1 for breakfast 1 for lunch and balanced meal. I think it made me lactose intol and gallstones!	Yet another situation where I have to just re-purchase something I need because my possessions are too disordered to find the one I have.
Composition: Complexity 'was it hard to follow?'	@User I use books to construct bookshelves. It's an elegant solution.	@User its quite confusing tho. like alot of things very unclear.
Valuation: 'was it worthwhile?'	@User You have valuable info. Hope that you'll follow us.	The dance sucked. my life is worthless and people don't give a fuck about anyone but themselves. Why do I even live?

Throughout this chapter and, indeed, this book, we will oscillate or 'shunt'[5] between a corpus and instance perspective on microblogging. For example, if we look closely at a sample of instances of the 5-gram, GOING TO BE A GOOD DAY, we find examples of sarcasm. For example, the following tweets construe negative appreciation about the day to come:

> You know its **going to be a good day** when your professor tells you at 8am that you have to 'pull yourself together.' Thanks thursday night.
>
> You know its **going to be a good day** when you wake up to a kid covered in puke.
>
> You know its **going to be a good day** when a crazy person starts to crap themselves in line

The sarcastic meaning is not directly retrievable from a word list or n-gram analysis without qualitative post-processing via manual inspection and annotation of concordance lines.

APPRECIATION and link sharing

One of the social functions of Twitter appears to be sharing interesting links that users find on the web. APPRECIATION is often deployed in HERMES to evaluate a weblink that the user has deemed noteworthy and wishes to share with his or her followers. The APPRECIATION *great* was often used in these instances:

> a great article! http://point5design.wordpress.com/2010/02/19/positive-thinking/

The target of APPRECIATION in this example is a blog post about positive thinking. Indeed, noteworthy weblink sharing is a function inscribed in the Twitter home page (as manifest in 2009) under the heading 'Nifty queries, along' with the suggested query 'cool filter: links'. This query will return tweets containing the string 'cool' along with a weblink. The assumption made by the designers appears to have been that users will like to find links that have been positively appreciated by others. Certainly tweets frequently occur in HERMES that contain weblinks coupled with inscribed evaluation, most often APPRECIATION. For example (POSITIVE APPRECIATION is marked in bold):

> **Amazing** hobby!! watch all the way.. very **cool** http://bit.ly/agU1Sb

The link in this tweet points to a gallery of photographs of life-like miniature models built by the owner.

In many tweets the APPRECIATION is not inscribed but rather invoked by the context. For example, the following tweets contains no specific evaluative lexis directly appraising the weblink:

> Greek slump threatens debt plan, EU aid elusive (Reuters) http://bit.ly/9aS341

As this example shows, in place of such meta-evaluation there is often a quotation of the news headline itself (which may, in turn, contain evaluation but at a different order of abstraction to evaluation of the hyperlinked text). In these cases we might suppose that the act of posting indicates that the link is deemed noteworthy. APPRECIATION could, however, be construed in language (although not necessarily as inscribed appraisal), for example, via imperatives such as 'check out', 'read', 'see' or 'go to':

> Need a #vacation? Check out http://br.st/8IK for a travel agency

Tweets containing these kinds of imperatives were often marketing by corporations and news services.

The JUDGEMENT system

Instead of making an aesthetic assessment, the JUDGEMENT system critiques human behaviour: what people say and believe. This can be further regionalized into two areas of meaning: social esteem and social sanction:

> **Judgements** of **esteem** have to do with 'normality' (how unusual someone is), 'capacity' (how capable they are) and 'tenacity' (how resolute they are); **judgements** of **sanction** have to do with 'veracity' (how truthful someone is) and 'propriety' (how ethical someone is). (Martin and White 2005, p. 52)

Social esteem can be further delineated into NORMALITY, CAPACITY and TENACITY (Table 4.5). NORMALITY considers behaviour in terms of deviation from the status quo, CAPACITY in terms of ability and TENACITY in terms of endurance. For instance, the social relationship of Twitter 'following' attracts judgement of social esteem in microposts:

> Once you get **good** followers that are happy with you, then you have a solid business online

In the example the followers are appraised with the system of TENACITY in terms of loyalty. Similar examples are shown in the bottom row of Table 4.5.

Table 4.5 Judgement, social esteem. Adapted from Martin and White (2005, p. 53)

Social esteem	Positive [admire]	Negative [criticize]
Normality 'How special'?	Night Twitter ^^ and all the cool people who were talking to me too	What is @User doin with this weirdo lmfao
Capacity 'How capable?'	RT @User: just had a lightbulb moment. emailed clever people to see what they make of it. More soon. :) [*checks email*]	@User There are alot of dumb people in the world
Tenacity 'How dependable?'	@User Congrats on the win, but what is the point of you Twittering if you aren't going to let your loyal followers know in advance ;-)	unfaithful followers have no life especially if they follow a billion ppl they get mad cuz you aint wasting time entertaining them

Table 4.6 Judgement, social sanction. Adapted from Martin and White (2005, p. 53)

Social sanction	Positive [praise]	Negative [condemn]
Veracity [truth] 'How honest?	Richard Balls of Balls Bros reports City bankers are discretely quaffing fine Burgundy rather than popping Champagne.	I really really really really really really don't like you. You are honestly the most untactful person I have ever met in my life. Poo.
Propriety [ethics] 'How far beyond reproach?'	Just backed my truck into a woman's car at Starbuck's. I appreciate that she was polite and friendly about it.	@User he should respect your opinion, and value your friendship enough not to be rude. I'm sorry :(

Social sanction delineates behaviour as truthfulness or decorum (Table 4.6). As we will see in Chapter 7, many people use Twitter as a platform for complaining about daily life, and often this includes critiquing the people around them. For example, the hashtag #petpeeve is a meme in HERMES used to label behaviours deemed to contravene social decorum. Sometimes the behaviour is presented with no INSCRIBED JUDGEMENT and instead a hashtag is used to invoke JUDGEMENT; for example,

> #petpeeve: people that drive 20mph

In other cases INSCRIBED JUDGEMENT is present, prosodically reinforcing the INVOKED JUDGEMENT made via the hashtag; for example (inscribed judgement marked in bold),

> Why must adults drag their feet? Actually, why must PEOPLE in general drag their feet? It's a **rude** habit! #petpeeve

In general, there seems to be a tendency in social media to avoid directing negative judgement at another user, in contrast to the kind of 'flaming' seen in forums and chat rooms earlier in internet history. For example, as we will see in Chapter 7, many slang terms that were originally used as insults via web 1.0 (when anonymity was still a possibility) have softened interpersonally over time and come to be used for light humour in social media.

A note on invoked attitude

Evaluative meanings can be made using a variety of resources, many of which are indirect, relying on connotation. Thus, alongside considering the type of ATTITUDE, we need to account for EXPLICITNESS; that is, whether or not the ATTITUDE is INSCRIBED in specific evaluative lexis that can be identified in the text. For example, the following tweet deploys unambiguously evaluative lexis (inscriptions in bold):

> @User I **LOVE** YOU! Thank you for being so **sweet** & for being so **POSITIVE**! YOU are the **best**! :)

On the other hand, evaluation can also be implied when 'the selection of ideational meanings is enough to invoke evaluation, even in the absence of attitudinal lexis that tells us directly how to feel' (Martin and White 2005, p. 62). In these instances the appraisal is said to be INVOKED. For example, we can infer an expression of AFFECT, most likely anger or frustration, in the following tweet from the act of imagined violence described:

> RT @User: I can see myself putting my fist through the tv any minute now . . . #6nations

There is, however, no explicit lexis in the tweet inscribing AFFECT and the target of the negative appraisal is not directly indicated. Instead, the hashtag '#6nations' is used to indicate that the Six Nations Championship (an international rugby union competition) is the item that is negatively judged (for an exploration of hashtags functioning as the target of appraisal, see Chapter 5).

The ENGAGEMENT system

Clearly attitudes are not expressed in isolation. ENGAGEMENT is the region of meaning concerned with managing the linguistic resources available for adopting a stance in relation to other positions in other texts. We may use this system to construe solidarity or to distance ourselves from these texts. Poynton (1990) argues that we should consider solidarity along two simultaneous dimensions:

> 'Solidarity' then can be analysed as incorporating two distinguishable dimensions of social relations: a distance dimension and an affective (strength of feeling) dimension, where the attitude or affect may be directed not towards other people but towards the shared activity of shared point of view. (p. 92)

The lack of obligation to reply in microblogging problematizes the notion of reciprocity directly applied to expression of online solidarity. The non-reciprocal nature of Twitter following relationships means that solidarity may be marked differently, for example, through in-group language such as slang (see Chapter 7).

The development of appraisal theory in the area of ENGAGEMENT has its origins in notions of intertextuality:

> Our approach is informed by Bakhtin's/Voloshinov's now widely influential notions of dialogism and heteroglossia under which all verbal communication, whether written or spoken, is 'dialogic' in that to speak or write is always to reveal the influence of, refer to, or to take up in some way, what has been said/written before, and simultaneously to anticipate the responses of actual, potential or imagined readers/listeners. (Martin and White 2005, p. 92)

The system network for ENGAGEMENT is shown in Figure 4.3, with examples of tweets containing each of the most delicate features. The most basic choice is between presenting something as bearing a relationship to other positions or as absolute. Where the meaning made is the former, there is a choice between contraction, closing down an opposing voice, and expansion, opening up the potential of that voice. More delicate choices in the network depend upon the particular position a text is taking up in relation to another text. For example, following the 'expand: attribute: distance' pathway in Figure 4.3, the text may choose to disalign itself from another text while still offering the opposed text as a potential alternative position.

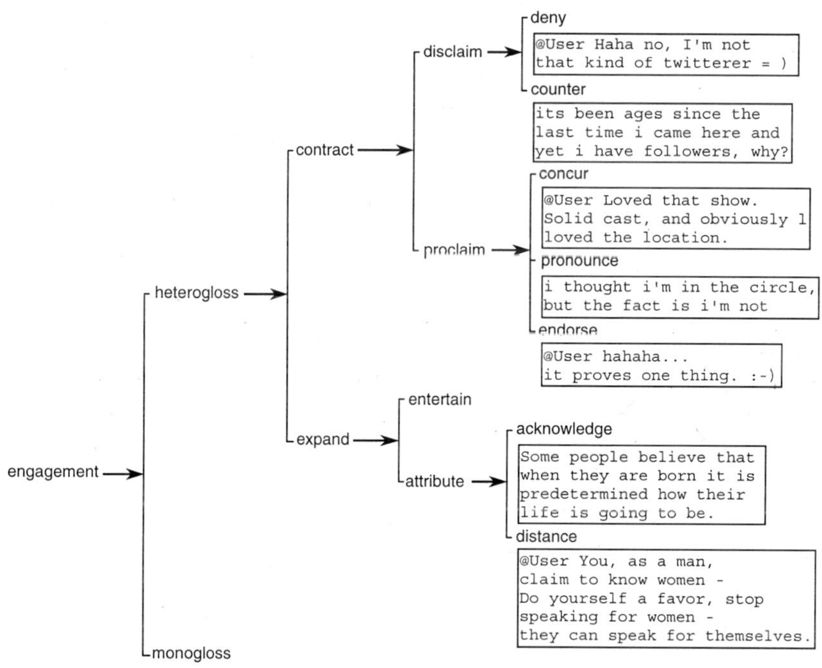

Figure 4.3 A system network for engagement (based on Martin and White 2005)

An important engagement resource at the level of lexicogrammar is projection. For example, mental processes such as *think*, *believe* and *suspect* can be used to project a user's opinion in a micropost, as we see with the most common 3-gram for 'think' in HERMES (Table 4.7):

> i think it's great that Justin Bieber trends like every single day.

The modalization in this example 'acts to construe a heteroglossic backdrop' (Martin and White 2005, p. 107) that indirectly acknowledges the possibility of other co-existent subjectivities. N2 in Table 4.7 is an example of a very common use of engagement whereby a user will ask the ambient audience for an opinion with a tweets, such as:

> What do you think of my new #etsy banner? http://leoandjunie.etsy.com

This practice is known as 'asking the crowd' and, as we will see in Chapter 5, often uses a hashtag to direct attention to the tweet.

Retweeting is an engagement resource that incorporates another text within the current text as a form of quotation. An example from the corpus is the following:

> **RT @user:** I'm not afraid of death. I'm afraid of missing everyone I love. #morbidthought

Table 4.7 The most frequent 3-gram for 'think' in HERMES

N	Cluster	Freq.	Example
1	I THINK I	15,357	@user LOL! now I get it! I think I missed a whole day of tweets because of it.
2	DO YOU THINK	8,320	@user Do you think we'll ever see the day when Premiership footballers come out? Or, maybe more radically, ones from small teams?
3	I DON'T THINK	7,930	RT I don't think anyone but programmers understand that the best code comes out when everyone else is asleep #truestory #code #dev
4	I THINK I'M	5,411	I think I'm gonna have to cheat to keep your eyes on me.
5	I THINK THE	4,152	I think the weatherman just wanted to give all the groupies a chance in Dallas this weekend!!

The RT@User structure is an example of ENGAGEMENT: HETEROGLOSS. However, we cannot determine a more delicate classification of the type of heteroglossic engagement due to the nature of the typographic convention. In most instances no metacomment is made on the retweeted text; instead, retweeting, as with hyperlinking, implies positive evaluation (in the sense of noteworthiness of the retweeted post). However, tweets such as the following were possible:

> Love it. RT @user: The Audacity of Bi-Partisanship: My Personal Letter to President Obama http://shar.es/makvT #p2 #tcot

In this example 'Love it' appraises the retweeted text, suggesting that RT, in this instance, could be thought of as ENGAGEMENT: HETEROGLOSS: PROCLAIM. Such meanings can only be made via the coupling of RT with evaluative lexis and some convention for indicating that the evaluation is not part of the retweeted text. The convention for indicating a simple retweet is usually RT directly preceding an @mention followed by a colon; for example:

> **RT @User**: People who get plenty of vitamin D can cut their chance of developing heart disease or diabetes by 43% – http://bit.ly/91me5f.

In order to add some metacomment, an additional convention is usually employed that includes special characters, such as the characters preceeding the RT @mention structure in the following:

> EXACTLY! Priorities Fucked Up! – **RT @User** So how many of you actually watch the news any other day??? Yeah, that's what I thought.

Here the negative appraisal at the beginning of the tweet preceding the – is a metacomment.

The GRADUATION system

ATTITUDE is a gradable system. We may express degrees of evaluation using the systems of FORCE and FOCUS, with the graduation system operating 'across two axes of scalability – that of grading according to intensity or amount, and that of grading according to prototypicality and the preciseness by which category boundaries are drawn' (Martin and White 2005, p. 137). At the coarsest level we may upscale or downscale each kind of graduation, as suggested by the simultaneous system at the bottom of Figure 4.4.

For example, the most common L1 collocate of 'follower*' is 'more':

> i need 4 **more** followers then i'll hav 55 please follow me!!! :-)

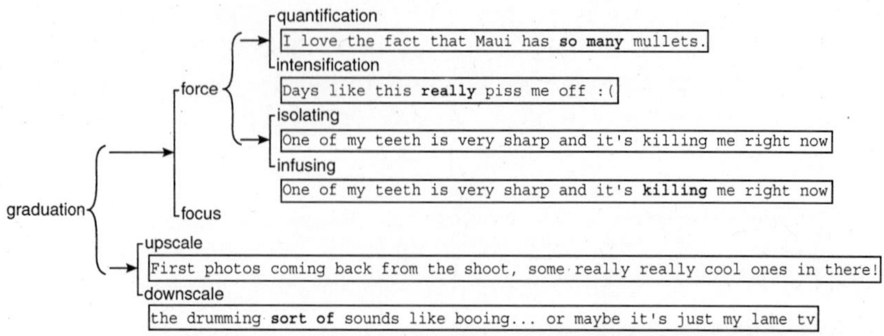

Figure 4.4 A system network for graduation (based on Martin and White 2005)

In this example '4 more' is an example of QUANTIFICATION via the FORCE system since it grades the followers by amount. Another common collocate of 'follower' is 'newest':

> A BIG Welcome and Thank You to my **newest** followers! :-)

By way of contrast, 'newest' is an example of the alternative option, INTENSIFICATION, since it grades the followers from newest to oldest.

In construing graduation, we may choose between INFUSE and ISOLATE.

Graduation may be realized with a specific feature or imbued within another feature. In other words, it may be 'realised by an isolated, individual item which solely, or at least primarily, performs the function of setting the level of intensity' rather than 'fused with a meaning which serves some other semantic function' (Martin and White 2005, p. 141). Infusion is best shown with a series of examples. Consider the increasing intensity of nibble → eat → gorge in the following tweets:

Half warm half cold all feeling rotten. Might just	**Nibble**	on some cereal and crawl right back into bed. Zero energy, zero strength
Fun adventure to start the day. About to	**Eat**	some really good food.
Made a gazillion pancakes last night and didn't eat one. Does that mean I can	**Gorge**	on everything I want for lent?

In these examples the meaning of intensification is embedded in the material processes about eating rather than realized by a separate intensifier such as 'more'.

The tendency to upscale

Social media discourse makes heavy use of upscaled GRADUATION, tending to intensify interpersonal systems as a way of increasing solidarity through emphasizing both positive and negative appraisal as shared experience. Users deploy playful typography and punctuation to assist with this upscaling, for example, repetition of characters supporting lexical evaluation:

> @User as long as the weather holds up, I should be back tomorrow. I would LOOOVE a makeover! :-) let me know!!

These type of resources are usually likened to the paralinguistic dimensions of face-to-face communication:

> As computer-based communication went online (initially through email, and then through listservs, newsgroups, and chat),[3] these same devices have appeared – especially in informal communication. While they are technically forms of writing, most varieties of online communication have often been thought of as forms of speech, with creative punctuation and typography substituting for paralinguistic cues (such as volume, proxemics, and facial expression) for expressing emotion. (Baron 2009)

The tendency appears to be towards these typographic resources acting in the service of intensifying rather than tempering, perhaps with the exception of the kind of interpersonal softening seen with emoticons, discussed later in this chapter.

A simple pattern that is a very common in HERMES is repetition of the exclamation mark to upscale the interpersonal meaning made. For example, it may support an expression of gratitude in the verbiage:

> Awe thank you Joe!!!!!!!!!!!!!!!!!! @User

Any of the myriad of evaluative meanings possible in language may be intensified when coupled with orthographic emphasis of this kind. For example, the negative attitude in the following tweet is intensified by the repeated exclamation marks and co-articulated negative emoticon:

> It is crazy up in this club!!! I can’t stand it!!!! :(

Herring and Zelenkauskaite (2009, p. 30) have noted a gender difference in the use of non-standard orthography such as this form of emphasis in SMS messages, where the character constraints involved are similar to microposts, with women tending to be ‘more economical and more expressive’.

One of the most common environments where two or more exclamation marks occurred in the corpus was preceding LOL, coordinating with resources construing humour and solidarity:

> I like driving:) But i parked kind of werid:P Its like an all saturdaaaay thingg!!lol

In a similar way, other punctuation, such as the full stop, could be used for upscaling both positive and negative appraisal. For example, repeated full stops were used to approximate the kind of dramatic pause which would be realized with intonation in spoken discourse:

> User **oh. My. God.** You are the most awesome person ever :D THANK YOUUUU!!! :D :D

> 'because you are so awesome, outside of room checks & being on duty, feel free to take the rest of the week off.' . . . **BEST. WEEK. EVER.** :):)

> Cutting out of Rep early . . . **feel. like. crap.**

The punctuation suggests one tone group per word and therefore one information unit per word; hence, each word is the focus of new information. This offers orthographic support to the meaning being made that the appraisal expressed is noteworthy. Other ways in which a similar effect was achieved included use of caps lock[6]:

> Work UNtil 00:00 AND then heading to Dj Party!! **LOVE MY LIFE**

This kind of hypergraduated construal might be read as overcompensation for the absence of paralinguistic cues afforded in other modalities. However, such a position suggests that CMC is the poor cousin of spoken discourse rather than a semiotic mode in its own right. While CMC may generally tend toward approximating features of spoken discourse (Baron 1998; Crystal 2006), it operates within different contexts of situation to most spoken discourses. Internet culture has stabilized to an extent that it is more useful to consider the kinds of genres that are evolving rather than to compare across modes.

Patterns of ATTITUDE in HERMES

Manually annotating for appraisal the 100-million-word HERMES corpus is beyond the scope of any sane linguist. In order to gain a small snapshot of the level of appraisal in the tweets, a randomly selected sample of 100 tweets from the corpus was annotated for ATTITUDE using the simple schema shown in Figure 4.5 and the software application UAM Corpus Tool (O'Donnell 2008). The schema is based on Martin and White's (2005)

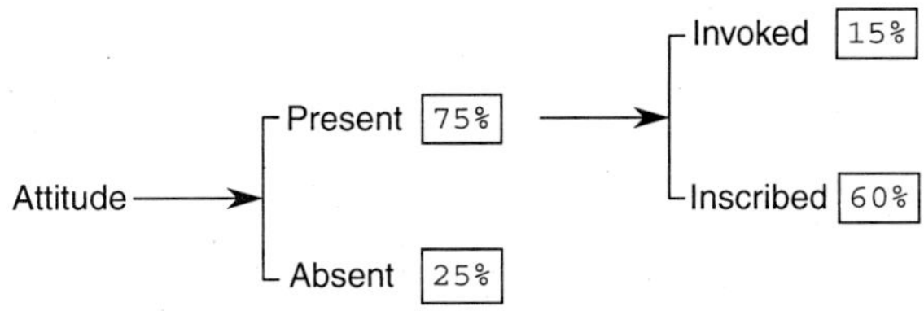

Figure 4.5 Attitude in a random sample of 100 tweets

definition of ATTITUDE, explained in the previous section. Where ATTITUDE was present in a tweet, it was further categorized as either INVOKED or INSCRIBED. The number of instances of ATTITUDE within each tweet was not annotated although many tweets contained multiple instances.

The results of the annotation (shown as percentages in Figure 4.5) demonstrate a very strong tendency for tweets to construe inscribed attitude. As many as 75 per cent of tweets contained some form of ATTITUDE. Page (2011) found a similar degree of ATTITUDE in Facebook status updates. Examples of tweets conforming to each annotation class are as follows:

- INSCRIBED ATTITUDE: @User Woaaaw :O you're so preety! :D
    - *preety* is an instance of INSCRIBED APPRECIATION. (Here the emoticon may also suggest POSITIVE AFFECT or may be an expression of solidarity).
- INVOKED ATTITUDE: they are left wing
    - While this tweet does not use any inscribed attitudinal lexis, left wing invokes either positive or NEGATIVE JUDGEMENT, depending on the political discourse in the cotext.
- ABSENT ATTITUDE: off to my aunts.
    - No attitude regarding the activity is expressed.

While such a small sample cannot be said to be representative of the patterning of ATTITUDE in the entire corpus, as we will see, it accords both with the qualitative analysis of evaluative language and with the general trends in linguistic patterns in the corpus described in this chapter. At the very least, it provides some support for the general claim, made repeatedly in this book, that interpersonal meaning is important to understanding microblogging.

Complaining with 'I have to'

Microblogging affords previously unavailable opportunities to complain about the details of life to a large audience. This will be evident across most of the chapters in this book! As we saw in Chapter 3, the second most frequent 3-gram in HERMES was 'I have to'. This cluster also expresses the interpersonal meaning of modal obligation:

> ugh **i have to** go to school in a few min . . . **i have to** walk all over snow to get to my bus stop . . . not fun!

Most of the tweets containing this cluster were a form of complaint and, as such, saturated with negative evaluation. Complaining can invoke solidarity via the potential for commiseration as people bond around shared irritations, as we will see with the fail meme in Chapter 8. Many Twitter hashtag memes function in this way; for example, #petpeeves, #idontunderstandwhy, #unacceptable, #nevertrust and the like.

Common semantic domains of complaint were work, school and sleep. For example, many tweets expressed NEGATIVE AFFECT about the obligation to leave for work:

> It's snowing! But **not loving** the part where **I have to go to work** now in all the traffic

Indeed, complaint regarding work could occur along with invoked and inscribed negative evaluation about sleep:

> 18 hours of no sleep. **I have to go to work** and i`m still going out tonight. **FAIL!**

Table 4.8 Most frequent items occurring in R1 for the cluster 'I have to'

N	R1	Example
1	GO	GM all, damn I have to go to work!! Lol
2	SAY	I have to say, I am VERY impressed with Windows 7 so far
3	GET	I have to get more friends . . . This is no fun . . .
4	BE	It's time to sleep, I have to be at my uncle's house at 11 tomorrow morning . GOODNIGHT TWITTER :D xo
5	DO	i am freaking sick of group projects where i have to do all the work because everyone else is too freaking lazy to do anything.
6	WORK	nite all I have to work in the am
7	WALK	blurgh, I have to walk the sister to school tomorrow, its like 2 blocks away, pretty sure she can make it without dying, she's in grade 5
8	ADMIT	I have to admit . . . there are few pleasures in life that beat a good shopping day.
9	START	@User yess I amm!! :(I have to start a diet plan.

The same pattern was possible when complaining about school:

> It's almost 2:30 in the morning and I can't sleep . . . **and I have to wake up to go to school** at 6 something **ughh** . . . !! :/

Table 4.8 shows the most common occupants of R1 in the cluster 'I have to'.

N2 and N8, are examples of grammatical metaphor[7] and as such they do not construe the same type of meaning as the other items. This structure was typically deployed to express an opinion, as in the second example in Table 4.8.

Emoticons

A common feature in microposts is the emoticon. These are stylized textual representations, predominately graphological realizations of facial expression[8]. Emoticons are associated with affective discourse. Their use, alongside other forms of non-standard graphological expression, can be seen as membership markers with 'CMC environments are virtual "linguistic markets" (Bourdieu 1977) in which language use, including nonstandard typography and orthography, is the symbolic currency' (Herring and Zelenkauskaite 2009, p. 3). In simpler terms, employing an emoticon signals that the user is familiar with electronic discourse and its conventions.

Many studies conclude the emoticons serve a role in discourse analogous to non-verbal cues in face-to-face communication (Derks, Bos and von Grumbkow 2008; Derks, Fischer and Bos 2008); in other words, they act as a form of paralanguage. However, some scholars have questioned why emoticons have appeared as a semiotic resource at this particular point in history and the validity of the popular notion that they have arisen to disambiguate meanings that would otherwise be made with paralanguage. Crystal (2006) and Baron (2009, p. 14) have noted that ambiguity can occur in written discourse but 'the lack of paralinguistic cues in traditional written language such as letters has not caused many authors to feel the need to insert substitutes for facial expressions or bodily stances'. Crystal instead suggests that emoticons have arisen due to the immediacy of internet interaction and the close association of electronic discourse with features of speech. A more important reason may be, as I will suggest in the rest of this chapter, the significant semiotic energy put into affiliation by internet users and the role of emoticons in assisting interpersonal connection.

Emoticons support the basic function of social media to connect with others in convivial, friendly and generally interpersonally positive ways. They often collocate with other, more elaborate, lexical expressions of emotion. The smiley was the most frequent emoticon in HERMES, as it appears to be in CMC in general. Some other frequent emoticons that occurred[9] in the

Table 4.9 Frequency of some common emoticons in HERMES

Emoticon (nose optional)	Frequency	Example
:-)	304,284	@User LOL I wasn't going to go there :-)
:-P	68,540	Haha set a cup on that booty! :-P
:-(	64,826	Where'd the sun go?:-(

corpus are shown in Table 4.9. Further examples (highlighted in bold) seen in HERMES include:

> @User I'm listening to it right now!!!! **:-)**
>
> @User oh right, of course **:)**
>
> I said 2010 was going to be an amazing year. But now im not so sure **:-(**
>
> Dear God, please take me with you. I can't stand this anymore . . . **:(**
>
> @User same thing you on lol **:-p**
>
> Love me, hate me, say what you want about me but . . . you know the rest **:P**
>
> I am such big spender this weekend **:-o**
>
> @User WOAAAHHHHH! How'd you do that with yr pic?! **:o**

Most users would be able to quickly group these emoticons via polarity (e.g. :-) as positive and :-(as negative). They will likely suggest that, for example, :-) represents happiness. However, as we will see, the situation is far more complicated, and emoticons cannot be said to straightforwardly express sentiment. Instead emoticons couple with other linguistic resources to make meaning, as I will elaborate later.

Emoticons can be seen as a form of discourse marker, produced in text as they are needed to aid in interpersonal negotiation. They have also been viewed as punctuation. For example, Knox (2009) sees emoticons as part of an ongoing evolution in punctuation to support the ever-more complex demands placed on language. Knox explains this progression in terms of the way systems of punctuation have developed to perform more interpersonal functions, evolving from their original textual (organizing discourse) function:

> The trajectory for interpersonal punctuation . . . begins with boundary marking, moves to punctuating speech function, and then to punctuating attitude and identity. At the same time, the prosody of punctuation spans (potentially) longer stretches of text, with the punctuation of attitude and identity through emoticons now able to spread over entire messages.

This ability to interpersonally charge extended stretches of text, imbuing them with evaluative meaning, is indicative of the way that emoticons are a resource that is realized prosodically. They might be compared to prosodic patterns of intensification where the impact extends over neighbouring discourse and line intensification 'is similar to the use of loudness and pitch movement for highlighting in phonology (as noted by Poynton 1984, 1985, 1996)' (Martin and White 2005, p. 20). The previous section noted an association of intensification with features (such as repeated exclamation marks) that have a paralinguistic style function. These features often support other interpersonal meanings made in verbiage, working in conjunction with emoticons. For example, upscaled graduation coupled with negative attitude in the coupling of the exclamation marks and the negative emoticon in the following serve to express a kind of amplified negative affect:

> tomorrow another exam!!!!!!!!!!!!!!!!!!!!!!!!!!!!! :(

Arguing that emoticons manifest prosodically is not to say that their placement in a text is random. Indeed Provine et al. (2007) suggest in a quantitative study that the patterning with which emoticons 'punctuate' a text is itself meaningful and cooperative with the phrase structure of the text, occurring 'at highly predictable and linguistically significant positions' (pp. 302–03).

Figure 4.6 is a system network showing the articulation potential for emoticons. In other words, it shows the choices that a user can make on the expression plane for constructing a face-style[10] emoticon. I will explore this articulation before turning to investigate the kinds of interpersonal meanings supported by emoticons.

The emoticon network[11] consists of a number of simultaneous systems (systems related by an AND relation, rather than an OR relation). For example the following emoticon :-)))))) selects the following features from this network:

- Eye: Open: Unpronounced
- Nose: Present
- Mouth: Closed: Curved: Up curved
- Forehead: Absent
- Repetition: Many
- Aspect: Horizontal: Right

Example realizations of each of the most delicate systems are given in Table 4.10. While the network systematizes the main instances of emoticons and since emoticons are an emergent, unstable system, there are likely to be

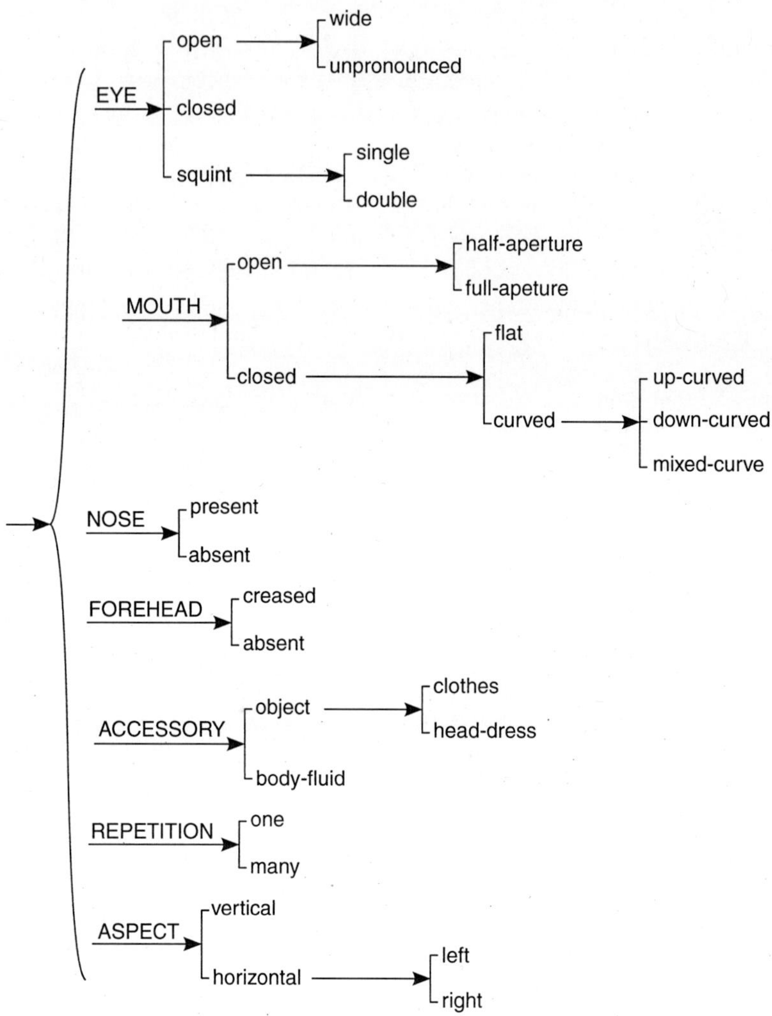

Figure 4.6 Articulation network for facial emoticons

many exceptions that do not conform to the choices presented. Consider, for example,

˘\(°_o)/˘

While emoticons that graphologically realize facial expression were most common, non-face emoticons were also seen in HERMES. The most frequent of these was the heart emoticon, formed with the less-than sign and the number three, as follows:

<3

Table 4.10 Example realizations of articulation systems for emoticons

System		Example
Eye	Open: Wide	0_0
	Open: Unpronounced	:-)
	Closed	-_-
	Squint: Single	;-)
	Squint: Double	^_^
Mouth	Open: Partial aperture	:-D
	Open: Full aperture	:-O
	Closed: Flat	:-|
	Closed: Angled	:-/
	Closed: Curved: Up	:-)
	Closed: Curved: Down	:-(
	Closed: Curved: Mixed	:-S
Nose	Present	:-)
	Absent	:)
Eyebrows	Furrowed	>:-(
	Absent	:-)
Accessory	Object	*<:-)
	Body fluid	:_(
Repetition	One	:-)
	Many	:-))))
Aspect	Vertical	^_^
	Horizontal: Left	:-)
	Horizontal: Right	(-:

Given the Valentine's Day skewing of the corpus already mentioned, this emoticon is likely over-represented in HERMES (54,302 instances) compared with general microblogging discourse, though anecdotally it appears a common feature in general. Examples include

Love is in the air. <3

Table 4.11 Example of the most frequent occupants of L1 for <3

N	Word	Example
1	I	'you want some potatos with that salt?' hahahahahahahaha I <3 my brother
2	<3	<3 <3 <3 the rain
3	YOU	@User i miss you <3
4	:D	@User awww thanks that means a lot :D <3 much love lol
5	DAY	OMG THIS MADE MY DAY <3
6	ME	@User waheeeey, and yeah do ring me <3 xxxxxxxx
7	LOVE	My day is over!! Thanks for the love <3
8	IT	it's going to be a great day!! i can feel it <3
9	THANKS	@User Thanks <3
10	LOL	my baby cusion is stealing the laptop lol <3

The most common collocates in L1 before a <3 are shown in Table 4.11. The first example is related to popular use of the word 'heart' as a verb in internet discourse in place of 'love':

> @User i heart the name Liam.

This perhaps derives from use of the Unicode heart[12]:

> Me and @user1 knew every single song that was performed by @user2 and @user3 we never sat down . . . **I ♥ them**

Emoticons and solidarity

We can look at emoticons from two perspectives: as graphological realizations of facial expression and as involved in the interpersonal work of negotiating exchanges, where they have a more pragmatic function (Dresner and Herring 2010). This section focuses on the latter function, where emoticons were frequently seen in HERMES to support interpersonal connection and solidarity.

A history of origin of the smiley emoticon has been offered by Scott E. Fahlman, the popularly acknowledged 'inventor' of this emoticon. This history suggests that a pragmatic function motivated emoticon inception. Fahlman describes how an emoticon approximating two eyes, a nose and a smiling mouth came to be used in the 1980s by the computer science community at Carnegie Mellon in their online bulletin board system as a kind of joke marker. A means for indicating when a post was intended to be humorous had been deemed necessary due to the lengthy discussions they would typically engender and given that in 'at least one case, a humorous remark was interpreted by someone as a serious safety warning'. He continues,

> This problem caused some of us to suggest (only half seriously) that maybe it would be a good idea to explicitly mark posts that were not to be taken seriously. After all, when using text-based online communication, we lack the body language or tone-of-voice cues that convey this information when we talk in person or on the phone. Various 'joke markers' were suggested, and in the midst of that discussion it occurred to me that the character sequence :-) would be an elegant solution – one that could be handled by the ASCII-based computer terminals of the day. So I suggested that. In the same post, I also suggested the use of :-(to indicate that a message was meant to be taken seriously, though that symbol quickly evolved into a marker for displeasure, frustration, or anger.

Fahlman's account suggests that development of the early emoticon was closely related to managing the interpersonal needs of the computer-mediated semiotic environment of the time. The phylogenic development since this time has seen them become an almost ubiquitous resource in electronic discourse, and they are highly prevalent in social media communication. Emoticons have retained some of the original interpersonal softening function suggested by Fahlman in terms of tempering potential interpersonal conflict and have gone on to develop further as markers of solidarity.

Tweets in HERMES addressed to other users were likely to employ emoticons to increase interpersonal closeness and solidarity. For example, while the emoticon in the following example could be read as expressing pleasure at drinking pleasant tea, it is also functioning to solidify the interpersonal work done in the exchange and support the inscribed lexis of agreement in the reply by User 2:

> User1: Earl Grey tea is amazing
>
> User 2: @User1 I agree, it's much nicer than normal tea :-)

Clearly it is not possible to neatly compartmentalize emotion and solidarity. Emotion is involved in the way solidarity is expressed since alignment with others is generally a positive emotional experience. Indeed 'AFFECT will always be present as the "emotional charge" (interpretable variously as want or desire, ideological commitment, belied, the conviction that something matters or is of importance) which the individual speaker both brings to discourse, seen as both experiential and interpersonal, and produces as a reaction to discourse' (Poynton 1990, p. 93). Page (2011) has explored the role of affective discourse in constructing sociality in Facebook, where emotional language is prevalent in status updates.

As well as invoking solidarity, an emoticon can be used to diffuse tension. This is in the general tradition prompted by Fahlman's bulletin board emoticons, whereby they were used as 'joke markers' to avoid what was intended to be comical being interpreted as rude. Often they will function somewhat redundantly with an explicit explanation by the user that he or she is joking:

> @User Thats funny cause I thought he kinda favored you . . . LOL nah just joking :)

For example, the main function of the smiley in the following tweets is about negotiating the relationship construed in the reply and avoiding offence, rather than clarifying specific emotion:

> @User jeezzzz I really hope I haven't offended you.if I have I'm really sorry :-)
>
> @User I don't agree with that, but you're entitled to your view :)

Clearly in these examples the emoticon does not construe affectual pleasure regarding the opposing viewpoint, but it is lessening the interpersonal awkwardness of making such a direct statement of challenge. Emoticons, however, 'are no more univocal than are words in ordinary language, and therefore cannot be assumed to unambiguously clarify user intention or emotion' (Baron 2009, p. 14). As Crystal notes:

> The emoticons can forestall a gross misperception of a speaker's intent, but an individual smiley still allows a huge number of readings (amusement, happiness, delight, joke, sympathy, good mood etc.) which can only be disambiguated by referring to the verbal context. (Crystal 2006, p. 39)

Alternatively an emoticon might occur where there are no explicit meanings made about possible offence to the other speaker and the emoticon simply construes a generalized amicability. Greetings are a common context in which emoticons are used to construe this type of friendly stance, for example, the widespread practice of greeting one's followers in the morning on Twitter:

> i am so hungry . . . about to go find some food . . . morning tweeps :)

Table 4.12 Most common occupants of L1 for :-)

N	Word	Example
1	YOU	@User Hiya, thank you too, lovely to Tweet you :-)
2	IT	@User thanks, we all are deserving of it :-)
3	ME	@User ok I will and you should follow me :-)
4	LOL	@User So I'm kicked off the list, just like that? lol :-) #kidding
5	DAY	@User Very GM to u too . . . Have good day :-)
6	THANKS	@User phew! thanks :-)
7	TOO	@User I want that hat too :-)
8	NOW	@User I am fighting hard to remain positive and Zen . . . that's all I've got right now :-)
9	TODAY	Wide awake. Need to do laundry. Gtl. Minus the t. Gonna visit mom today :-)
10	THAT	@User Morning . . . oooh, you have cold hands, I like that :-)

In this example, the user is conveying a friendly disposition rather than directly expressing affect.

As the examples in Table 4.12 suggest, :-) is most often employed dialogically and seems to be used to express camaraderie.

Emoticons and coupling

Emoticons do not afford the kind of delicacy of meaning potential possible with other linguistic resources, such as the systems of evaluative language outlined in the beginning of this chapter. In other words, they are able to activate less meaning potential than emotional lexis, a property which Martin (2008c) explains as the level of 'commitment', that is, 'the amount of meaning potential activated in a particular process of instantiation' in terms of 'which meanings in optional systems are taken up and, within systems, the degree of delicacy[4] selected' (Martin 2008c, p. 45). Zhao (2011, p. 132) advises caution in theorizing commitment in multimodal environments 'since it is not clear how the degree of commitment can be measured accurately since instances of different semiotic systems are not necessarily comparable'. Acknowledging this tempered view of commitment, we can argue that emoticons make meaning by co-patterning with other, potentially more committed features in texts, such as emotional lexis.

Emoticons couple with the patterns in cotext to realize interpersonal meanings. Viewed alone, emoticons display a high degree of 'fuzziness', for example, a smiley could express a range of positive emotions from happiness to satisfaction. The interpersonal meaning is more readily studied when we look at how emoticons work in tandem with evaluative meanings made in the verbiage. For example, a smiley may be motivated by a co-occurring instance of inscribed AFFECT such as the POSITIVE HAPPINESS in the following tweet:

> And in this moment i am **happy, Happy** =)

Similarly, it might be used to suggest AFFECT where there is otherwise no evaluative lexis present, for example, suggesting that the wine and television in the following tweet have engendered a positive affectual state:

> Glass of wine and Sex & the City 2 :)

Table 4.13 shows examples from HERMES of emoticons coupling with each of the AFFECT systems.

Emoticons may also support meanings made across other systems of appraisal. They may support the APPRECIATION system, for example:

> @User :) My Nana went there and she said it was **Beautiful :)**

In addition they may support JUDGEMENT:

> i took Citizenship thinking it would be easy . . . boy i really am an **idiot :(**

Table 4.13 Examples of couplings of affect and the smiley emoticon

Affect	Positive	Negative
Dis/inclination	Has her tix 2 c the phonics in glasgow & jst booked to go to Cardiff 2!!! Can't wait :)	This weather is going to drive me up the wall . . . I can't stand it :(
Un/happiness	@User what do you think about Brazil ? hahaha :) luv u :)	@User umm . . . i would be sad :(
In/security	Been practicising for my theory test which is coming up soon, feeling slightly confident :)	Theres some paranormal activity goin on in my house right now . . . Im freaking out :(
Dis/satisfaction	@User Thanks for listing me on your Personalities list. Flattered :) xx	fckn sick of takin these nasty ass pills! ughhhh :(

Emoticons may also support the realization prosodies of graduation. In these instances the emoticon is usually also supporting the attitude system that is being graduated, for example, the upscaling of ATTITUDE via INFUSION (consider the infused meaning realized by 'awesome' compared with 'good' and 'great') in the following tweet is supported by the repetition in the smiley emoticon, itself signalling upscaled AFFECT (though, as I have mentioned earlier, emoticons do not directly instantiate simple AFFECT):

@User oh that is **awesome :))))**

In cases where attitude is explicitly upscaled, the emoticon appears to support the overall attitudinal meaning:

Vampire diaries is **so so so good :)**

In this example the smiley works in tandem with the upscaled graduation to strengthen the general positive attitudinal stance taken up.

Emoticons and humour

As a result of their role in invoking solidarity, emoticons are often involved in the way microposts construe humour. A playful, lightly humorous tone is commonly suggested with the following emoticon, representing a face with a tongue poking out:

:-P

As Table 4.14 shows, this emoticon frequently collocates with LOL (Laugh Out Loud), an initialism associated with humour, although, as already mentioned, also often having a phatic function. The example N1 is an

Table 4.14 Most common occupants of L1 for :-P

N	Word	Example
1	LOL	@User Why u got ur son playin in the snow naked? Bad parent . . . Lol :-P
2	IT	@User ewww thats actually so wrong . . . I like it :-P
3	THAT	@User lmao u gunna tell him that :-p
4	ME	@User lol i do what i please!!! ur not the boss of me :-p
5	YOU	@User I'm going to pretend like you're dogging Justin Bieber jokingly. If it was it was serious . . . i'm unfollowing you :-P

instance where the :-P emoticon is supporting a playful 'just teasing' meaning, reinforced prosodically by the LOL. The micropost involves humour about parenting norms and presents what Knight (2010c) terms a 'wrinkle' to be laughed off by the interactants. The :-P is motivated by this 'laughing off' function usually realized as actual laughter in convivial conversational humour seen, for example, among friends in casual conversation:

> Humour is a way to present these clashing bonds as laughable, so that the interactants may laugh this off together in favour of shareable bonds from common social networks (around which they commune). (p. 48)

Knight (p. 47) gives examples in the casual conversation of three young female university students of a bond of heavy eating (of 'good pie' during the holidays) being laughed off in references to another competing bond of thinness which these interactants share. This deferring process of affiliation allows these students to negotiate conflicting identities. In this way laughing off a bond has a solidarity-enhancing function.

In the case of microposts, emoticons can flag the potential wrinkle. For example, N5, sarcastically invokes the bond network associated with the many fanatic Justin Bieber fans that populate Twitter. It leverages mock offence (i.e. threatening to unfollow a user) to construe intimacy and to solidify the relationship with the user, addressed by the @ mention. The :-P emoticon supports this ironic meaning and the general humour. In Knight's terms it also suggests the potential wrinkle in the bond network.

This section has provided a brief discussion of the importance of emoticons to affective discourse and construals of solidarity in microblogging. Emoticons are involved in expressions of personability, emotional closeness and camaraderie through couplings with other meanings made in the verbiage of microposts. The support that emoticons give to affective discourse is characteristic of the foregrounding of the interpersonal by social media where making social connections is an imperative function of the discourses produced.

CHAPTER FIVE

Ambient affiliation

In Chapter 1, I introduced the concept of semiotic studies of affiliation, where language patterns are used to understand interpersonal bonds. Throughout this book I have referred generally to processes of ambient affiliation. I will now look in more detail at a particular instance of ambient affiliation, a form of online communion through hashtagging and explore this practice using a specialized corpus of tweets containing hashtags, hereafter, the hashtag corpus.

The hashtag corpus was derived from the HERMES and consists of all tweets containing hashtags[1] (962,156 tweets, 14,488,307 words), a Twitter convention introduced in Chapter 3. Briefly, hashtags are a form of metadata labelling the topic of a tweet. For example:

> #tcyasi getting full brunt of storm now. Sheltering in bottom room. Nature doing its worst outside. Worried-might lose the roof. Pups scared

The hashtag in this tweet, #tcyasi, refers to Tropical Cyclone Yasi, a category 5 cyclone that was causing extensive damage in northern Queensland, Australia, at the time. This cyclone came just weeks after the state experienced dramatic flooding around Brisbane. Both natural disasters have seen social media deployed to communicate news, share personal stories and assist with coordinating the relief effort. The cyclone was a trending topic on Twitter on the day it hit, with users posting live updates of the cyclone's progress:

> The winds are roaring like a freight train here. Unbelievable. We're bunkered down. #TCYasi

An ambient audience following #tcyasi accumulated.

As well as eyewitness accounts (see Chapter 9 for discussion regarding an emergent eyewitness report microgenre), there was speculation, rumour, correction and censure regarding what was happening:

> RT @User: Rumors that the Innisfail evac centre lost roof are FALSE – LIES, do not believe the weirdos spreading rumors. #TCYasi
>
> I might add, it is not helpful to spread rumours, this is an extremely serious situation. Please Twitter, don't start rumours. #TCYasi

After the cyclone had passed, fortunately inflicting less damage than was expected, descriptions of the aftermath together with expressions of relief were posted using the tag. Throughout the period users from other locations expressed support, sympathy and concern:

> I'm scared to wake up tomorrow to find out what's going on in north qld. I really hope that everybody took care of themselves!! #tcyasi

There were also tweets, such as the following extensively retweeted tweet, commenting on the media coverage of the cyclone itself:

> Our thoughts today are with the media, struggling to cope with the terrible lack of casualties #tcyasi

Many tweets provided clues that users had been actively following the progress of the cyclone live via Twitter. For example, the point at which the eye of the cyclone was expected to hit corresponded with the time users were likely to go to bed:

> @user: I need to go to bed, but I'm scared of what I'm going to wake up to. #TCYasi

The tweets that I have just presented give a glimpse into the potential role that hashtags play in aligning users during crisis events so that they can track information, share stories and coordinate resources. The sections which follow explore how the language of hashtagging supports processes of affiliation that are at the heart of the kind of solidarity shown during natural disasters.

Twitter hashtags

Hashtags set up an attributive relationship between the tweet as a tagged token and the label as its type (e.g. a tweet about Python). Halliday and Matthiessen (2004, p. 219) define *attributive relational processes* as relationships where 'an entity has some class ascribed or attributed to it'. In other words, hashtags assign a keyword to a tweet in the form of metadata referencing the topic of the message as specified by the user. The 'tag as type' relationship assumes that other users will also adopt this tag and use it as a keyword for a tweet on the same topic. Thus hashtags are also broadly involved in construing heteroglossia (Bakhtin 2008) in the sense that their use presupposes a virtual community of interested listeners who may or may not align with the values expressed together with the tag.

This type of in-line metadata is different from the way metadata is usually deployed in other contexts, such as information cataloguing, since the labels are directly visible to the user as part of the text of the tweet. While metadata rendered in markup languages, such as extensible markup language (XML), will typically separate form from content, social tagging on systems such as Twitter collapses this separation. Hashtags will often occur at the beginning or end of a tweet:

> #rte #ireland Looking forward to – Samuel L Jackson, Dionne Warwick, Michael Fassbender, Gerry Adams and much more besides!
>
> If there is Magic on this planet, it is contained in water. -Loren **#quote**

Hashtags are also interesting, as they may occur inside clauses, as follows

> Listening to **#Meatloaf** Greatest hits CD, been ages since Ive listened to him.. 'Paradise by the Dashboard Light' Classic !

Thus hashtags, unlike other metadata, can visibly mark functional roles in the linguistic structure to highlight what the tweet is about without interrupting the discourse. The tweets in Table 5.1 are examples of this potential where classifiers, things and processes[2] are marked (Table 5.1).

Table 5.1 Examples of the hashtags marking units with different grammatical functions

	Tweet	Function marked
1	Interesting take on the debate over the #apple iPad - http://bit.ly/aXmLB2 @User @User2 This is for you!	Classifier
2	in charge of the #cake for my mom's birthday. What's the best #bakery in Chicago? She likes the icing.	Thing
3	Ppl tht play the dumbest music in public like get sum head phones or #gohomeanddothat	Process
4	Ok #apple now your just pissing me off. We wouldn't have to jailbreak if you gave us multitasking!!! http://yfrog.com/4iyiqcaj	Vocative

As multiple users begin to follow a hashtag, they are able to share values and information relating to a common interest. Examples of some of the common collaborative uses afforded by hashtags include:

- Participating in internet memes – internet memes are explored in Chapter 6. A subset of memes use hashtags allowing users to contribute to the stream of responses for what are often very topical memes but also are often ongoing, such as the following example:

> **#idontunderstandwhy** why they took naps out of school they should add it back and add it to work

- Tracking and participating in events – Often conferences, particularly technology-related conferences, will define a hashtag that participants can use when tweeting about the presentations, in effect creating a back channel (McCarthy and Boyd 2005; Reinhardt et al. 2009) to the live event.

> What should I check out at **#pycon**? I've been too busy to even glance at the program.

- Monitoring and offering support in crises – Hashtags have been used during disasters to coordinate the relief effort and to allow people to share their experiences (Hughes et al. 2008).

> West Wood is still not open. Cops are still turning people away. **#sandiegofire**

- Asking the crowd – Hashtags are often used to ask the ambient audience for their opinion on a new purchase or any number of decisions that users make in their social lives.

> Lease is up, time for a new car. What should I test drive? Who has a great lease offer? **#carshopping**

These social processes are all forms of ambient communion facilitated by the tracking function of the hashtag. They are ambient in the sense that they are open to all comers; anyone can 'opt onto' the conversation at any point in the unfolding.

It should also be noted that some users adopted hashtagging for their own more personal purposes, such as:

- General recall and recall of tasks – A hashtag can be used to create an ongoing list of tasks that need to be completed or have been completed or of information that needs to be remembered for some purpose:

#todolist get phone fixed, go to the bank, pay bills, go to the post office, finish new zine, get a job . . .

- Archiving milestones and memories – Hashtags can be used to group items so that they can be archived by topic, allowing the users to, for example, to record milestones for their various children as they develop:

Name's second tooth came through yesterday #Name #milestone

These less social uses of hashtagging leverage the tracking power of hashtags together with the brevity of the medium as a useful mechanism for self-monitoring and personal documentation. For this reason questions about how to retrieve one's own Twitter feed so that a user can save it to his or her local computer are quite common in forums offering technical advice about Twitter usage. Services have also been developed for mining one's own tweets and other instances of social media use. For example, one such service makes the following claim:

> On the path to greater knowledge, Grafitter makes it easy to report daily personal behavioural information by connecting with various social media in different contexts. The tool automatically culls data from these sources so that users may reflect on visualizations of their collected behavioural information, and perhaps get to 'know thyself' just a little better. (Ian et al. 2009, p. 13)

Thus I posit two dominant functions for hashtagging: ambient affiliation and personal reflection, with the latter being part of how we form our online identities and narrativize self-representation (Page 2011; Rettberg 2009).

Tweets and the hashtags that they contain may thus be thought of as two different orders of experience: a tweet is an instance of language use, while a hashtag is language about language, performing an affiliative (or reflective) function. The function is not static, as hashtags will shift with users' interests over time as they respond to their social world. Cottingham (2010) suggests a fairly short half-life for hashtags:

> . . .on Twitter, hashtags can live that entire lifecycle in the course of a day or two. A news story breaks, and competing hashtags vie for dominance. Then a few influential folks adopt the same one. Suddenly the conversation coalesces around it, the term trends, the spammers start using it, and then the conversation peters out as we move on to the next topic. (Cottingham 2010)

While this may be the case for some hashtags, such as those based on current events in the news media, other tags are more enduring. Sarita et al. (2009)

explore Twitter spam by tracking the life cycle of the 'endogenous' – that is, native to Twitter – meme #ROBOTPICKUPLINES. They described activity using this hashtag as follows:

> Most activity occurred in the first 24 hours of the hashtag's lifecycle and then trailed off over the next few days. After about two hours, the hashtag was placed on Twitter's top 10 trend list and stayed there for three–four hours, at which point it was replaced by other topics.
>
> Using whitelisted Twitter accounts, we tracked the hashtag over the next four days and captured 17,803 tweets from 8,616 unique users. User participation followed a power law distribution where 6,021 users tweeted one time, 2,595 tweeted two or more times, and a dedicated 205 tweeted 10 or more times using the #robotpickuplines.
>
> Spammers started to use the hashtag when it became a trending topic, and the spam lifecycle mirrored the meme lifecycle, with a slight lag.

These kind of endogenous hashtags emerge from grass roots usage in a kind of organic 'survival of the fittest' struggle. They can also result from imitation of high-profile users such as celebrities. Though multiple labels are possible for the same topics, usually a single hashtag will dominate. There thus seems to be some stability in hashtag choice and persistence despite the absence of high-level prescription as to use. This persistence is, however, relative, and hashtags relating to news events are likely to be more stable than other forms of tags (such as those used for personal documentation identified earlier):

> It is a fascinating yet not so well understood phenomenon that even though there is no entity regulating the hashtags assigned to tweets, there seems to be only a small number of hashtags for a particular news topic. In fact, a simple clustering just based on the similarity of the hashtags yields surprisingly good cluster quality, and this simple idea forms the basis of services such as Twitter Search [21], Twist [20], Monitter [15], Hashtags [7], Tweetmeme [19], and others. (Jagan et al. 2009, p. 44)

Third-party services have also been developed that attempt to visualize the diachronic progression of hashtags as they ebb and flow in the tweet stream. For example, at the time of writing, hashtags.org produced line graphs that showed the frequency with which individual tags were being used on Twitter.

Having provided a brief introduction to hashtagging as a general social practice realized in language, I will now explore hashtags from a corpus-based perspective and investigate patterns of use. The aim is to understand the kinds of meanings that are made, particularly the types of interpersonal meaning involved in hashtag-related affiliation.

The function of frequent hashtags in HERMES

Figure 5.1 shows the five most common hashtags in HERMES. The most frequent hashtag, #nowplaying, is a meme (see Chapter 6 for a study of memes), whereby users share the music that they are currently listening to. In 2009, approximately 650,000 tweets were posted per day containing this hashtag along with the name of the song (Boutin 2009). For example:

> **#nowplaying** Ain't Nobody by Rufus

The patterns connected with this tag show users sharing their musical preference with the ambient audience, contributing their selection to a communal pool of song choices. A common evaluative cluster in the hashtag corpus, 'I love this', co-occurred with #nowplaying. For example:

> **#nowplaying** One Time. **I love this** song it was 1st JB song I've heard and it was love at the first heard ;)

N	Word	Freq.	Description	Example
1	NOWPLAYING	51,738	Meme – specify the song that you are currently listening to	#nowplaying prices on my head by young buck and Lloyd banks. Lloyd wrecked it!
2	OLYMPICS	17,922	2010 Winter Olympic Games	is anyone rooting for canada? yeah, i didnt think so. #olympics
3	FB	15,234	Automatically updates the status on Facebook	Watching a Michael Jackson concert from 1994. I miss him so fucking much. #fb
4	JOBS	10,404	Job advertisements	Lead Rational Tester job in Fort Lauderdale, FL at CDI Corporation http://bit.ly/atQKbY #jobs #tester
5	IDONTUNDER-STANDWHY	9,558	Meme – note something that you find puzzling (humorous)	#Idontunderstandwhy women bring millions of clothes wit them for a 3 daygetaway.?Someone please explain!!?!?

Figure 5.1 The five most common hashtags in the Twitter corpus

> **#nowplaying** Merry Christmas, Mr. Lawerence. I think I'm gonna faint cause **I love this** music so much! #fb

However, the tag was most often used without any explicit evaluation in the cotext. Instead positive appraisal of the song choice is invoked via the use of the hashtag itself. In other words, appending the hashtag suggests that the song is worth listening to. Alternatively, it may suggest the aesthetic value of the song by reflecting the user's current mood state, which has also been invoked in the song choice itself. The practice likely arises from early blog services, such as Livejournal, where users appended information about their mood via an emoticon together with a song choice to their journal entries.

Memes were the most common type of hashtag. They are often seen in the list of trending topics because of their viral nature, where a 'user who observes the rise of a compelling trending topic micro-meme may be inclined to take the tag associated with the meme and compose his or her own tweet on the subject' (Huang et al. 2010, p. 173). Common memes included FOLLOWFRIDAY (recommend an individual worth following), CONFESSION (post a personal confession), and INHIGHSCHOOL (post a memory from high school). The other major class of hashtags were political and news hashtags such as TCOT (top conservatives on Twitter), IRANELECTION (protest and comment regarding the 2009 Iranian election), NEWS (newsworthy reports). These were generally topical in contrast to memes which are humorous and interpersonally charged. For example, consider #CONFESSION, a hashtag meme in which users post personal revelations, such as the following:

> #confession I **miss** dating hood/thug dudes
>
> #Confession I **have a crush on** a girl . . . but I'm not gay, does that make sense? Lmao

The most common example of this class of memes is N5 in Figure 5.1. Most contributions to the confession meme involved expressions of AFFECT (bold). The other major type of appraisal coupling with the hashtag invoked SOCIAL SANCTION, where the entire meaning of the body of the tweet implies negative JUDGEMENT:

> #Confession i love to talk on phone when im using the bathroom x]
>
> #confession I cant Drive on the Highway And Not Punch it to 120MPH . . . its impossible

As a result of the corpus generation occurring during the 2010 Winter Olympics, the second most frequent hashtag in the HERMES was the topical hashtag Olympics. This ranking is indicative of the time sensitivity of hashtags. APPRECIATION of sport and the Olympics as an event frequently occurred in these tweets, alongside expression of AFFECT surrounding the experience of watching the games:

> **#olympics** are so **exciting!** so **happy** for HK, shannon, bryon wilson, vonn, mancuso . . . good luck to shaun white tonight! **can't wait** to see it

The most common evaluative 3-gram was I LOVE THE. For example:

> Watching the opening ceremony and attempting to start my three papers. **I love the** #olympics!

The topical hashtag allows users to share bonds around a particular ideational focal point. I will now consider how the affiliative function of the evaluative language seen in the tweets by investigating the role of hashtags in couplings of evaluative and ideational meaning.

Hashtags as ideational labels

This section will demonstrate how hashtags enact the social relation: 'Search for me and affiliate with my value!'. These hashtags allow users to search topics that interest them and share associated values. As users share values and thereby affiliate with each other, prosodies of positive or negative evaluation as tweets unfold in time. The concept of coupling (introduced in Chapter 1) is central to affiliation. Coupling is illustrated in the following tweet posted on Twitter during the 2010 federal election as part of a stream of tweets about the election, labelled with the hashtag #ausvotes:

> Just Heard Tony Abbott interviewed on rn . . . The man really is an idiot! #ausvotes #justsaying

Here the then leader of the Australian Liberal Party is coupled with explicit negative appraisal (NEGATIVE JUDGEMENT highlighted). This type of coupling could also be invoked, as in the following tweet negatively appraising Abbott without using explicit appraisal lexis in the body of the tweet (JUDGEMENT is also playfully suggested in the hashtag #deargodno):

> Finding my passport in case I need to follow through on promise to leave the country if Abbott is PM #deargodno #ausvotes

Posts such as these realize a social bond by rejecting Abbott, creating a kind of semiotic anti-Abbott community that might be populated by supporters of opposing political parties sharing their political values.

We have thus far considered hashtags as a typographic convention used to mark the topic of a tweet. We may also think of these tags as indicating the target of the appraisal in the tweet. For example, consider the use of #FLASH[3] in the following (instances of negative appraisal, both inscribed and invoked, have been marked in bold):

> #Flash can be useful for making fun browser games with though. Outside of that, **we really should be moving away** from the technology.
>
> With all the backlash from #Apple about #Adobe ‘s #Flash I am starting to HATE those **ridiculous** and **difficult to close** banners . #design
>
> #flash is DEAD. Why? **Closed, heavy, anachronistic** in respect to html5._

In these examples #FLASH is the target of the appraisal; in other words, it is the entity being evaluated. We can think of this in terms of coupling as a binding of ideational meaning ‘about Flash’ with various instances of evaluative meaning. The value that ‘flash is ineffective’ is shared. The presence of the hashtag expands the affiliative meaning potential of the tweet when compared with the similar examples that do not contain hashtags:

> No wonder some ppl **hate** Flash. Some ads can be **fucking annoying**
>
> Is it weird that I **hate** Flash but love Adobe AIR? (JavaScript & AJAX AIR of course, not that flash **crap**).
>
> wow i agree with Steve Jobs on Flash, i think it’s going the way of the dodo. flash is **non-standard** and **sucks** on every platform.

While these tweets negatively appraise flash with a similar degree of hostility, the coupling is rendered ‘louder’ in the presence of the hashtag. This is because it links itself to other texts featuring similar complaint. It is also more likely to be automatically followed by those subscribing to thc tag interested in flash. In addition, the use of the hashtag intensifies a call to affiliate with these values by rendering the tweet more searchable by those who may be attracted to the general topic.

Hashtags and play

What I have presented so far is the simplest type of axiologization strategy used in hashtagging. Reiterating, the archetypal example already covered is the case where the hashtag labels an ideational target; for example, the following tweet taken from the Obama Win corpus used in Chapter 9 relating to the 2008 US presidential election contains the hashtag #obama:

> I just typed the words ‘Obama presidency.’ It felt good. **#obama**

However, the other major strategy deployed, a play on this former approach, is to insert some form of appraisal in the tag. This requires bridging on the part of the reader in order for them to unpack the underlying ideational target. For instance, using the Obama example once again, we have two tags positively appraising Obama using evaluative terms central to his campaign:

> Prediction: Obama as powerful leader starts within month, big speech, call for economic legislation **#hope #change**

This type of strategy invokes greater solidarity with the putative audience, as it assumes that they possess the cultural knowledge to understand the implicit references made in the tags.

Another kind of play related to the example just given is seen in a genre of memes to do with complaining about life. These memes use tags such as #IHATEITWHEN, #AREYOUSERIOUS, #DONTJUDGEME, #GETOVERIT and so on to express a kind of universal complaint about daily events. Using a hashtag flags the universality of the complaint, as it suggests that others share the same experience (and hence would use the same tag). In these instances expressions of appraisal occur in the hashtag rather than simple ideational topics. Some of these reverse the appraisal-ideation coupling normally seen. For example, the appraisal may occur in the hashtag with the function of invoking evaluation in the body of the tweet:

> **#iHATEitwhen** ppl edit their faces on pics and think that they really look like that pic lol

In this tweet, the AFFECT in the label, #iHATEitwhen, marks the invoked NEGATIVE JUDGEMENT of the behaviour (digitally altering a photograph for vanity). This might be contrasted with a tweet that negatively appraises the target in the hashtag, for instance:

> I **hate** #googlebuzz I think google have **totally fkd this up**.

Another hashtag meme, #THUGLIFE, is similar to #CONFESSION but more focused on amusing instances of playful INVOKED JUDGEMENT signalled by the hashtag. For example,

> just used dads good pen to scrape bird poop off the bottom of the cage #thuglife

The playful and humorous nature of this hashtagging is an example of interpersonal foregrounding on Twitter. Here the hashtag is not being used as a means to share ideational meaning; in other words, we are not going to use #CONFESSION to retrieve information. Instead we are likely to subscribe to this hashtag as a form of entertainment; in the case of this particular tag, humour, which seems to construe the social bond 'we all do things that aren't particularly socially acceptable but which aren't truly socially irresponsible; let's laugh at them'. In other words, Knight's (2010c) terminology, we 'laugh off' the unacceptable bond. Wolk (2010), commenting on #THUGLIFE, notes the important social role of humour in this kind of hashtag meme:

> The main thing to note here is that, unlike many of the Silicon Valley and Alley Twitterati, who take themselves and their tweets oh-so-seriously, this crew is having fun. The tweets are meant to be funny, and the funniest and most outrageous of them will wind up getting retweeted. Yet despite the fun and the humor, the flow of the hashtag is uniquely Twitter-like in that it mixes people who already know each other with strangers who are interested in the same topic – or joke, as the case may be.

The humorous play arises from the hope of being perceived as witty within the meme community and hence being retweeted. In this way it is a form of identity performance. An example of a hashtag meme employing a retweet is the following, with the hashtags and initialism acting as a metacomment on the original tweet:

> Lmao! #ghetto #thuglife RT @user: I just used a Sharpie as eye liner in the airplane bathroom.

Thus we have a classificatory system that is very different from the principles that would be employed to categorize a reference collection using subject keywords. From the perspective of information science, this may be perceived as a degradation of classification. However, the social function of the classification is not so much to facilitate efficient recall of relevant items but to allow people to bond around common experiences or themes.

As the meme examples suggest, hashtags are often very funny. Iterations of hashtag memes often result in accumulated displays of wit. The inline nature of #tag usage opens up the possibility of play with users creating tags that are unlikely to be used as search terms and which instead seem to function to intensify the evaluation made in the tweet. For example, returning to the #Obama example, during the 2008 US presidential elections, the following hashtags were used:

> #racialjokeswecanmakenow
>
> #presidentsIhavetheslightestshredofrespectfor
>
> #finallyicansleepatnight
>
> #americastillhasabrainandaconscience

This play is possible because of the close relationship of hashtagging to evaluation, where, as mentioned earlier, hashtags are usually evaluative targets. The final two hashtags listed are part of a single tweet:

> Yes! #f*ckin-A #obama #finallyicansleepatnight #byebyebush #americastillhasabrainandaconscience #whew!

Here the repetition of hashtags functions to upscale the positive evaluation of Obama's victory via the system of GRADUATION. Without the hashtags this tweet would lose some of its humorous hyperbole.

Searchable talk

The expansion of meaning potential seen in hashtag usage on Twitter is the beginning of searchable talk. Searchable talk is online conversation where people render their talk more findable and hence more affiliative. Talk using this kind of graphological expression amplifies the potential for users to connect with each other and so establish interpersonal bonds. In this way it becomes 'louder' and more bondable. We affiliate with a co-present (Goffman 1963), impermanent community by bonding around evolving topics of interest. This function is directly inscribed in the web interface to users' Twitter accounts as the list of trending topics. In increasing interpersonal reach in this way, hashtags mark meanings that have become hypercharged with an additional semiotic pull that may be likened to a gravitational field. They render searchable the coupling that occurs in the tweet and act as a label for the potential discourse community that they establish.

Searchable talk is the linguistic corollary of Morville's (2006) concept of 'ambient findability', where information can be found in any location. Now information can be found anywhere you have access to online talk, and the wealth of online discourse renders Twitter an interpersonal search engine. The search interface invites you to 'see what's happening – right now'. In other words, Twitter is the place you can go when you want to find out what people are saying about a topic right now and in order to involve yourself in communities of shared value that interest you in this given moment.

Searchable talk is supported by graphological conventions, allowing different features of the discourse to be retrieved by search (e.g. topic, addressee, etc.). This is both a product of the reduced affordances of the character-constrained mode and part of a 'multiplication of meaning' (Lemke 1998) affording new kinds of sociality. It is electronic discourse explicitly encoded as searchable. Like an index to talk, hashtags technicalize classes of tweets. Using the #obama tag is, for example, analogous to saying, 'If you are interested in values about Obama, search for me'. The social function of the hashtag is to provide an easy means of grouping tweets and, in turn, creating ad hoc social groups or subcommunities. Being searchable opens up a new kind of sociality, where microbloggers engage in ambient affiliation. The affiliation is ambient in the sense that the users may not have interacted directly and likely do not know each other and may not interact again. It also could not occur without adequate search functionality. Users searching to explore online conversations produced on social networking sites in this way is a new cultural process.

While Twitter has developed a search facility whereby a user can search via a range of parameters, this does not override current hashtagging practice. In fact, Twitter has incorporated a hashtag field into its search form. The utility of the hashtag can be seen when considering searches; for example, a search for 'election 08' will only return results containing this exact string. A tag such as #Election08, used in the 2008 US presidential election, becomes very useful for quickly retrieving a range of tweets about a topic that does not necessarily reference the topic as a word in the body of the tweet. In addition, it inscribes a form of intentionality in the tweet via the 'token of a type' relationship, described earlier in terms of relational processes in the lexicogrammar. This is because the user has explicitly indicated that the tweet is a token of the category labelled by the tag.

Developing models of ambient affiliation

As I have suggested in the examples in this chapter, hashtags invite an ambient audience to align with the values with which they are coupled. The 'hypercharge' of the hashtag locates the tweet within a bond network of values. For example, we might think of the search window for the tag #Obama as creating a momentary, ambient affiliative network of tweets in which this tag is a potential target of evaluation (Figure 5.2). Other available bonds temporally related to #Obama are marked by concurrent hashtags, such as #McCain.

The tags shown in the blue circles within the grey search window might correspond to the following tweets:

> Tears of joy! Tears of joy! #Obama
>
> Oh yeah, this needs to be said. EPIC WIN #obama
>
> Damn, just watched #obama speech again with @User. Amazing.
>
> @User Go for it. Obama is an includer, not an excluder. :-) #obama

The inscribed positive evaluations highlighted are examples of appraisal represented by the red circle in the model tweet in the figure. The group of tweets within the given search window, that is, a particular temporal

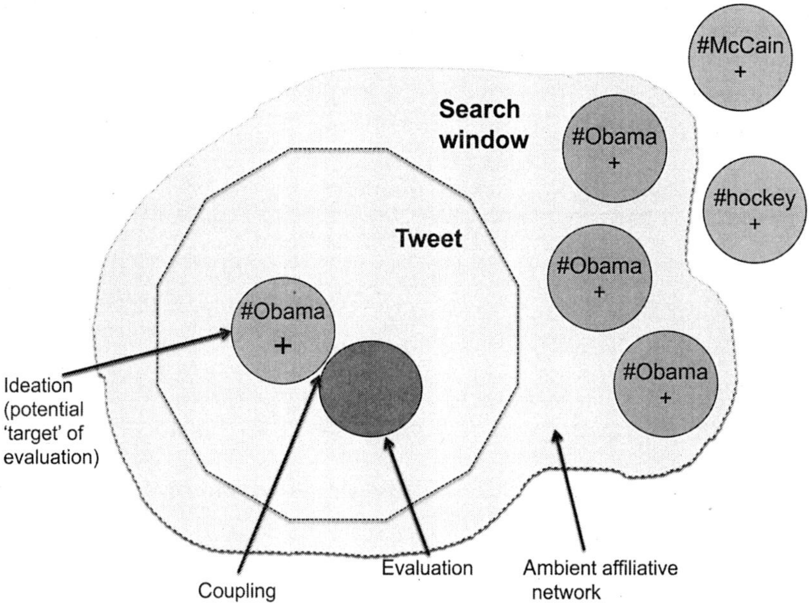

Figure 5.2 Search creating an ambient affiliative network for the '#Obama tag'

snapshot of the Twitter stream, is in effect a potential ambient affiliative network of these values. Competing or alternative values are marked by different hashtags (pictured outside the grey area in the figure).

Of course, for the sake of simplicity, the representation in Figure 5.2 factors out time, perhaps the most important dimension in Twitter discourse. This omission means that the tweet starts to look like an artefact rather than a text unfolding dynamically over the Twitter stream. We can, however, gain some insight into what a more time-based representation might be if we consider Figure 5.3, a StreamGraph (Havre et al. 2002; Byron and Wattenberg 2008; Clark 2008) showing the unfolding of tweets that contain the string 'happy'. This graph was produced using Clark's (2008) system Twitter StreamGraphs, a text visualization technique which was introduced in Chapter 3.

Examples of the tweets represented in the streamgraph in Figure 5.3 include

> Wow, I'm so **happy**, bring it home **Obama.**
>
> **Obama** :) I'm so **happy** that I'm crying! Hahhaa. Yes. He got his daughters a puppy. :) He is an amazing person and has well deserved this.

The stream along the bottom of the graph shows the coupling of 'happy (POSITIVE AFFECT) and 'Obama' unfolding over time (represented as

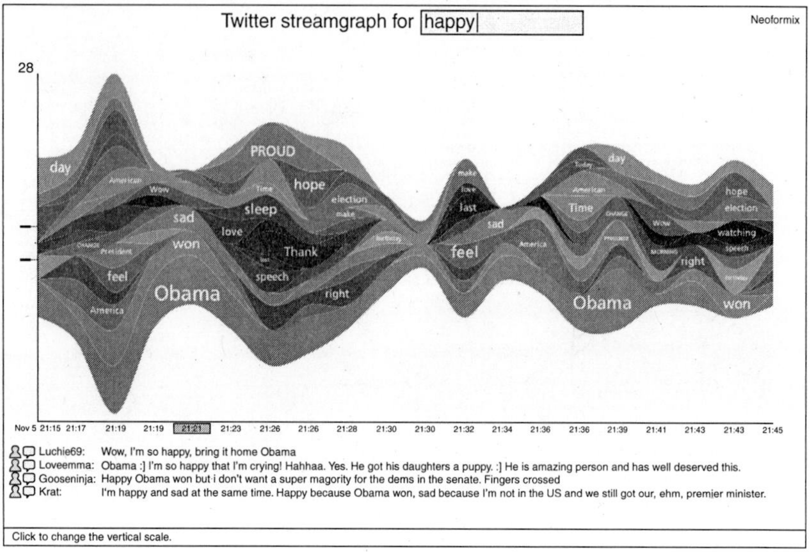

Figure 5.3 StreamGraph of the query 'happy' after the Obama election win (produced using Clark's 2008 system, Twitter StreamGraphs)

intervals along the *x*-axis). The other coloured streams present in the graph are lexical couplings within temporally related tweets. There is a fairly consistent relationship between 'happy' and 'Obama' in the time window graphed. Other evaluative items in the environment of 'Obama' and 'happy' were: 'proud', 'sad', 'feel', 'hope', 'right', 'won', 'love' and the like. Given that tweets unfold over time along private and public streams, considering them from this dynamic perspective is crucial when making claims about the discourse.

The argument that has been made in this chapter about the construction of ambient community assumes a dynamic perspective; communities shift as hashtags shift and different couplings of ideational and interpersonal meaning are established depending on what people are talking about at a given time. Theoretically, some topics might remain fairly constant, such as, for example, the 'microgenre' of complaining about something, usually technological, that is not working for a user, marked by the #fail tag (see Chapter 8 for analysis of the fail meme). The following is typical of complaints regarding software problems, an issue likely to persist for much time to come:

> Vista spent 45 minutes installing updates . . . only to say after rebooting that the update has failed and all changes are rolled back. **#fail**

Other tags will be more transient and dependent on political and social factors as they change in the context and hence are involved in more transient communities of value. For instance, the tag #election08, while it may have a fair degree of internal consistency (i.e. used consistently across a population of users), is unlikely to persist beyond that election period:

> Local TV reports: newspaper stands allover San Francisco more or less sold out. Everyone wants an Obama souvenir. #election08

Thinking about affiliation and microblogging in this way overcomes some of the problems that researchers have recognized regarding defining what constitutes a virtual community. By analysing how people use language to share values and considering their language from a functional perspective, we have a way of viewing community as unfolding discourse semantics rather than a static entity defined by non-semiotic attributes, such as whether profiles are linked. Some studies suggest that reciprocity in the following relationship on Twitter is not prevalent (Kwak et al. 2010) and the follow relation does not necessarily imply direct interaction between people:

> Many people, including scholars, advertisers and political activists, see online social networks as an opportunity to study the propagation of ideas, the formation of social bonds and viral marketing, among others. This view should be tempered by our findings that a link between any two people does not necessarily imply an interaction between them. As we showed in the case of Twitter, most of the links declared within Twitter were meaningless from an interaction point of view. Thus we need to find the hidden social network; the one that matters when trying to rely on word of mouth to spread an idea, a belief, or a trend. (Bernardo et al. 2008)

I argue, on the other hand, that the 'hidden' network is a semiotic network of meaning-making. The analysis of hashtagging practice undertaken in this chapter is a small step towards understanding the linguistic strategies in electronic discourse for construing community, where we apply a semiotic rather than purely interactional definition of community. In other words, Twitter and its hashtags practices allow an associative community to emerge through microblogging. This associative community is not necessarily formed through dyadic, reciprocal interaction but through searchable talk.

CHAPTER SIX

Internet memes

@User omg is dawkins ultimately responsible for all your base and lolcats? I hope that's on his cv.

Social media memes

The term *meme* was coined by Richard Dawkins in *The Selfish Gene* (2006) to suggest that we think about culture in a similar way to genes. According to his perspective, influenced by evolutionary theory, cultural units replicate and mutate as they are shared:

> Just as genes propagate themselves in the gene pool by leaping from body to body via sperms or eggs, so memes propagate themselves in the meme pool by leaping from brain to brain via a process which, in the broad sense, can be called imitation. (Dawkins 1989, p. 192)

Dawkins (p. 35) proposes that a successful meme has a number of key attributes contributing to its survival and proliferation: high longevity (the endurance of a copy), high fecundity (the rate of copying) and high copying fidelity (the amenability of the idea to copying). Culture is formed via natural selection as memes compete for semiotic survival.

The internet is a medium of communication that allows copies of multimedia to be quickly generated and transmitted. In this way it facilitates fast meme production, allowing, in Dawkins's terms, high fecundity memes, although not necessarily supporting longevity. Viral sharing of multimedia content occurs on the many different platforms and networks available via the internet, particularly social media networks, the focus of this chapter. Electronic texts can be easily remixed (Kate et al. 2010; Mitchell and Clarke 2003) through image, verbiage, audio and video manipulation to produce many derivatives of an original concept. Remixing is a popular activity in social media (Hill et al. 2010). ‘Memeing’ is inherently heteroglossic (Bakhtin 1981), as users affiliate around intertexts derived from both popular culture and trendily obscure sources.

This chapter is not, however, an investigation of memes in the sense that Dawkins and the field memetics propose. Instead it will employ a linguistic perspective[1], in essence adopting a semiotic lens on formulaic language that users themselves mark as memes, often with typographic devices such as hashtags. This popular sense of meme, appropriated by internet discourses, refers to online trends or fads, sometimes also described more generally as internet phenomena. The multimedia shares spreads virally through the various networks that constitute the internet. Particularly popular are image macros (image-text combinations). The focus of this chapter is on the involvement of language in the social affiliation central to meme making (hereinafter memeing) and the kinds of interpersonal meanings made using memetic phrasal templates.

Internet memes are deployed for social bonding rather than for sharing information. Humour is a very common strategy supporting this bonding, and memes are most often humorous, involving a witty observation or simply the absurd but catchy. Humour has been theorized as a factor in maintaining social and institutional boundaries (Davies 1982; Vine et al. 2009; Holmes and Marra 2002). Indeed a commonly cited reason for producing a meme is for the ‘lulz’, an act associated with humour that solidifies an ingroup (Tajfel 1970) by ridiculing others. Manifesting a kind of Schadenfreude, the phrase ‘I did it for the lulz’ is itself a meme, perhaps derived from ‘I did it for the laughs’. I will explore this kind of humour further in the study of the fail meme in Chapter 8.

The humour of widespread memes has generally developed from niche usage in a small community to general use in social media. Internet humour typically involves some form of inside joke, with general users using the joke as if they are part of the original, and often defunct, subcommunity. In this way memes that evolved within the culture of boutique communities, such as communities of online gamers, spread more generally to the point where the inside joke is a joke shared throughout the ‘internets’. Participating in inside jokes can increase what Lankshear and Knobel (2006, p. 242) refer to as one’s ‘cool quotient’. Participation in internet-mediated affinity spaces, spaces likely to use self-referential language and in-jokes, functions to amplify displays of cultural awareness of the latest trends (Lankshear and Knobel 2006). Within internet culture high status is given to being privy to an inside joke before it becomes well known:

> Online, contributing directly to spreading a new, mutating meme is considered cool, and generating an entirely new meme is even cooler. Being among the first to spot a potential online mutating meme is perhaps coolest of all. (p. 242)

Humour appears to be one of the attributes involved in increasing the fecundity of a meme: 'some element of humour, a rich kind of intertextuality, and the use of anomalous juxtaposition' (Lankshear and Knobel 2006, p. 221). The role of intertextuality will be seen in many of the examples used in this chapter. The term *internets*, which I used in the previous paragraph, is an example of memetic usage that functions as a high profile in-joke. Internet is an intertexual allusion to technological illiteracy. The text referenced is the following 'Bushism'; that is, a faux pas made by former U.S. President George W Bush[2] which spawned many online parodies and general lampooning of conservative identity:

> I hear there's rumors on the Internets (sic) that we're going to have a draft. (Commission on Presidential Debates 2004)

Internet users wield this inside joke to suggest that they are part of the cognoscenti rather than the 'illiterati' of which, by their view, Bush is an exemplar. The following are examples from HERMES:

@User Obviously. I made up all the awesome on	**teh internets.**	
@User Can't you watch it online? Where is	**the internets**	when you need it?
Wow . . . an athlete died training?? That's what I get for being unplugged from	**the internets**	for the past 30 hours or so
@User You do not observe	**the internets, the internets**	observe you
@User you should secretly record suzi and post it all over	**the internets**	

Additional cachet is acquired by using the form, seen in the first example, 'teh internets', a self-conscious reference to a common typological error made when typing 'the'. However, the phrasing of the internets meme is now largely outdated. Most online memes are fads in the sense that they rise and decline rapidly. Applying a meme beyond its semiotic used-by date is undesirable, lowering status. Part of the memetic lifecycle is this point at which a meme is declared to be passé by subcommunities, who go on to adopt other memes with which to distinguish themselves. Complaints such as the following can be found in message boards, blogs and comments:

(Yes, the Internet. The next moronic fucker geek-wannabe I hear say 'internets' or 'interwebs' is going to get an earful from me.) (Mobius 2009)

The following user discusses more explicitly the social expiry date of a meme which originated in a small community:

'This meme was then used to death and abandoned by the forums, at which point it was picked up by the rest of the internets and from there became the utterly retarded LOLcats meme. http://encyclopediadramatica.com/I_Am_In_Your_Base_Killing_Your_D00ds

Thus, it is useful to think of the kind in-group/out-group structuring that the inside joke invokes as a process rather than a static product. Online memes, and culture defined more broadly, continually evolve. Particularly in the case of social media, where recency is so important as a communicative principle, status is achieved by using the most recent meme, and being too slow on the uptake is status reducing. In other words, there is a kind of infinite regress of cool.

Some non-topical memes may endure for longer periods due to their wide appeal. An example is the popular LOLcat meme. LOLcats are a form of 'image macro' (sometimes called a cat macro). Images macros superimpose verbiage on an image as form of caption. The superimposed verbiage is typically humorous. LOLcat image macros usually feature a photograph of a cute cat and a short phrase in LOLspeak, a parody of internet slang. These memes populate image-sharing boards, such as the infamous 4chan, where they are claimed to have originated[3]. A well-known example is Happy Cat (Figure 6.1), the image which inspired the title of the website 'I can haz cheezeburger', a popular website that achieves millions of visits per day. It relies on user-driven content, with users contributing their own custom-made LOLcats. Some derivatives are absurdist, such as 'long cat' (a cat with an excessively long torso that has spawned an accompanying faux-mythology) and 'monorail cat' (a cat depicted running along monorail tracks). Others invoke a cheeky cat persona performing human activities, often technology related, with formulaic captions, such as 'WHATZ UR NAME ILL ADD U ON FACEBOOK' (Unknown 2007) or 'I made you a cookie but I eated it' (Unknown 2007).

Generating an image macro and submitting it to a website or posting it to a blog or forum is an act geared toward fashioning semiotic belonging. In this way LOLcats are skewed towards the interpersonal; in other words, they are used for social bonding rather than purely information sharing. They mark awareness of a particular aesthetic where 'Participation signals solidarity with the spirit of the phenomenon

Figure 6.1 Happy Cat, an example of a LOLcat image macro (Unknown 2007)

("I get it; I'm part of this" or "I am like you") rather than any particular attention to the information value of these images' (Knobel and Lankshear 2008, pp. 28–9).

Another enduring memetic form, also a common component of image macros, is Engrish, a parody of grammatical errors in non-native English, most often Japanese English. The most famous Engrish-based meme is 'All your base are belong to us'. This meme is sufficiently well-known to have its own Wikipedia page detailing its history (Wikipedia: The Free Encyclopedia 2011). Its origins are in poorly translated text from the introductory animation of a Sega Mega Drive console game, Zero Wing, produced in 1991:

Captain: What happen?
Operator: Somebody set up us the bomb.
Operator: We get signal.
Captain: What!'
Operator: Main screen turn on.
Captain: It's You!!
Cats: How are you gentlemen!!

Cats: All your base are belong to us.
Cats: You are on the way to destruction.
Captain: What you say!!
Cats: You have no chance to survive make your time.
Cats: HA HA HA HA!
Cats: Take off every 'zig'.
Captain: You know what you doing.
Captain: Move 'zig'.
Captain: For great justice. Don't even try to make sense

The meme became popular in the form of image macros derived from an animated GIF (Graphics Interchange Format) (a bitmap image format) of the opening scene to the game. Appropriation of content, such as the screenshot of the Zero Wing game, is a form of remixingthat results in 'a resonance set up in the viewer: a simultaneous recognition of the familiar and a noticing of the different' (Mitchell and Clarke 2003, p. 342). The screenshot remains familiar while the iterations of amusing captions set up the resonance with new meanings. The practice of generating this kind of resonance can be generalized as the communal activity of customizing a memetic template by 'riffing' on a theme.

This chapter focuses on social media memes; that is, memes that are propagated via social media. Huang, Thornton and Efthimiadis (2010, p. 174) term memes associated with particular hashtags 'micro-memes', suggesting that as 'more users adopt the hashtag, they add to an asynchronous, massively multi-person conversation by tweeting their thoughts about the topic prompted by the hashtag'. Replication arises via sharing among friends or as part of the larger exchanges through social tagging within communities of users. For example, as we saw in Chapter 5, some memes seen on Twitter are marked by hashtags that allow users to follow the topic indicated by the tag and, in so doing, form an ad hoc ambient community.

Social media memes are realized by a range of different features, including the following:

- phrasal templates – phrases with 'slots' available to be modified (e.g. In Soviet Russia, [object] [plural verb] you!);
- catchphrases (e.g. 'This is relevant to my interests');
- image macros (e.g. LOLcats);
- initialisms – an invitation to respond to a theme (e.g. WDYDWYD [Why do you do what you do?], TGIF [Thank God it's Friday]).

I will deal primarily with the first type of structure, using specialized corpora of phrasal templates captured from Twitter to explore the way users commune around the shared experience. This communion is a type of affiliation where shared knowledge of the frame marks inclusion in an ambient group of the initiated. The contributions represent something beyond mere parroting of a phrase. Instead users manipulate a template, adapting it in a paradigmatic way by inserting their own meanings into the template slots and experiencing the pleasure of intertextual play.

Phrasal templates

This chapter focuses on a set of social media memes involving a particular kind of formulaic language: the phrasal template. These memes are structured as frames with slots that can be modified, allowing the meme to 'mutate' as users add their own elements to the slots. The 'casing' of a phrasal template is a kind of formulaic scaffolding, while items that occur in the slots are customizable. For example, the simple template 'X is the new Y' is often cited as an archetypal instance of a phrasal template (McFedries 2008). It is also an example of what Whitman (2004) refers to as a 'snowclone'; that is, 'a kind of phrasal cliché, with some assembly required, that journalists adapt for use and re-use over and over again' (Liberman and Pullum 2006, p. xi).

A phrasal template's frame is not usually subject to a large range of variation, although there will always be users who seek to show off their skill by witty modification, metareference and inversion. Different entities may fill the slots depending on the semantic domain and context. 'X is the new Y' is a template often seen in media discourse and discourses of fashion and design. The final slot is most likely to be occupied by the word *black*, as in 'Pink is the new black'. The following news headlines selected from a search engine results for the query 'is the new black' (restricted to news pages) are examples of this kind of usage:

White	**is the new black**	in home décor http://articles.sfgate.com/2010-08-08/home-and-garden/22209122_1_home-decor-spelling-bee-white
Handmade in the UK	**is the new black**	http://fashionunited.co.uk/fashion-news/fashion/handmade-in-the-uk-is-the-new-black-201008209329
Is grey really	**the new black**	www.express.co.uk/posts/view/191351/Is-grey-really-the-new-black-
	The new black is	a $100 suit www.dailytelegraph.com.au/lifestyle/the-new-black-is-a-100-suit/story-e6frf00i-1225907020933

The template has also been appropriated by other discourses. Thus, instances such as the following title for an article on financial risk are also possible:

> Risk **is the new black** in world turned upside down www.smh.com.au/business/risk-is-the-new-black-in-world-turned-upside-down-20100804-116pe.html

This type of structure is perhaps related to Pawley's (1986, pp. 62–3) concept of a speech formula as 'a conventional pairing of a particular formal construction with a particular conventional idea or idea class'. It exists at the strong end of idiomatic expression (Sinclair 1987) since the casing of the template is a fixed frame that cannot readily be reverse engineered from its components. In essence, phrasal templates are a form of collocation since they involve 'syntagmatic association of lexical items, quantifiable textually' (Halliday 1961, p. 276). Indeed they have been referred to as 'phrase long collocations' (Smadja 1994, p. 149).

Both corpus-driven and corpus-based approaches to formulaic language have been undertaken in Corpus Linguistics, the former exploring predefined linguistic patterns and the latter inducing patterns from the corpus (Morley and Partington 2009). Renouf and Sinclair (1991) use the term *collocational framework* to refer to 'a discontinuous sequences of two words, positioned at one word remove from each other; they are therefore not grammatically self-standing; their well formedness is dependent on what intervenes'. This chapter uses phrasal template corpora to investigate what commonly occupies such intervening slots. The semiotic occupants reveal the preoccupations, desires and fears of users of social media and the fun to be had in customizing meaning.

Using the social media corpora to understand phrasal templates

In this chapter I will consider five memetic phrasal templates which represent a range of use, from a LOLcat-inspired meme (1), a joke-based meme (2), memes based on popular TV series (3 and 5) and a meme based on an event in popular culture involving a celebrity (4):

1. Im in ur [noun] [present infinitive verb] ur [noun].
2. In Soviet Russia, [object] [plural verb] you!
3. I for one welcome our [classifier] overlords.
4. Look/Yo [vocative], I'm really happy for you, imma Let you finish, but [noun] is the [superlative] of all time.

Table 6.1 Frequency of phrasal template memes in HERMES

Meme	Number
'Im in ur'	8
Russian reversal	9
'I for one'	6
'Imma let you finish'	96
Pimp my ride	3

5 Yo sup dawg, I heard you like [noun X], so I put a [noun X] in your [noun Y] so you can [simple present verb X] while you [simple present verb Y]

The focus will be on how these templates are used by microbloggers in the service of ambient affiliation. For each template I will consider two types of data: instances from HERMES and instances drawn from specialized corpora generated by automatically scraping the phrasal templates from Twitter using regular expressions. Table 6.1 displays the number of instances of each meme in HERMES, giving an indication of their relative frequency over 100 million words. As can be seen the 'Imma let you finish' meme is the most frequent, perhaps because it is the most temporally topical.

As I analyse these memes I will approach them in terms of ambient affiliation from two perspectives:

- frame level – bonding around the aesthetic pleasure of adding items to a phrasal template's customizable slots;
- slot level – bonding around the values expressed in the particular iteration of the meme that has been generated by inserting items into the template slots.

In general, phrasal templates seem to have a 'rallying' (Knight 2010c) function, inviting affiliation simultaneously at these two levels.

The 'im in ur' meme

The phrasal template 'im in ur' is a meme alleged to have originated in online gaming discourse, reportedly an exchange between a noob gamer (see Chapter 7 for a discussion of the term *noob*) and a more experienced user, 1337h4x, playing Starcraft:

> dude, where are you?
>
> im in ur base, killing ur d00ds

The template has the following form, borrowed from the second move in the exchange:

im in ur	noun	present infinitive verb	noun

For example:

> @User O hai! im in ur fazbook defacing on ur walls! kthxbye

While this description of the origin of the meme makes a neat picture, it is most likely urban legend perpetuated by media reports that do not take a critical etymological or historical perspective using primary texts. Given the scope of the internet, it is unlikely that the true origins of a meme can be uncovered with certainty.

The casing of the template is usually written in a form of lolspeak, using its characteristic morphology (e.g. nouns ending in z). It also applies a form of pseudo-'textese' (Crystal 2008) (abbreviation used in SMS text messaging), with shortened words such as 'ur' for 'your'. Sometimes a mix of uncontracted and shortened orthography will be deployed: for example, 'I am' together with 'ur'.

As with most of the examples covered in this chapter, this meme has an ongoing association with image macros, particularly LOLcat macros. Captions include text such as 'im in ur fridge eatin ur foodz' with a picture of a cat raiding a fridge (Unknown 2006), 'I'M IN UR WIKI RVRTIN UR EDITS' (Unknown 2008) with a picture of a cat sitting on a laptop, and 'I am in ur dictionaries verbing ur nounz' with a picture of a cat sitting on a dictionary (Unknown 2006). These macros do not function as serious censure and instead are self-consciously humorous, drawing on the incongruence central to the amusing aesthetic of a cute kitten behaving badly. In other words, they are funny because they present an unexpected coupling pattern. Most posts using this phrasal template retain this lightly humorous tone and rarely express any genuine irritation with another user. They have moved away from, or 'de-coupled' from, the original contextual meaning of the template, in this case, the combative jibe 'im in ur base, killing ur d00ds'.

Table 6.2 Instances of the 'im in ur' meme in HERMES

1		Im in ur	code, decoupling it. For I am the astronaut you've been looking for.
2	@User Dude everyone knows *I* invented math which is what physics is based on, I win! Also	Im in ur	interwebz eating ur nrgz!
3	I'd say I've been on the phone all morning but . . . [MUAHAH! THIS IS AT&T!	I'M IN UR	CELL NETWORK, EATING UR CALL. FAILED!]
4		I'm in ur	Kitchen, bein' domestic. Homemade Valentine cookies for the win!
5	Starcraft 2 beta to be released this month.	I'm in ur	Base killin ur doodz http://bit.ly/bLcL0H
6	@User	I'm in ur	Tweets stalking your locations.
7	Had a swim. Now	I'm in ur	bespoke code applying #rule35 #drupal
8	@User do'h – at least it's a human response, better than	I'm in your	Bank hoarding all your moniez

This movement toward humour and away from negative interpersonal charge is characteristic of the semiotic progression of most internet memes as they come to be used in social media. The memes tend to be benign possibly because they operate in an environment in which anonymity is not readily supported and their discourse may be publically traceable to their offline identity. A notable exception to this friendly semiosis is where a meme is aimed at ridiculing a public figure such as a celebrity or politician (as we will see later in this chapter with the Kanye West meme).

There were eight instances of the phrasal template in HERMES shown here (Table 6.2) as concordance lines for 'Im/I'm in ur/your':

As these concordance lines show, the dominant semantic domain of the template is technology (interwebz, code, tweets, bespoke code). Preoccupation with technology is a recurrent feature of social media possibly because social media users as a demographic contain a large population who wish to construct a 'tech savvy' identity. These users are likely to enjoy discussing technology and displaying their technical knowledge.

Consider, for example, the technical lexis in the first instance, 'Im in ur code, decoupling it. For I am the astronaut you've been looking for'. This lexis is relatively specific to the software development community. 'Code' refers to the instructions written by a programmer in a particular programming language telling the computer what to do. 'Decoupling' refers to the software design practice of reducing the number of dependencies between different sections of a computer program in the hope of reducing the errors that occur when another part of the program is altered. 'Astronaut' refers to a particular kind of identity, an 'architecture astronaut' (Spolsky 2001); that is, a programmer who tends to think too abstractly, concerned more with technical purity than practical solutions, and hence one who is metaphorically 'up' in the stratosphere rather than on earth getting things done.

Play with such technical lexis is a kind of inside joke. While not intrinsically amusing, the play is witty because it references ideas that are well known in one community in an unexpected way. This builds solidarity with a putative ambient community of other users who understand the technicality. Framing this lexis in a phrasal template highlights the terms as identity markers – in effect, saying 'because I am part of this subculture I can play with these technical terms in this frame, look at me!'. As I will explain further in the discussion of humour in Chapter 8, humorous references are often homophoric (Halliday and Hasan 1976), requiring insider knowledge of the culture to unpack their meanings.

The 'Im in ur' meme plays with the metaphor of being 'on the inside'. However, instead of breaching an enemy's defences, as suggested by the original phrasing, other kinds of phenomena are infiltrated – from cars to space centres. The most common entity to be breached was some form of internet-related technology, particularly social media services, as in the following example, which refers to the location-referencing 'geotagging' capabilities of Twitter:

> @User I'm in ur tweets stalking your locations

The processes undertaken in the infiltrating are generally negative, for example:

- Theft:

  Thankfully there's one person left in the neighbourhood who doesn't realize they're OPEN so 'Im in ur router stealingz ur internets'

  @User Im in ur panel stealing ur memes

- Unauthorized change:

  @User im in ur pooter, loggin ur passwds

im in ur app bundle, re-signing ur b1nar13z

im in ur phone, compilin ur kernel

im in ur live SQL queries, editing ur where clausez.

- Unauthorized use:

  Im in ur interwebz, downloading picz of michelle rodriguez ;)

- Unauthorized monitoring:

  @User I'm in ur tweets stalking your locations

- General harassment:

  im in ur forums. trollin ur threadz.; @User O hai! im in ur fazbook defacing on ur walls! Kthxbye

However, some instances did involve benign processes, such as the following example about providing another user with assistance in solving a problem with the open-source web browser application Firefox:

> Im in ur tweetz helping you wiz Firefox problemz! ;) ^TM

Lolcat humour was also prevalent:

> LOL WUT. Investigated intermittent alarm. Found: 'O hai im in ur L33TT car settin off ur alarms' http://twitpic.com/2e0me8 [picture of a dog looking out the window of an expensive car]
>
> Im in ur sinkz steelin ur wataz . . . http://yfrog.com/ndnl0oj [picture of a cat in a sink]

The meme was also deployed, though less frequently, in a wide range of semantic domains, such as fashion:

> @User_yelp Im in ur dress, wearin ur applez. http://yfrog.com/mhsbzj [link to a picture of the legs of someone wearing a dress with apple pattern print]

News and current affairs:

> IM IN UR CITEHS KILLIN YOUR BIODIVERSITEH! http://bit.ly/cssQjl [interesting concern & comment on 'sustainability', despite the pic!] [link to an article about urban biodiversity]

Communication:

> @User Im in ur face, steelin ur werdz

and industry:

> Im in ur mine taking ur coals.

The kinds of social relationship construed when using this phrasal template are twofold. There is a frame-level pleasure of being involved in mass-customization of a meme and being part of a community of users all editing the phrasal template slots to suit the particular meaning they want to make or joke they want to crack. Simultaneously, at a content-level, the users are also bonding around the values they insert into the slot, typically using the APPRECIATION system to express aesthetic evaluation. A common evaluation that is invoked is technical process, for example, the tweet discussed above about helping with a Firefox problem or the tweets about unauthorized change to technical artefacts such as passwords and SQL queries. The meaning made via the humour appears to project an identity for the tweeter as technically proficient. In addition, the template increases solidarity, suggesting that, 'we are so familiar I can tease you about invading your space without actually being offensive and instead being humorous'.

The overlord meme

> One thing is for certain: there is no stopping them; the ants will soon be here. And I for one welcome our new insect overlords. I'd like to remind them that as a trusted TV personality, I can be helpful in rounding up others to toil in their underground sugar caves. (Springfield TV anchor Kent Brockman in 'Deep Space Homer', *The Simpsons* [Mirkin 1994])

The quotation from *The Simpsons*[4] shown above is the likely origin of the Overlord internet meme. However, it is entirely possible that this episode itself may be making an obscure reference to USENET (a threaded internet discussion system) discourse. In this episode the Springfield TV anchor Kent Brockman mistakenly believes earth is under invasion by giant alien ants and begins a speech to appease the invading overlords. The phrasal template has the following structure:

I, for one, welcome our classifier overloads

The meme invokes a kind of mock deference used for humorous effect. At one level it can be read as ironic, taking the form of a snowclone used to 'ironically indicate that one really isn't all that pleased that X has so much power but is resigned to the fact because nothing can be done about it' (McFedries 2008, p. 27). However, the meaning made with this template is not necessarily straightforward. The irony is often double layered (mock ironic deference!), particularly where the classifier is something relatively benign, such as:

> @User I for one welcome our new rabbit overlords.

The main function of deploying such irony is affiliation rather than simply an evaluation of the particular 'overlord' specified in the template slot. For example, consider the following exchange, in which a user points to an image of a child's dinosaur colouring on a page on which amusingly incongruent speech bubbles, such as 'What do you mean Polaroid is discontinuing instant film?!' have been appended:

> @User Nothing is worse, however, than a hipster dinosaur. www.forkparty.com/hipster-dinosaurs/
>
> @user1 @User2 I, for one, welcome our new hipster dinosaur overlords.

The reply in this exchange acts as show of alignment with the original post rather than expressing any serious fear of the specified overlord. The mock deference serves to heighten the solidarity via humour; the reply construes complicity in the imagined world populated by dinosaurs who can speak and express 'hipster' opinions. In general, the frame of the overlord phrasal template itself prefabricates an expression of solidarity with the possessive pronoun 'our', defining an ingroup united under the oppression of the specific type of overlord.

The template is most frequently used in response to a current event in the news. For example, this tweet was posted on Twitter at the time that a ruling overturning a ban on same-sex marriage was made by a federal judge in the United States:

> I, for one, welcome our new married homosexual overlords.

The tweet can be read as positively evaluating the judge's decision if we read 'married homosexuals' as a hyperbolical inversion (i.e. something benign construed as something malignant), possibly a humorous dig at conservative objection to gay marriage.

The most frequent substitutions possible for this template are shown in Table 6.3, which provides the five most frequent collocates of 'overlords' in a corpus of 895 tweets containing the string 'I for one welcome'.

Table 6.3 The five most common collocates of 'overlords' in the 'I for one welcome' corpus

Alien (67)	e.g. www.vgtv.no/?id=27553 Portal opens over northen Norway . . . Good luck surviving the invasion.	I for one welcome our	New alien overlords.
Robot (45)	e.g. Aussie and Finnish Scientists create single-atom transistor http://tinyurl.com/ylosyrs	I for one welcome our	New robot masters
Butterfly (40)		I, For One, Welcome Our	New Space Butterfly Overlords http://bit.ly/4GyNMe
Google (37)	e.g. Google Chrome is out for Mac.	I, for one, welcome our	Google overlords.
Space (34)	nasa.gov's alexa ranking (as read by the toolbar in firefox) is 666.	I, for one, welcome our	space demon overlords.

'Space' almost always collocated with 'butterfly'. This appears to be a reference to a media report at the time about painted lady butterflies that were hatched in space.

As the examples given indicate, the meme is often used as a comment on a news item in tweets with a deictic function, pointing to web content that the user has found. The first example, 'alien overlords', refers to new reports of an apparent failed Russian missile launch that resulted in a blue spiral formation in the night sky above Norway. Some other examples of this usage are:

I, for one, welcome	our new alien overlords.	#norwayspiral
I for one welcome	our new alien overlords,	and commend them on their choice of Norway. They obviously like death metal.
What is up with that spiral UFO sighting over Norway? I for one welcome	our new Alien masters,	or the CERN boys have some explaining to do.

This collocate 'robot overlord' usually refers to a news items about advances in robotics or amusing or interesting incidents involving existing robotic technology. These news stories sometimes had titles such as 'his breakdancing robot is going to destroy us all' (http://guyism.com/2009/12/this-breakdancing-robot-is-going-to-destroy-us-all.html) that echo the invasion motif of the meme:

RT @user: I, for one, welcome	our new break-dancing robotic overlords	http://bit.ly/5UB0Ty
Aussie and Finnish Scientists create single-atom transistor http://tinyurl.com/ylosyrs I for one welcome	our new robot masters	
I, for one, welcome	our new robot overlords.	Protect us! http://bit.ly/5iF71Q[5]

Where a headline or weblink collocates with a phrasal template containing a related classifier in the template slot, the structure functions to invite readers/followers to bond via the APPRECIATION system. The pre-packaged mock deference offers a witty way of saying, 'hey, look at what I noticed in the news' and evaluating the following link positively as pointing to noteworthy content. Chapter 4, on evaluative language in microblogging, provides further discussion on this type of coupling of deixis and positive evaluation in tweets. By construing the positive evaluation as a phrasal template, the tweet taps into the existing social bond created by this structure, in other words, the collective rallying around contributing iterations of the template to the communal pool of instances of this meme. In this way, the tweet contributes to the frame-level affiliation mentioned earlier. This bond is then leveraged to direct attention to the link being appreciated.

The meme could also be used in the kind of conversation-like structure that Twitter affords. The following is an example of the meme used in a conversational exchange about peas:

1		User1	@User2 Don't make me shoot you with my pea gun!
2	9 minutes later	User1:	@User2 Mmmmmmmm . . . Peas . . . nom nom nom
3	1 minute later	User2:	@User1 There's nothing wrong with peas, they just don't belong in tuna macaroni salad!
4	2 minutes later	User1:	@User2 Peas belong everywhere, and I, for one, welcome our new pea overlords.
5	2 minutes later	User2:	@User1 Pea lover! Pea lover! *points and laughs*

In this exchange the use of the template in exchange 4 is clearly humorous. The repetition of pea in this conversation is hyperbolic, as is the grand assertion made in exchange 3. The choice to use the phrasal template is part of the humorous play of finding ways to insert the lexical item into the exchange. Using 'pea' as a classifier both in the phrasal template and in the exclamation 'pea lover' (exchange 5) is humorously absurd and also gently mocks, in a very generalized way, ideas about identity and food preferences.

But why choose a phrasal template as a mode of expression? The answers seems to centre on the way that humour is being used affiliatively to connect with an imagined community of users with similar attitudes. We find the template amusing and bond around the value being expressed while also experiencing a Bahktinian intertextual pleasure when we are able to pick out any popular culture references made (in this instance, the original Simpsons reference of the meme). Interestingly, the meme still appears to be funny even if you do not work out the Simpsons reference. This may point to a layering of intertextuality that increases the complexity of the humour. Wit and cleverness seem to be at stake with this meme, fuelling the verbal play.

The Russian reversal meme

The Russian reversal meme is a phrasal template in which the subject–object structure is swapped alongside an optional mismatch in subject–verb agreement. The template has the following form:

In Soviet Russia	object	plural verb	you

The subject–verb mismatch is optional in Twitter versions of the meme, with most instances choosing agreement:

> In Soviet Russia, Status Updates You!!!!

The original joke upon which this meme is reportedly based is attributed to the comedian Yakov Smirnoff, whose political humour in the 1980s contrasted life in the United States with the then Communist Soviet Union. His joke is as follows:

> In America, you can always find a party. In Soviet Russia, the party always find you.

The structure of the joke is an instance of antimetabole; that is, a device where grammatical order is reversed. For example, this line from Keats's 'Ode on a Grecian Urn' is an example of antimetabole:

> Truth is beauty, beauty truth

Here the poet leverages the aesthetic appeal of the grammatical symmetry for rhetorical effect.

The original prefacing of the phrasal template with the marked theme 'In America' to make a satirical comparison between nation states is not usually retained in current usage. Thus, some of the political nature of the original joke is lost when it is deployed via social media.

This phrasal template was more likely than the other template discussed in this chapter to operate at frame level, with users simply bonding around contributing iterations that did not involve particular evaluative couplings. For example, many posts did not give additional context, and the template was instead used purely for wordplay. The following example is from a corpus of 657 instances of the meme:

> In soviet russia, car drives you.

The most common verbs in R2 position after 'Russia' in the corpus are shown in Table 6.4. As this table shows, the verbs range across a wide variety of semantic domains such as motoring, food, technology and entertainment. Much like the other memes discussed in this chapter, technology is a common semantic domain for this phrasal template (e.g. 2, 4 and 8).

Tweets such as the following require some technical knowledge from the user to unpack:

> RT @User: In Soviet Russia, iPhone jailbreaks you!!

In this example the process of 'jailbreaking' is domain-specific lexis for referring to unlocking a smartphone so that it can be used with any phone carrier. Often phrasal templates about technology had a similar deictic function to the overlord meme directing the reader to a website or news story. For example, this tweet directs the user to an article about the author of a game:

> in soviet russia interview drives you: http://tinyurl.com/2dkzy22 (http://gamestar.ru/article/1607.html)

Specific couplings of evaluation and ideation characterizing a particular world view are not obvious in most instances in the corpus. Nevertheless, the memes seems to have an affiliative function, operating at frame rather than slot level; in other words, focused on the play of the phrasal template itself

Table 6.4 Most common items in R2 in the Russian reversal meme corpus

N	R2	Example
1	DRIVES	In soviet russia, car drives you.
2	RELAXES	RT @User: In Soviet Russia Database Relaxes You: http://bit.ly/br76bG [link to a Russian website on the Apache Couch database which has the motto 'Relax']
3	IS[6]	in soviet russia, lactose is intolerant of you!
4	FOLLOWS	RT @User: In soviet Russia Twitter follows you.
5	EATS	@User in Soviet Russia, falafel eats YOU!!
6	HAVE	@User in soviet Russia, birthday have you!
7	WRITES	Roses are red, violets are blue. In Soviet Russia, poem writes you.
8	TWEETS	In Soviet Russia, Twitter tweets YOU.
9	KILL	Alex: 'In soviet russia, zombie kill you!' Me: 'They do that here in America too stupid!'
10	DRINKS	@User In Soviet Russia, vodka drinks you.
11	WATCHES	In soviet russia tv watches YOU!

rather than the items that are inserted into the template's slots. As mentioned earlier, this type of meme usage, rather than inviting the reader to share a particular value, is part of a communal rallying around a surface texture: the fun of playing with the template and making your own iterations.

This is not to say that there were no instances where the user had inserted his or her own value-coupling into the template, construing a social bond to be shared. For example, consider the following:

> In Soviet Russia, Budgies smuggle Tony! #ausvotes

This tweet, posted prior to the 2010 Australian federal election, embeds a political inside-joke within the template that would be shared by consumers of Australian news media. The reference is to the Australian politician Tony Abbott, who was photographed wearing 'budgie smugglers', an Australian expression referring to scant male swimwear. During this election campaign Abbott was frequently mocked for his swimwear choice, with word play on his desire to stop 'people smugglers' from bringing illegal immigrants into Australia often deployed:

> My action plan for australia. Stop illegal budgie smugglers #ausvotes

Why package this kind of play as a phrasal template? The original comparison of the United States and Soviet Russia is not the point of these structures. An important motivation is ambient affiliation. As asserted elsewhere in this chapter, these meme templates offer a humorous way of creating a bond through implied shared knowledge, in the above case, affiliating around a particular perception of a political figure. The humorous nature of the template frame in which the ideation-value coupling is inserted, charges the bond to be shared in the sense that it primes or makes more likely an opportunity for Twitter members to affiliate. For the budgie smuggler example, the value is negative appraisal of Tony Abbott and, by association, the Australian Liberal Party. The template frame charges this bond in the sense that it leverages humour as a mechanism for increasing rallying around the value expressed. In other words, if you laugh at the meme, you may become complicit in the value it is espousing. As we saw in Chapter 5, the hashtag #ausvotes also has a charging function, increasing the likelihood that people reading election updates will see this post and share the bond.

Pimp my ride meme

This meme references the catchphrase of the rapper Xzibit, the host of *Pimp My Ride*, a TV show on American MTV. The Encyclopedia Dramatica (2009) gives the following synopsis:

> Each week, Xzibit jacks a white boy's car, takes it to his crib – West Coast Customs – strips it, sells the parts to his homies and paints it neon green with a roller.
>
> Before returning it to the unsuspecting dupe, he replaces the interior with stupid shit relevant to the owner's interests (according to the dupe's so-called friends) but mainly for maximum lulz . . .

Under the username 'mrxtothaz', Xzibit initially rejected the meme publicly on Twitter:

> Everybody with the 'sup dawg' shit can find the highest place in your house and jump on something sharp to kill yourselves. it's fucking old.

Later, he attempted to embrace the meme:

> come on guys! I DO have a sense of humor! Some of the 'SUP DAWG' shit is actually funny!!! Im not mad @ you!! Have at it! LOL

The original image macro which allegedly precipitated the meme featured an image of Xzibit with the caption YO DAWG I HERD YOU LIKE CARS

SO WE PUT A CAR IN YO CAR SO YOU CAN DRIVE WHILE YOU DRIVE. The resultant phrasal template seen in microblogging takes the following form:

> Yo sup dawg, I heard you like [noun X] so I put a [noun X] in yo/your [noun Y] so you can [verb X] while you [verb Y]

The meme manifests a kind of play with the idea of phenomena within metaphenomena. It also demonstrates a play with the idea of inside in a related way to the 'Im in ur' meme. A similar preoccupation with the semantic domain of technology and a self-indulgent reflexivity seen in the other phrasal template in this chapter is also prevalent in the way the pimp my ride meme is used. For example:

> Yo dawg, I heard you like Twitter. So I put a Twitter in your tweet so you can tweet while you tweet.
>
> Yo dawg I herd u liek reading facebook feed so I liked a page of spam on your fb feed so you can read while you rage.

However, the meme overall had much less semantic consistency than the other memes and was employed over a diverse range of domains.

This semantic variation may be due to one of the functions of bonding at the frame level being finding increasingly absurdist items to occupy the slots of the template. Consider the following:

> @User yo dawug, I herd you like speakin in ebonics so I put double negs in yo double negs so you can be black while being white.
>
> @ballsybalsman Yo dog, I heard you like explosions, so I put C4 on your tank so you could explode while you tank.
>
> I heard you like pushing up so I put a bra in your gym so you can push up while you push up

One user uses the template to parody the preoccupation with popular culture reference seen in most meme usage:

> Yo dawg, I herd you like pop culture, so I put some pop culture in your pop culture so you can explode from all the popular you've cultured.

This meme was much less common than the other memes described in this chapter, and this may be due to the time frame in which they were collected coinciding with declining interest in the TV programme *Pimp My Ride*.

Like the Russian reversal meme, this phrasal template more often is used for frame-level rather than slot-level bonding (though both were simultaneously possible). In other words, what is at stake is the virtuosity demonstrated in playing with the template rather than the particular values inserted into the slots. As with most of the phrasal template memes, cleverness is the dimension that is socially valued, as the following two examples suggest:

> RT @User: Yo dawg I heard you like deadlines so I put a deadline in your deadline so you can stress while you stress.
>
> @User Yo dawg, I heard you like blisters, so I put a blister on your blister so you can hurt while you hurt? Sorry! D:

In both of the instances there is no particular ideation-value coupling construed. Instead the textual enjoyment of these iterations of the meme is inherently metatextual. In other words, the pleasure is similar (though the artefact is much less complex) to that invoked by looking at an Escher drawing. We bond via the mutuality of this pleasure.

'Imma let you finish' meme

The 'Imma let you finish' meme is a phrasal template that arose after an outburst, possibly staged rather than spontaneous, by Kanye West at the 2009 MTV Video Music Awards during Taylor Swift's acceptance of an award. He is reported to have declared,

> 'Taylor, I'm really happy for you. I'll let you finish, but Beyonce had one of the best videos of all time! One of the best videos of all time!'

The interruption was widely reported in news media and sparked an outpouring of image macros with captions based on the following template:

Look/Yo [vocative], I'm really happy for you. Imma let you finish. But [noun] is the [superlative] of all time!

The template is the most popular of the memes covered in this chapter, with a corpus of 1,499 instances created. Iterations included image macros:

> Yo Firefox, I'm really happy for you, I'll let you finish, but Safari is one of the best browsers of all time. (picture of Firefox window with an error message displayed)

> YO I KNOW WWII JUST ENDED AND YOU ARE GLAD TO SEE EACHOTHER, I'M REALLY HAPPY FOR YOU, IMMA LET YOU FINISH, BUT BRITNEY SPEARS AND MADONNA HAD ONE OF THE BEST KISSES OF ALL TIME. (picture of Alfred Eisenstaedt's 'The Kiss')
>
> Yo Darwin, I'm really happy for you, I'm gonna let you finish, but Lamark had one of the best theories of all time! (picture of Charles Darwin)
>
> Yo you ONTD, I'm really happy for you. I'm gonna let you finish, but 4chan has started some o the best memes of all time!
>
> YO KATHERINE HOWARD, I'M HAPPY FOR YOU AND I'M GONNA LET YOU FINISH BUT ANNE BOLEYN HAD ONE OF THE BEST BEHEADINGS OF ALL TIME.
>
> YO OBAMA, I'M REALLY HAPPY FOR YOU. IM GONNA LET YOU FINISH, BUT CANADA HAS THE BEST HEALTH CARE OF ALL TIME! (picture of President Obama at a health care forum)

In keeping with the cultural location in which the meme originated (the VMA awards), it is typically used in the corpus to refer to people in the domain of film, music or general celebrity. The most common occupants of the vocative slot (Table 6.5) and the five most common occupants of the

Table 6.5 The five most common items occupying the vocative slot in the Kanye West phrasal template corpus

N	L2	Example
1	SPENCERPRATT	RT @user: Yo @spencerpratt, I'm really happy for you, imma let you finish . . . but @kanyewest is the most entertaining douchebag of all time. OF ALL TIME.
2	SELENA	RT @OfficialJONATO: Imma let you finish selena, I'm really happy for you. . . . But Demi has the best Tv actress comedy OF ALL THE TIME.
3	BELIEBERS	RT @user: Yo Beliebers, I'm really happy for you and Imma let you finish but the Jonas Brothers are the best JB of all time. #TheOriginalJB
4	COLE	Yo, Chris Cole, I'm really happy for you and imma let you finish, but Nyjah Huston had one of the best runs of all time! #robbed #MMC.
5	KANYE	@kanyewest Yo Kanye, I'm really happy for you and imma let you finish but Muse had the best VMA performance of ALL TIME!!!!!!! Sorry had to.

Table 6.6 The five most common items in R1, after 'but', in the Kanye West phrasal template corpus

N	L2	Example
1	@KANYEWEST	RT @spencerpratt: Yo @spencerpratt, I'm really happy for you, imma let you finish . . . but @ kanyewest is the most entertaining douchebag.
2	MRS. DOUBTFIRE	RT @TWITTERWHALE: Yo @tylerperry . . . Imma let you finish but Mrs. Doubtfire was one of the funniest cross-dressers of all time.
3	ALL (THE GIRLS AROUND THE WORLD)	RT @user: Kayne: 'Yo Timberlake, I'm happy for you & imma let you finish but all the girls around the world are actually More #hornyforjustin bieber'.
4	@JUSTINBIEBER	RT @user: aye @kanyewest imma let you finish but @justinbieber has the best Twitter of all time, OF ALL TIME. (:
5	DAVID ARCHULETA	RT @user: Hey TWILIGHT, imma let you finish, but DAVID ARCHULETA has the most fanatic fans of ALLL TIME!

R1 slot, after 'but', are all referenced figures in popular culture such as celebrities or film characters (Table 6.6).

Again, with a kind of self-indulgent reflexivity, technology and social media were a major semantic domain for the template. For example:

> 'Yo Facebook, I'm really happy for you and Imma let you finish, but Twitter is one the best social networking sites of all time.'
>
> User: Windows imma let you finish, but Ubuntu is the best Ass kicker OS of all time! Twanye.com
>
> RT @User: 'imma let you finish, but . . . Consolas is one of the best programming fonts of all time. OF ALL TIME!!!' Agreed

The social play at work in this memetic phrasal template at a slot level is that of the humour of customization. The meme invites users to add their own humorous cultural observation and so to bond with other users. This might involve bonding around common holidays:

> User: Yo Halloween, imma let you finish your special day and all, but Christmas us the best holiday of all time!!!!!

Or a kind of playfully competitive rallying around support for celebrities with different types of fan base, for example, Justin Bieber fans parodied as Beliebers:

> RT @user: Yo Beliebers, I'm really happy for you and Imma let you finish but the Jonas Brothers are the best JB of all time. #TheOriginalJB

In addition, it might reference a current news story or display knowledge about a historical figure or incident. For example, the following tweet, in somewhat poor taste, references a news story about parents who deliberately hid their child in order to become minor celebrities and Anne Frank, a young girl who kept a diary during the Holocaust and was killed in the Nazi camps during World War II:

> User: RT @User2: RT @User3: Yo Balloon Boy, Imma let you finish, but Anne Frank had the best attic hideout of all time -_- really?!

The meme also plays upon the humour of hyperbole. Most instances employ hyperbolic praise via the APPRECIATION system, using superlatives to indicate that something is the maximal example of a class. Most of this appreciation is satirical. However, the following tweet is an example of the phrasal template directly inscribing negative evaluation, in this case criticism of a particular brand of crib note:

> 'Yo, I'm very happy for you and Imma let you finish that Shakespeare fact, but Cliff Notes has the best useless info of all time.'

Celebrity scandals were also a popular area for this meme. The most common example in the corpus was the Tiger Woods scandal; the celebrity golfer was found to have had a large number of extramarital affairs and publicly humiliated in the popular press. Reference to this scandal was combined with the semantic domain of the Olympics (which due to the timing of the corpus collection was a frequent topic) to produce the following amusingly witty tweet:

> Imma let you finish Olympics, but the best mens downhill of all time was Tiger Woods.

Why are internet memes humorous?

The Tiger Woods tweet with which I ended the previous section exemplifies frame-level bonding via humour. We are impressed by the author's capacity to fuse two semantic domains (celebrity scandal and Olympics coverage) to create a witty iteration of the template, where wit is defined as the ability to wield intertextual resources for play. The phrasal template iteration deployed also has the additional humour of a pun on 'downhill' to reference both skiing and a decline in celebrity status. Most internet phrasal templates such as this example are lightly humorous in tone, particularly when they are used in social media. Humour is integral to their memetic function (Lankshear and Knobel 2006). It aids the viral proliferation of the meme, as users share items that they find funny with their followers.

Where a meme's original instantiation involved negative appraisal (for example, the 'Im in ur base killing your doods' meme), social media memetic templates shed this type of meaning through a kind of interpersonal 'lightening'. I will explore this kind of interpersonal lightening further in Chapter 8, on internet slang, where I investigate how slang terms are used more benignly than in the vitriolic days of forum flaming and trolls. The humour of internet memes thus seems to be a humour closely associated with the APPRECIATION system rather than the JUDGEMENT system (explained in Chapter 4). In other words, it is largely a humour of aesthetics rather than of serious social censure, and framing something as a phrasal template is an exercise in the display of wit, often involving an element of self-indulgence. Liberman (2004) suggests that these phrasal templates differ from Whitman's (2004) snowclones because of such indulgence, arguing that they 'are self-conscious and ironic evocations of a pattern viewed as intrinsically funny, rather than serious uses of a pattern that is felt to be intelligent and perhaps even original'.

A meme typically starts off as an inside joke and progresses to a wider community, where it becomes humorous in a more generalized sense, and then is rejected by the original host community, who go on to define themselves via other means. Before a meme reaches its semiotic expiry date, users will add increasingly obscure intertextual references to the template slots in displays of template skill. As Lankshear and Knobel (2006, p. 220) note, this kind of mutation seems 'in most cases to help the meme's fecundity in terms of hooking people into contributing their own version of the meme'. Services, such as MemeTracker, have arisen that track how template from a variety of sources such as news media and blogs mutate over time (Leskovec et al. 2008). Memes often involve hashtags: as social creatures we appear to derive pleasure in tracking our own semiotic play. We might define 'play' here from a social semiotic perspective as disruptions in the more typical couplings of a particular culture, for example, reversal in the subject–object configuration in the Russian reversal meme or increasingly improbable figures occupying the slots of the Kanye West meme.

CHAPTER SEVEN

Internet slang

Social media facilitate different kinds of casual, interpersonal interaction. There are many avenues for informally checking in with and chatting to other users. In this environment slang proliferates, as it does in casual conversation (Eggins and Slade 1997). This chapter explores examples of slang in microblogging, suggesting the role this kind of language plays in invoking solidarity while contributing to the construal of ambient affiliation. As we will see in a detailed study of 'noob', many instances of social media slang have shed their initial negative interpersonal loading and are used mostly jovially in social media. This seems indicative of a general shift in terms of the ATTITUDE system away from JUDGEMENT toward APPRECIATION in social media. This chapter seeks to systematize the kinds of slang used in social media with evidence from HERMES.

The popular conception of internet slang centres on salient non-standard orthography, such as initialisms (e.g. LOL, 'laughing out loud'; BRB, 'be right back'), used frequently in many kinds of computer-mediated communication where brevity is advantageous. As one tweet quips:

> I made this new internet slang today, LMBOSHMSFOAIDMT – Laughing my butt off so hard my sombrero fell off and I dropped my taco.

Definitions of slang are often circular and imprecise, and there is no widely accepted model of slang (Nunnally 2001). It is typically described as a form of non-standard or informal language.

> What linguists and lexicographers alike seem to agree on is that slang includes words that are *below the level of stylistically neutral language*, and that, in addition to being group-related, it is innovative, playful, metaphorical and short-lived. (Stenström et al. 2002, p. 67)

Early work on slang was prescriptive and exclusionary, suggesting that slang was substandard usage not appropriate in formal contexts. For example:

> Slang is a kind of speech that belittles what it conveys. It was developed to express a few widely prevalent attitudes and therefore lacks precision and variety. You should avoid it because it is inadequate to critical thinking and because it imposes a cynical or flippant tone on your serious ideas. (Milton 1952, p. 309)

The view presented in the quote is clearly outdated. However, recent concern over the impact of internet slang on youth literacy is the product of this kind of preoccupation with slang degrading more formal written expression. Thus, research endeavouring to determine whether text speak is harmful to general literacy has flourished (De Jonge and Kemp 2010; Drouin and Davis 2009; Kemp 2010; Plester and Wood 2009; Pleste et al. 2009; Powell and Dixon 2011; Rosen et al. 2010; Tagliamonte and Denis 2008). Fear about eroding literacy is encouraged by media exaggeration of the differences between computer-mediated and face-to-face discourse (Thurlow 2006).

According to Moore (2004), 'basic slang' can be distinguished from other forms of slang by its pervasiveness and longevity. In a study of two long-standing slang terms, 'swell' and 'cool', Moore suggests that a slang term will endure while it is linked to a particular identity arising from sets of values that the younger generation at the time find appealing:

> Speakers who utter the term cool suggest that they understand and approve of the attitude of knowingness, detachment, control, and rebelliousness that comprises the core meaning of this term. Despite being widely used over a period of decades, the core value that cool expresses is still positively valued by the baby boom generation and the cohorts following it, and this core value gives this slang term its quality of undiminished freshness. (Moore 2004, p. 83)

Halliday's concept of an 'anti-language' is useful for thinking about the kinds of slang that have come to populate the discourses of different subcultures:

> The principle is that of same grammar, different vocabulary; but different vocabulary only in certain areas, typically those that are central to the activities of the subculture and that set it off most sharply from the established society. (Halliday 1976, p. 571)

Slanguage

Corpus-based approaches to slang often consider slang among a particular group of speakers, often young people such as teenagers and college students. Stenström and her colleagues (2002) explore a range of 'slangy' phenomena, which they broadly term 'slanguage', in teenage talk. The focus is predominately on slangy lexis, including proper slang words (slang that may be found in a dictionary), dirty words (such as swear words), vogue words (words that are popular for short periods of time), vague words (such as fillers and set markers), proxy words (used in place of quotative verbs), and small words (such as softeners). Examples of each of these kinds of lexis can be found in HERMES (see examples in Table 7.1).

Most of the lexis discussed in this chapter is not present in traditional dictionaries or print-based slang dictionaries, since the language is largely 'ephemeral language' (Adams 2000). One non-scholarly, collaborative resource that is available, however, is UrbanDictionary.com. This is a web-based dictionary of slang and popular internet-related expressions that uses a voting system for editorial filtering whereby an accepted term receives a certain proportion more 'accept' than 'reject' votes from users. In this way the terms present in the dictionary conform to a community-determined definition of slang:

> The flexibility afforded by UD's online format and idiosyncratic approach to the contributions of its thousands of often-disparate users makes a rigorous definition of slang a moot point. While traditional print slang dictionaries determine a definition, isolate a corpus, and abide by physical

Table 7.1 Instances corresponding to categories of slanguage in teen talk (Stenström et al. (2002)

Type of slanguage	HERMES example
proper slang words	RT @User: nothing quieter than your hotel room after a great show. peaceful and **spooky** at the same time.
dirty words	i've really had enough of seeing america. said it before, but it all looks the exact **fucking** same.
vogue words	Went to the toboganing park too it was **mad** =D
vague words	Today just reminds me of the hellish week i have ahead of me. No emoticon face **thingy** would do it justice.
proxy words	And she **goes** 'pinch, leave an inch and roll' lmfaooo
small words	i'm gonna get 2 tigers and call em rose and fred like on animal planet **innit**. birds luv cats **innit**

> parameters determined by publishers and their deadlines, UD grows with the language and with the evolving notion of what the contributors themselves consider slang to be. (Damaso and Cotter 2007, p. 22)

While not a typical academic resource, Urban Dictionary does afford insight into slang practices and their contexts of use, useful for obtaining a starting point for exploring a given instance of slang and also for assessing its stability.

Most research into slang suggests a relationship between slang and notions of identity, community and group boundaries. There has been ongoing work on the study of college slang and the slang of young people and teenagers (Stenström et al. 2002).

Solidarity and involvement

The features that Stenström, and colleagues (2002) have identified as slangy language can be usefully approached using the system known as involvement in systemic functional linguistics. Involvement is a system heavily involved in negotiating group identity. It works together with the appraisal resources explained in Chapter 4, complementing them 'by focusing on non-gradable resources for negotiating tenor relations, especially solidarity' (Martin and White 2005, p. 33). Table 7.2, adapted from Martin (1992, p. 532), shows involvement resources across the strata of discourse semantics, lexicogrammar and phonology as theorized by SFL. As Martin notes, this table is not intended to be exhaustive but to give a indication of the kinds of resources in play. Involvement offers 'interactants ways to realize, construct and vary the level of intimacy of an interaction' (Eggins and Slade 1997, pp. 143–4).

Unpacking involved CONTACT (the 'involved' column in Table 7.2) can be especially difficult since its discourse semantic patterns tend to be homophoric. So whereas, endophoric references can, by definition, be resolved with the cotext, homophoric reference require specialized cultural knowledge to unpack. This knowledge may be further specified by the permutations of the relationship between interactants which allow them to draw on a shared semantic history (e.g. inside jokes etc.). One of the main ways of heightening solidarity is via humour, particularly boundary-marking humour, as we will see in Chapter 8.

Involved CONTACT tends to invoke rather than inscribe meanings, drawing upon assumed networks of social meaning to unpack the relevant connotations. For example, the following tweet uses core lexis that the general audience of users is likely to understand:

> My computer keyboard isn't working. What am I supposed to do.

Table 7.2 'Tenor – aspects of the realization of contact' (Martin 1992, p. 532)

Contact proliferation/contraction [phonology foregrounded]	Involved	Uninvolved
phonology	pre-tonic delicacy marked tonality marked tonicity varied rhythm fluent reduction processes native accent range of accents acronym	basic tone unmarked tonality unmarked tonicity constant rhythm hesitant full syllables standard accent single accent full form
grammar	minor clauses mood ellipsis mood contraction vocation range of names nick-name	major clauses no ellipsis no contraction no vocation single name full name
lexis	specialized technical slang general words	core non-technical standard specific words
discourse semantics	dialogue homophoric implicit conjunction	monologue endophoric explicit conjunction
interaction patterns	experiential metaphor	experiential congruence

We might compare this, however, to the specialized lexis (shown in bold) and the technical lexis (shown underlined) in the following:

> @User Reason for **power cycle** is that you do need to **drain** so it **resets** all the <u>persistent registers</u> on the <u>i82574L's</u>.

Martin (2007) provides the following definition of the difference:

> Technical lexis can be defined as lexis which has to be learned by definition, though language (typically in institutionalized learning); specialised lexis on the other hand is lexis that can be learned by observation, though gesture (it is ostensively 'defined') . . . like everyday lexis, specialized lexis is concrete; but like technical lexis it belongs to specific walks of life

> (and similarly enacts the boundaries between common and less common sense discourses). (Martin 2007, p. 41)

The contrast between the extent to which these two tweets call on common sense or specialized knowledge held by communities is the basis of most jokes about the unhelpful nature of IT helpdesk assistance:

> 'You're not seriously going to tell me to **turn it off and on** again are you?' – 'Nope . . . Could you just **re-cycle the power** please? *grin*'

Here the joke involves play around the common-sense and specialized meanings for restarting the computer in order to fix a problem.

The affordances of Social Media corpora in studies of slang

Social Media corpora allow researchers to study internet slang in its social context, providing a ready means for collecting high volumes of naturally occurring examples of usage. In contrast, offline slang typically occurs in contexts that are difficult to record, such as casual conversation between friends. Search functionality also means that specific terms can be queried, enabling the researcher to build up a substantial specialized corpus despite very narrow selections of criteria (see, for example, the fail corpus in Chapter 8). However, while mainstream Social Media slang is readily studied with corpora scraped from publically available SNS feeds, the niche slang of particular subcommunities may be more difficult to isolate and access, being more likely to occur in private forums.

Many social media platforms have geotagging capability whereby users can either manually (via Facebook) or automatically (e.g. Google Latitude) indicate their geographical location. Making use of this type of information is the focus of the domains known as geotagging (Eisenstein et al. 2010) and location-based social networking (Lee and Sumiya 2010). Users are often posting in the field via a mobile device and thus are able to respond almost immediately to events around them and as 'citizen microbroadcasters use their mobility and understanding of their community's needs to provide broad-ranging and timely information to that community' (Erickson 2010, p. 1202), likening them to citizen journalists. Twitter optionally collects metadata regarding the location from which a tweets was posted. This functionality means that slang researchers have a means for studying regional variation. For example, in a study of lexical variation using a geotagged Twitter corpus, Eisenstein and colleagues (2010, p. 1285) found that 'A large number of slang terms . . . have strong regional biases, suggesting that slang may depend on geography more than standard English does.'

As the discussion of the term *noob* below will exemplify, there appears a general trend in internet slang, as it deployed in social media, away from negative judgement and the kind of derisive slang usage identified by Dumas and Lighter (1978), towards slang as a social lubricant for increasing solidarity.

Twitter slang

With the development of a new social technology comes associated development of medium-inspired slang that comes to be part of how communities of users express particular identities and form what might be likened to weak versions of anti-languages (1976). This slang allows users to bond around shared use of the medium, 'over-lexicalizing' (1976) aspects of this experience. For example, alongside linguistic creativity similar to that seen with SMS (e.g. shortening of words with numbers, initialisms etc.), Twitter users have generated a lexicon of playful, self-parodying slang involving the prefixial accretion 'tw', derived from the word Twitter, appended to a commonplace word. For example, we can refer to other users as 'tweeps' (a variation of 'peeps', i.e. people), the entire Twitter community as the Twittersphere (similar to the way 'blogosphere' refers to the collective semiotic space occupied by bloggers as a community), face-to-face meetings with other users as 'tweetups' (meetup):

> @User Let's keep the conversation going here in Twittersphere!

This kind of slang is often seen in naming practices on Twitter, where it acts as a playful solidarity marker. Naming is widely acknowledged to play a part in both construing solidarity and solidifying ideology (Kress and Hodge 1979; Poynton 1984; Martin and White 2005; Knight 2010b). Brown and Gilman (1960) introduced the concept that the use of certain pronouns for example the *tu* and *Vu* forms in languages such as Italian and French, are an expression of power or solidarity. Knight (2010b) suggests that naming is helpful in interpreting implicit attitude in couplings of value and ideation (see Chapter 3) often seen in conversational humour.

The kind of tw-based naming slang seen with Twitter has a convivial, lightly humorous function, likely because the terms generated sound somewhat ridiculous and are in this way self-parodying. There are a number of tw-based naming slang for the collective of followers that an individual has accrued. For example, users may refer to their collection of followers as 'tweeps', 'tweepz', 'tweeple'. One environment where this slang frequently occurred was address to a user's followers, particularly

Table 7.3 Examples of tw-based naming slang.

tweeps	Goodmorning tweeps, lol don't you hate when ppl say that . . .
tweets	Goodmorning tweets happy cupid sucks day lol . . . Somebody skype and sing happy bday to me!
tweeple	#Goodmorning Tweeple! Anybody out there miss me? lol
tweeties	goodmorning my tweeties!
tweeters	Good Morning Tweeters . . . Have a Great and Productive Day!
tweethearts	Good morning tweethearts!! I had a dream y'all all left me! Whew . . . Glad it was just a dream!!!
tweetheads	Good morning tweetheads!
tweetlanders	Good Morning Tweetlanders!! Cloudy cool day here in NH, how is your part of the world?
twit fam	Good Morning Twit Fam!!! Eating & Tweeting on the go while stuck in traffic :/

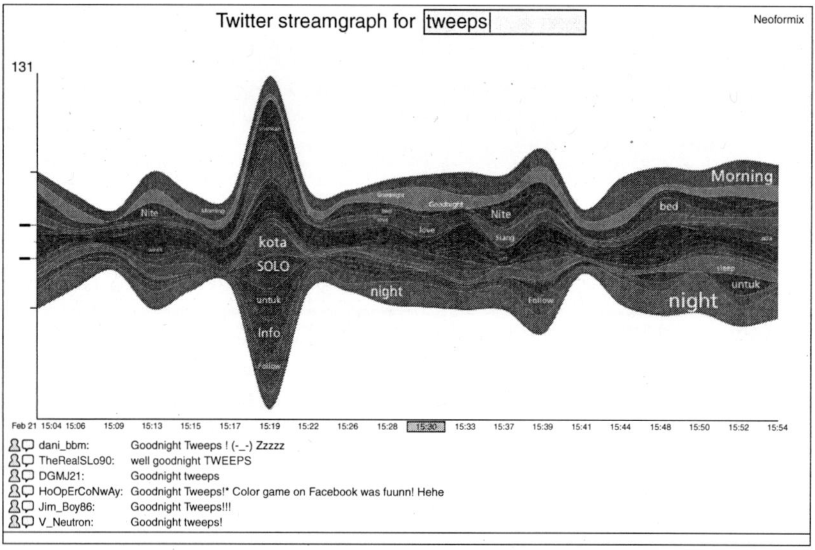

Figure 7.1 Twitter StreamGraph for 'tweeps', created using Clark (2009)

as a first tweet of the day (see the instances of collective noun slang in Table 7.3). This association is also shown by the StreamGraph for tweeps (Figure 7.1). For example, tweeps often functioned as a vocative.

The most common 3-gram involving tweep in HERMES was 'GOOD MORNING TWEEPS':

> Good morning tweeps ! Busy day today. Let's get it started, shall we . . .

Variations can become increasingly tongue-in-cheek, with 'twit' replacing 'tweet' in terms such a 'twithead', invoking humorous associations of idiocy:

> good mornin' twitheads and #Twittercrushes LOL

The proliferation of tw-based terms is related to Halliday's ideas about anti-languages through the notion of 'overlexicalization', an accumulations of terms for an area of experience that is important to a subculture. In the case of Twitter as a culture, creating a relationship with the ambient audience is clearly of significance, hence this overlexicalization. Similarly this kind of prefixial accretion is seen when referring to the audience as an ambient space with terms such as TWEETLAND/ TWITTERSPHERE

> Good morning Tweetland. Weatherman got it wrong, no snow. Darn!
>
> Morning holds such promise, like a blank canvas waiting 4 yr 1st inspired brush strokes! Good morning Twittersphere!

However, the overlexicalization does not seem to have the function of making the anti-language impenetrable to outsiders that is seen in subcultures such as hackers. Instead it mainly functions to enhance 'the possibility for verbal play and display within the anti-society' but remains small with distance (Montgomery 1995, p. 98). Poynton (1990, p. 80) has noted 'proliferation' as a feature of increased solidarity 'where address provides the clearest example of proliferation, as the range of potential choices increases with intimacy but remains small with distance'. The proliferation of tw-based naming slang suggests that users are displaying a form of intimacy with their followers.

The kind of address, while in part directed at a given user's base of followers, is also an address to an unknown audience. This bears some relation to the 'generalized other' of unaddressed YouTube vlogs (Wesch 2009). Oulasvirta and his colleagues (2010, p. 243) argue a stronger position, suggesting that microblogs are not directly addressed at anyone but instead 'are made available for others' response, without the obligation of response'. The address 'goodmorning tweeps' is unlikely to be met with replies from other users, but instead functions to indicate ambient presence in the absence of other types of indicators of online presence (such as online status markers in instant-messaging services, such as Google Talk). Lack of direct reply is generally not an indication of rejection in this context. 'In the context of microblogging, when replies are missing, it is easier for the initiating speaker to assume the audience is not present than to think there is non-interest or disapproval' (Oulasvirta et al. 2010, p. 243).

The tw-prefixing functions like a self-conscious, playful solidarity marker. It indicates affinity with a putative Twitter community, while the absurd-sounding nature of words formed simultaneously make fun of being an avid Twitter user. This is particularly seen in words such as 'twitastic' (fantastic):

> Hope everyone is having a twitastic day! /via @user / you know it, man!

It is also more explicitly inscribed with the kind of tw-based naming conventions mentioned earlier. Overlexicalizing 'followers', for example, liken themselves to a family with the term *twitfam*:

> Twit Fam what up! Who's up wit me

Self-parody is also achieved by referring to a user as a 'twit'. This term was also used to mean 'post'. The most common 3-gram for twit in HERMES was the title of the software, 'The Twit Cleaner', an application for removing followers from your Twitter stream.

Geek identity

As researchers have noticed the kind of typograhic innovation that has arisen with different forms of CMC, a common place to begin their investigations is an apparent geek or hacker slang (Blashki and Nichol 2005). These studies often claim to study 'l33tspeak', However, caution is needed, as what may be being studied is, in effect, a parody of a popularized hacker language. The true discourse of subcommunities conforming to the so-called hacker ethic likely has long since found other ways to fly beneath the radar of observers with ways of avoiding automatic detection. In addition, the linguistic features they use to distinguish themselves from other kinds of internet users is unlikely to resemble 'leetspeak' as appropriated by social media users. The half-life of niche-community slang is likely quiet short. More mainstream slang which is parasitic on niche slang has a longer shelf life.

There has been some interest in studying the geek as a subcultural identity (McArthur 2009). 'Geek' is a relative concept which is dependent on the perspective from which it is approached rather than on stable categories of identity:

> . . . nerdiness, like all identities, is a contested domain in which speakers struggle both over control of shared values, via positive identity practices (Who's better at being a nerd?), and over control of identity itself, via negative identity practices (Who counts as a nerd?). Such conflicts reveal the heterogeneity of membership in the community of practice – its constitution through the work of central and peripheral members alike. (Bucholtz 1999, p. 220)

In other words, one user's geek is another user's noob.

Construals of a geek identity are one of the most obvious identity patterns in the HERMES corpus. However, it is largely not the archetypal geek persona, an obsessive, expert programmer, but a much milder version, a kind of amatuer geek. In other words, these are general users taking on aspects of geekiness that are positively appraised. Often the effect is humorous and self-depricating. Urban Dictionary provides the following amusing definition of a geek that reflects the term's shift from a derogatory gibe to a positive evaluation:

> The people you pick on in high school and wind up working for as an adult. The geeky kid now owns a million dollar software company

The identity referenced in the example given has particular currency in popular culture, relating to a perception about various high-profile technologists who have achieved billion-dollar fortunes in their ventures. This kind of wannabe identity has also been noted by (Marwick 2010) in the context of the Silicon Valley technology scene.

However, when interpeting these construals of geekiness, it is important to read them within their context. The authentic geek identity relies on exclusivity based on particular expertise and originated as a kind of alternative, reappropriated identity in a similar way to other slang that began as taunts, such as 'wog'. When this kind of identity is deployed in a more mainstream way via social media, the original meanings are diluted. Genuine geeks would likely refer to these users as wannabes. Most of the slang discussed in this chapter is not the true slang of subcultures; instead it is much more widespread. In this way social media slang holds some similarity to Moore's (2004, p. 59) concept of basic slang, 'slang expression that emerges when a young generation or cohort takes on a set of values starkly opposed to the values of its elders and begins to use a positive slang expression that is semantically linked to its new value orientation'.

Table 7.4 The five most frequent realizations of 'geek' in HERMES

N	Word	Freq.
1	GEEK	1969
2	GEEKS	636
3	GEEKY	440
4	GEEKED	184
5	GEEKING	84

However, it remains to be seen whether most social media slang will meet the criterion of longevity that characterizes basic slang. Moore notes the mainstream cache of basic slang:

> Basic slang is probably used as much within mainstream society as among subcultures, but its usage still conveys a somewhat subversive message. (Moore 2004, p. 61)

Similarly, while 'geek' is used in this mainsteam manner in HERMES, users still summon some of the term's subversive edge, using it in a similar way to a fashion accessory to assert a particular kind of aesthetic in relation to technology.

Table 7.4 shows the five most frequent realizations of 'geek' in HERMES. An example is the following tweet:

> I am such a geek. My idea of romance is talking about the iPhone or my amazing Quad-Core Intel Xeon. & my hubby still likes me. I think. :D

Clearly, the original instantiation of the geek identity is unlikely to embrace the term of endearment 'hubby'. This tweet, as with most tweets adopting the quasi-geek identity, involves an element of humorous showing off. The humour plays on tension between the expectation that the described phenomena invoke negative appraisal but are instead highly positively appraised by the user, rendering him or her a geek and simultaneously slightly better than the rest of us who are not sufficiently geeky to appreciate the evaluation. The phrasing 'My idea of romance is' plays on the common cultural pattern of complaining about a partner's, usually male, lack of romantic tendencies; for example,

@User1 @User2 I've never seen someone get so excited and start speaking	**geek**	about apps! Amazing!
4,8,16,42.. . . The numbers that keep showing up. I'm a horid	**geek**	and always forget them.
binary for the word 'amor'.	**geek**	love. :D http://tiny.cc/8GKWe
Just started tethering my 3G connection from my rooted Android G1. Why did I buy a USB modem last month? I am happy back in my	**geek**	clothes!
Constant f2.8. Ohhh yeahhhh. :) My apologies for the	**geek**	speak. http://twitpic.com/13zaqq
@User . . . and I'm sure you can do that UBER	**GEEK**	;)
@User sent the link to a couple of BIG movie	**geek**	Friends. Their all up in a hizzy about it . . .

> #yourenotmyvalentine becuz my idea of romance isnt me playing with ur kid all day while ur playing ps3 #fail

The tweet reappropriates this pattern again deploying a humorous counterexpectation about what constitutes romance.

The following concordance lines for geek in HERMES show a similar pattern of expressing pleasure about positively evaluating something that is usually not the subject of positive appraisal.

A slang term often associated with geek is 'nerd'. As these concordance lines suggest, geek is closer to 'enthusiastic expert' than nerd, where the latter invokes negative judgement to do with a kind of endearing social awkwardness; for example:

> Nerd boy I see occasionally @ bus in a.m. wanted to brag about having a gf, but lacks social graces to do so not awkwardly. It was cute.

Nevertheless, geek is a term generally used in an environment of positive appraisal, as the concordance lines for geek suggest. McArthur (2009, p. 61) notes that geek has shed most of its orginial negative value to 'become an endearing term of affection (and perhaps jealousy) and label for those who demonstrate expertise in a certain field'.

The most common 3-gram for geek in HERMES was 'SUCH A GEEK'

Table 7.5 Most frequent collocates of 'geek* out'

N	Word	With	Example
1	OVER	geeking out	Geeking out over Mathematician Benoit Mandelbrot, he is the pioneer of fractals. [ps, he spoke at the first #TED in '84]
2	ON	geeking out	Geeking out on soil. It's so cool. +1 for future vineyard, matching soil to many successful Virginia Vineyards. http://bit.ly/dj0diM
3	WITH	geeking out	Geeking out with Joel at Courier Coffee on the glaring shortcomings of espresso grinder design. #don'tcallitmodern
4	ABOUT	geek out	I secretly geek out about my seminar class. I take this as a sign that research/academia is the path I should choose.
5	AT	geeking out	This is cool!! RT @User Have een geeking out at possibly the best thing on the internet in the whole of today: http://bit.ly/7m2nU5
6	ON	geeked out	@User Oh yes! Me too. I geeked out on that episode and watched the extra footage. LOL. Conan is okayy, a little anoyying though.

At an Apple Presentation! I'm such a geek!! ;-) love it

As with the examples discussed earlier, this usage relies on humourous counterexpectation. The pattern 'Such a' usually includes an instance of negative appraisal in the final slot; for example, 'I'm such an idiot' or 'I'm such a goof'. Here the phrase 'I'm such a geek' can be read as 'I'm an individual who stands out because I appreciate this obscure domain and I am pretending that this is bad'.

This kind of relationship between geek and positive appraisal is sustained in slang such as 'geeking out', used to refer to zest regarding a particular subject, often a technology-related domain requiring particular and detailed expertise. For example, the instances in Table 7.5 include domains such as historical figures in mathematics, soil science, coffee, education, chemistry and televsion. The Urban Dictionary entry for 'geek out' suggests that the term refers to '[t]he act of becoming emotionally and physically aroused by the sight or the thought of a technicality of a certain topic of major interest' (Urban Dictionary 2009). Indeed, 'geek* out' is often collocated with an inscibed POSITIVE AFFECT, such as excitement:

> I'm **GEEKING out** over being featured in print for @SFWeekly. Like, actual geek out, squeal, excitement. http://twitpic.com/13ud4n

Geek* out was often used with emoticons invoking positive affect and heightened solidarity. The term is associated with expression of pleasure that has been triggered by appreciating the esoteric. For instance, the following positively appraises the exclusive social position of becoming a beta tester for a game:

> I am **Geeking out** here. StarCraft 2 Beta released today. AND I got in to the first round of testing!!!!!!!!!!!!!! =D

Geek* out is also associated with upscaled GRADUATION that is somewhat humorous in nature due to the juxtaposition of a hyberbolic response and an obscure or at least unexpectedly domain-specific stimulus. The 3-gram 'totally geeking out' was common. For example,

> Streaming multi-camera video for the first time in years. Totally geeking out and loving it.

> Okay. The librarian in me is totally geeking out about the celebrity genealogy show NBC's advertising.

The slang word geek was furthermore seen as hashtags in HERMES. The most common geek-related hashtags in the corpus are shown in Table 7.6. This is a way of labelling a tweet as related to geeklike identity and perhaps more loudly broadcasting one's geekiness. Chapter 5 explored the way in which hashtags can label the ideation a Twitter community bonds around. Here instead we see the hashtag itself taking on a 'master value' around which other values will orbit. In other words, the hashtag indicates the kind of identity, or set of values, with which a tweet is associated and then appends its own set of more specific values, such as positively appreciating the televsion show *Doctor Who* (N7, Table 7.6).

'Geeked' has shed some of its relationship to the 'domain-expert' identity construed with label 'geek'. Instead it has retained the meaning of enthusiasm without the accompanying fascination with a subject. In other words, it is mainly used to express AFFECT. So, for example, in N5 (Table 7.6) the user is expressing excitement that her relatives plan to buy her a car, rather than conveying enthusiasm surrounding some expert knowledge about cars.

After 'geek', 'geeky' is the next most common form of the term. It is typically used as a classifier for geek identity. For example:

Table 7.6 Most frequent 'geek*' hashtags in HERMES

N	Word	
1	#GEEK	Olympics Opening Ceremony a Hit On BitTorrent #geek http://bit.ly/cXInIx
2	#GEEKIPAD	To win an iPad, I'd strip off my clothes and run around screaming Geeksugar rules :). RT @User http://ow.ly/13czw #geekipad
3	#GEEKSPAZZ	Physicist Discovers How to Teleport Energy http://bit.ly/cwnQzE #GeekSpazz
4	#GEEKERY	Just saw a Double Aortic Arch in a CT of an 8-y-o kid sent for bronchiectasis. Ah! It's tough to please a radiologist. #radiology #geekery
5	#GEEKED	just got off the phone with mommy . . . her and uncle eli are gonna buy me a car . . . #geeked
6	#GEEKS	Only 39 minutes until I can go to the library! #Geeks of the world rejoice
7	#GEEKALERT	Yay Doctor Who marathon on Sci-Fi channel #GeekAlert but I can't resist a bit of David Tennant action :D

> @User IT Crowd you can find on the torrents lol. Its pretty freaking hilarious. Lots of good geeky humor.

Other entities categorized as geeky in HERMES represent a wide range of semantic domians including tendencies, apparel, stuff, friends, shirts, blogs, graphics, fonts and theories. The classification of these entities as geeky provides the opportunity for bonding around the conglometaration of values expressed about the domain which are in turn linked to the overall positive appreciation of the geek ethos.

Noob

At the other end of the continuum from geek is *noob*, a slang term for 'novice', rather than expert. In a similar way to geek, noob, as it is used in microblogging, has lost much of its original vitriolic edge and is employed largely to mean 'newbie', that is, someone new to a particular domain and hence lacking in experience and skill. For example, the following is typical of its use in tweets:

> Setting up the blog now. I'm such a **noob** when it comes to Wordpress. D:

Here noob indicates a negative self-evaluation of capacity with regard to a particular piece of software for managing a blog. The humorous and self-deprecating nature of the evaluation is prosodically reinforced by the smiley emoticon at the end of the tweet.

The two most common spellings in the corpus were 'noob' and 'n00b', the latter is influenced by leet (1337 or l33t), an orthographic form developed on Bulletin Board systems in the 1980s to signify an elite status or cultural boundary. Leet has also been associated with gaming and hacker communities, where part of its original purpose, as a kind of antilanguage (Halliday 1976), was to bypass simple filters and keyword detection software. However, in current usage, leet is mostly sarcastic and, where genuinely employed, is likely to mark the speaker as a newbie or show-off:

> The language of leet is constructed via a participatory design process, even collusion, specifically intended to 'send itself up', and thus functions as a meta-textual commentary on the irony of its use! (Blashki and Nichol 2005)

By the time this type of language is used in social media, we have seen two cycles of ironic metadiscourse. Some Twitterers appear conscious that using leet-style terms such as n00b and w00t affords them a sarcastic cultural kitsch that indicates their awareness of the discourses in which they are involved. For example, the declaration that one possesses 'skillz' is an ironic negative appraisal (meaning one does not possess a skill) but also invokes an amusing, gentle mocking of 'noob speak' and some kind of imagined parochial community of naive internet users:

> Man I got skillz I can Speed and TWEET #danger!! Lol I am so #lame lol

Before developing this sarcastic edge, noob was employed as an insult. For example, consider one definition contributed to the Urban Dictionary,[1] a collaborative online resource in the form of an editable lexicon of popular terms

> derived from online video games[;] often confused with the term newb or newbie, but instead of meaning new to the game as the latter does, noob refers to people who have played the game for a while but still suck balls and are ignorant, selfish, and lack the most important skill of all, teamwork. (*Noob* 2006–07)

As this definition suggests, rather than negative capacity, some early uses of noob were to signal negative judgement in terms of social sanction. In other words, the term was used when someone contravened a social norm within a particular community. For example, used with older forms of communication media such as internet forums, particularly by online gamers, the term was often deployed as a direct insult, of which the following is a relatively tame example:

> Don't post pointless replies like this you fucking noob. If your post doesn't contribute anything, then don't even bother.

However, since social media in general does not afford the kind of anonymity enjoyed (and abused) in the era dominated by message boards and Internet Relay Chat (IRC), we see a softening in the kind of interpersonal meaning made with this and most other forms of internet slang. Consider, 'fucking noob', used as a vocative in the previous example. This form is rarely used in the Twitter corpus and generally has two functions:

- Self-deprecation

  E.g. How is the blackout gonna help me sleep? I'm a **fucking noob** :|

- Negative appraisal of an other (not present in the exchange)

  E.g. LOL RT: @User If you sing along to 'Don't stop believing' at a bar you're a fucking **n00b**

Self deprecation appears the most common function and is related to Leech's (1983) maxim of avoiding self-praise. There were no instances where fucking noob was used directly as a vocative in any way similar to the example forum post.

Indeed, these two functions of noob seem relatively stable when we inspect its targets as an instance of negative evaluation. For example, Table 7.7 shows the ten most common 3-grams for 'noob' in the Twitter corpus. As the final column of this table exemplifies, the self or a generalized, non-present other is a target of appraisal rather than any specifically referenced or addressed individual.

This is not to say that 'noob' could not occur as a vocative directed at a participant in an exchange. Examples of such usage include:

> @User alrighty then, **noob** who stays up til 4am to play words with friends.
>
> @User it's our wedding **you noob**, I need you, user1, and user2 all to dress up in same outfits too

In these instances the appraisal appears to be jovial and lightly mocking, rather than offensive.

Table 7.7 Ten 3-grams for 'noob'

N	Cluster	Example	Appraisal Target
1	SUCH A NOOB/ SUCH A N00B	The shit I go through just to fucking jailbreak an iPod. I'm such a n00b.	self
2	BE A NOOB	I support this #bfbc2 'Battlefield Bad Company 2 'How not to be a Noob' video www.youtube.com/watch?v=qk7QpNzLmNE	hypothetical other
3	A NOOB AT	#dontjudgeme because I'm a noob at this Twitter thing n I don't have a lot of followers	self
4	I'M A NOOB	Does anyone know anything about riding the LIRR? I'm a noob.	self
5	A NOOB IN	Hmm I guess uploading that picture of ringo had me hit 1500 tweets. I still feel like a noob in comparisson to some (@ user for example)	self
6	A TOTAL NOOB	This bus driver is a total noob driver. Terrible.	recounted other
7	WHAT A NOOB	I wondered why msn wasn't signing in . . . I hadn't clicked . . . 'sign in' what a noob!	self
8	A TWITTER NOOB	Its time to get up off my ass again and stop being a Twitter noob ;)	self
9	FEEL LIKE A	I feel like a noob. Tried to get a better parking spot after i was already parked. I'm parked in the same spot now. Haha	self
10	IM SUCH A	LoL using that program is fun but im such a noob on it . . . still learning but once i get the hang of it ill upload my 1st mix :D	self

An important social function of microblogging is the practice of probing the 'hive mind' for advice. This function is seen in the pattern 'noob question' (Table 7.7). This term is an example of nominalization (a form of grammatical metaphor where a verb is realized as a noun) in the service of the interpersonal. For example, in the following, tweet, it functions as a kind of interpersonal theme that we might gloss as 'I am a noob for asking a question like this'. As such, it is another strategy for generating a self-deprecating tone and for suggesting, perhaps to invoke a kind of solidarity that might prompt others to answer the question, that we are all in some way 'noobish':

> **Noob question**, can someone explain how image titles in wordpress effect search engine results (do they?)

These questions traversed a range of fields but were most often technology related, such as the following regarding Buzz, a failed microblogging service launched by Google to accompany it's Gmail service (a popular email service):

> @User so bztwt is up, how do u make it work? total **noob question** I know. I'm curious what my buzz name is supposed to be.

In this example noob is functioning as a classifier. Classifiers are usually realized by the word classes, noun and adjective, and function to indicate 'a particular subclass of the thing in question, e.g. electric trains, passenger trains, toy trains' (Halliday and Matthiessen 2004, p. 319). In the corpus noob was used to classify people:

> e.g. noob driver, noob student, Noob facebook users, n00b followers, noob tuber, noob senior, n00b idiot

and things:

> e.g. noob tie, noob sauces, noob city, noob phone, NOOB free stuff, Noob shit, noob number, noob accounts, n00b session, n00b tournaments, noob english

An abstract class of things was that of the 'pitfall':

> e.g. Noob traps, n00b errorz, noob mistakes, Noob screwup

Noob was also used as a hashtag; for example, in a welcome to a new user:

> @User welcome to the world of Twitter **#noob**

or to signal negative appraisal:

> By @User #Twitter is buggy #bug **#noobs** #fail #epic #-omg #wtf #rl #??? Twitter on the rocks!

As mentioned earlier, this negative appraisal is most often directed at self:

> leaving my ipod in lawrence **#n00bjitsu**

The examples of noob explored so far are, however, most usefully examined from the perspective of involvement rather than evaluation. They appear more concerned with invoking solidarity rather than construing a fine-grained evaluation of the nature of the target's ineptitude, though the two are closely linked. Benwell and Stokoe (2006) discuss the related term, 'newbie', in relation to membership categorization and online identity. What is difficult to define is exactly who or what is the target of the solidarity. While slang is often seen as a kind of identity marker, indicating affiliation with a particular group, here the social marking is quite subtle. It is more about appreciating a certain aesthetic rather than branding oneself as part of a particular social grouping. In other words, it is about recognizing the social value of using a once passé term and reappropriating it in casual, often flippant discourse, even though the next wave of sarcastic users may be secretly laughing at you.

Pwned

Pwning (pronounced 'owning') is slang for the process of defeating an opponent. It has the following origin story, as unverifiable as the popular myths surrounding the internet memes explored in Chapter 6:

> Originally dates back to the days of WarCraft, when a map designer misspelled 'Own' as 'Pwn'. What was originally supposed to be 'player has been owned' was 'player has been pwned'.
>
> Pwn eventually grew from there and is now used throughout the online world, especially in online games. (Urban Dictionary 2009)

While pwn may have originated in gaming subcultures, its use in social media is similar to the pattern we have seen with geek and noob where most of the original meanings have faded and the term has been reappropriated. Table 7.8 shows the most frequent forms of pwn in HERMES. The meanings construed seem to be a kind of humorous militant or oppositional identity. The humour centres around the non-seriousness of the expressed domination. For example:

> @User thumb wrestling? i'd still pwn you at that. ;)

Table 7.8 Most frequent forms of 'pwn*' in the HERMES corpus

N	Word	Freq.	Example
1	PWNED	353	MEwwee! pwned almost 30 halo players this week!
2	PWN	131	finally! WEEKEND, finally got all my homework done for the past week, it was so much so I am going to eat soon and pwn ppl's on my Phat NDS
3	PWNS	108	I just got the greatest package in the mail I think I have ever gotten in my life . . . CANDY. MY GRANDMA PWNS YOUR GRANDMA!!!
4	PWNAGE	65	sittin at home, tea is wielded as well as my mouse, uber pwnage initiated, 12 year olds on miniclip.com, GTFO!
5	PWND	50	oh dear, Square Enix. Looks like you just got PWND. Doctoring PS3 shots to have the 360 UI coz the 360 version is all compressed and shitty.
6	PWNING	50	#User is pwning! time to get some autographs! :D

A model of internet slang

As we have seen in the slang discussed in this chapter, social media slang, a subset of slang used on the internet, generally appropriates slang originally used within subcultures. The original meanings and identity patterns associated with this slang are recontextualized, realigning with the semiotic activity undertaken via channels such as microblogging.

If we return to the characterization by Stenström and her colleagues (2002) of the prominent 'slangy' features in teenage talk, we may add some of the notable features seen in HERMES and summarized in Table 7.9. Non-standard orthography of the kind seen in textese (Crystal 2008) is particularly prominent, perhaps reflecting the type of language that arises through the imposition of character constraints and the mobile capabilities of the medium (many users update their Twitter status via mobile phone or PDA). Some of these textese-type features have been noted by other researchers, who, as De Jonge and Kemp (2010) note, have 'have categorised textisms as logograms (e.g. c for see or 2 for to), letter/number homophones (e.g. m8 for mate) and emoticons (e.g. :-) for happy), among others (e.g. Crystal 2008; Plester, Wood and Joshi 2009; Thurlow and Brown 2003)'. These orthographic forms can be hybrid (Yvon 2010). For example 'bcum' is a mixture of a letter homophone and phonetic writing.

Table 7.9 Slanguage features relating to non-standard orthography specific to HERMES

Feature	Example
Phonetic writing	@user I didn't think u could . . . u already on top, just underrated rite now . . . its comin tho
Lolspeak phonetic writing	Muriel playz da same song on wuteva instrument dat iz
Vowel removal	off to wrk
Prefixial accretion	Hope everyone is having a twitastic day! /via @user / you know it, man!
Initialisms:	Well I'm going back to sleep ttyl:)
Leetspeak-like features[2]	Wakin' up in the mornin' feelin' like a n00b. w00t I feel l33t today! Goodmornoning yall!!! Thanks for waking up @user to take my ass to work.
Numbers homophones	@user thats a gr8t point, true 4 mentorship also . . .
Letters homophones	RT @user: when ur bestfriend tells u he likes u n he n watns u 2 dump ur bf now
Logograms	Dam yo u faker than a $3 bill!!! . . .
Emoticons	Mark my words: GL Live is gonna be off the chaaaaaainnnnnnn! :-) mali and richie are both amped! :-) let's do this!!!
Non-standard spelling	RT @user: Oi back down to 297 followers WTF? Come one gissa follow I wanna get 300 ;o)

Microposts are often a pastiche of different kinds of non-standard orthography alongside more standardized language. Phonological reduction via number and letter homophones, for instance, may be irregular. For example, the compressed form 'ur' and the full form 'your' commonly co-occur in tweets:

> @User thanks for trying us out and for **your** great feedback! Can you ensure to add **ur** feedback here – http://bit.ly/5ki4tm thanks! ^cw

Similarly '2' and 'to' and 'u' and 'you' are used simultaneously:

> @User will **you** reetweet or dm this **to** @justinbieber if he is following **u 2** get him **to** get him **to** see this plz – http://tl.gd/9q8h7

This type of shifting between abridged, non-standard orthographic forms and the full form of words may be symptomatic of a system of meaning yet to stabilize in light of the newness of the channel. It is also perhaps characteristic of the 'on-the-fly' format of microblogging in general, where users are generating microposts on mobile devices as part of other activities and will quickly deploy whichever linguistic resources can speedily be used to make a point. In this way, time plays an important role in the production of slanguage, as it does with the meanings made in general with microposts.

CHAPTER EIGHT

Internet humour and fail: 'The world is full of #fail tonight'

Man, only from himself, can suffer wrong;
His reason fails, as his desires grow strong:
Hence, wanting ballast, and too full of fail.
He lies expos'd to ev'ry rising gale.

Ambrose Philips, 'From Holland to a Friend in England, in the Year 1703'

Internet humour

Social media frequently uses humour as a resource for maintaining relationships. Many studies have noted the role of humour in displaying solidarity. For example, Norrick (1994) argues that mocking and sarcasm can have a solidarity-invoking function. Joking in casual conversation can function to negotiate affiliation (Knight 2010c; 2008) and construe relational identity (Boxer and Cortés-Conde 1997). However, while there has been much linguistic work on humour, suggesting its role in affiliation, internet humour has not been widely studied in linguistics. The small number of existing studies has covered areas such as gender in popular internet humour (Shifman and Lemish 2010), humour in USENET newsgroups (Baym 1995), humour and irony in travel blogging (Cappelli

2008), web-based election humour (Shifman et al. 2007) and presidential humour (Oring 2008). As with more established studies of humour in other media, a common theme in internet humour research is exploring humour as developing solidarity (Baym 1995).

This chapter employs Eggins and Slade's notion that humour is a 'semantic resource' related to appraisal and involvement (see Chapter 4), since 'humorous devices such as teasing, telling dirty jokes or funny stories, and using hyperbole enable interactants to negotiate attitudes and alignments, and provide a resource for indicating degrees of 'otherness' and 'in-ness' (Eggins and Slade 1997, p. 155). What is particular about the kind of in/outness construed via ambient humour is that the interaction is 'ambient' in the sense that it may occur indirectly, for example, via participation in a humorous internet meme.

Humour in social media is a subarea of internet humour research in which there has been little work to date. The kind of social-media-based humour I explore in this chapter will be referred to as *ambient humour*. Similar to social media memes explored in Chapter 6, ambient humour invokes a putative community of users who may have no direct virtual contact but share in the expression of certain values, often aesthetic values. Ambient humour produced via social networking services such as microblogging can be difficult to analyse since the character-constrained language means there is less opportunity for humourous references to be resolved in the context. In this environment homophora, meanings that require knowledge of the culture to unpack, abounds. Homophoric reference 'is used when interlocutor's membership in a particular community means that certain participants can be treated as inherently "given"' (Martin 1992, p. 122).

This chapter is a case study of the term *fail*, an example of internet slang and a very popular internet meme. As we saw in Chapter 6 on social media memes, a common form of microblogging humour is meme-related humour, involving playful use of phrasal templates. *Fail* has become increasingly common in microposts, where it is mostly used to make humourous complaints regarding everyday life. I will explore how fail functions both in HERMES and in the fail corpus, a specialized corpus consisting of 8,384,128 tweets (117,869,067 words) that contained fail hashtags.

Many studies suggest some essential incongruity or unexpectedness is at the heart of humour, with language playing the important role of making it 'possible for us to see the unexpected expectations we share, since while language itself is explicit its rules are usually not; it incorporates many expectations we overlook or allows many inferences we take for granted until they are violated' (Boyd 2004). While we may question that language is always explicit (see, in particular in Chapter 4, the way evaluative meanings may be invoked), Boyd makes a useful point.

The presence of an alternative, non-serious reading of a text facilitates humorous play and is the underlying idea encapsulated in Bateson's (1972) notion of a 'play frame', a concept often applied in humour studies. Play frames can be invoked by various means, such as word play (Norrick 1994). For example, fail invokes a play frame in the way that using the word *failure* does not.

Some studies suggest that internet-specific features such as emoticons are associated with the expression of online humour (Derks et al. 2008; Huang et al. 2008). Initialisms such as LOL (laugh out loud) may mark online humour and are associated with emoticons supporting humour (see Chapter 4). However, they can also have different interpersonal functions; for example, LOL sometimes 'functions as a phatic marker, meaning the equivalent of *OK*, *Cool*, or *Yeah*' (Baron 2009, p. 114). In addition, intialisms – such as LOL or any of its many variants, including ROFL (rolling on the floor laughing) may function to indicate group membership (Baron 2003).

The internet history of fail

The term *fail* achieved prominence via image macros depicting humourous calamity with the caption 'fail'. Subsequent usage of the term in status updates, blog comments and other channels see fail arise as popular slang and as a social media meme often marked by the hashtag #Fail. The term is usually deployed as a playful form of mockery, most often of the self, or an aspect of daily life. Users are typically complaining about trivial misfortune with various phenomena described as being a 'fail', 'made of fail, 'full of fail', an 'epic fail' or some other related iteration. For example:

> mornings are clearly made of fail, anyone know how to make mornings out of win?

This is in keeping with the propensity of microbloggers to express the mundane (Oulasvirta et al. 2010), as was discussed in Chapter 3.

Popular internet commentators have suggested the fail meme originated in a particular home console game titled Blazing Star developed by the Japanese company SNK for their video game system, Neo Geo (Zimmer 2009). This scrolling shooter game contains the following instance of 'Engrish' that is said to have given rise to the meme:

> You fail it! Your skill is not enough, see you next time, bye-bye!

However, this claim is largely urban legend (as we have seen with the alleged origins of the memes explored in Chapter 6) and is essentially unverifiable given the scope of the internet.

As fail has come to be used on Twitter in a more mainstream way, gaming associations have largely decoupled from the term, and it is doing different work in terms of group authentication. Nevertheless, the kind of popularized identity that users may be trying to invoke with fail bears some relationship to a persona who appreciates what is sometimes termed '8 bit retro'. Users adopting this identity are likely to enjoy the original instantiation of fail in the Engrish quotation from the console game in the same way that an art lover enjoys kitsch. Interest in retro console games is the technological equivalent of retro fashion appreciation and

Figure 8.1 An example of a fail image macro (Unknown 2009)

the kind of in-group that is established via ironic appropriation of tacky decor.

Beam (2008) suggests that fail has become the public corollary to private experiences of Schadenfreude, taking pleasure in someone else's misfortune. A catalogue of such pleasure is evident in the humourous website Fail Blog (http://failblog.org/), developed in 2008 when fail image macros grew in popularity. An example of a fail image macro is Figure 8.1, a photograph of the 1895 Granville–Paris Express wreck. These macros have become so mainstream that the Granville–Paris Express wreck image features on the Wikipedia page devoted to 'failure'. These types of image macros will usually involve some form of humour; for example, the visual unexpectedness in the train catastrophe image. The same caption on an image of an ordinary rail incident, provided it did not contain some element that might be construed as amusing or hyperbolic, would not be a genuine fail macro.

The opposite of fail is *win*. Many of the quantifications applied to fail can also be used with win; for example, 'full of win', 'made of win', 'bag of win', 'bucketload of win', 'total win', 'epic win', 'uberwin' and so on. The initialized exclamation FTW (for the win) is a kind of rallying catch-cry signalling positive appreciation of a target. For example:

> @User its Sunday, much more important than any other day, be it valentine's or some other. Sundays FTW!

The preoccupation with fail/win reflects a general concern with boundary policing, a central component of the discourses of winners and losers that pervade contemporary social life.

Fail and solidarity

Fail is often used as self-mockery in humorous microposts. As an interpersonal resource, self-mockery in conversation usually has a solidarity-invoking function (Ungar 1984) by showing 'goodwill' through de-emphasizing hierarchy (Hübler and Calhoun Bell 2003, p. 281). The self-deprecating humour associated with fail seems to echo this general function seen in offline conversation. Instances of self-mockery are often marked by the phrase 'I #fail', configuring fail as a hashtag, which, as we will see later in this chapter, invites affiliation with others who have experienced the problem described. For example:

> i was vegetarian for a week. then I gave up. I #fail

Indeed, complaining itself can build solidarity. An important function of the kind of hyperbolic self-denigration seen with fail is to complain and consequently to bond with an ambient audience which shares the complaint.

Chapter 4 briefly introduced complaining as a common pattern in HERMES with discussion of the common 3-gram 'I have to'. Complaining often occurs in conversational exchanges (Laforest 2002; Edwards 2005). Boxer (1993, p. 124) suggests that 'at least one speech act sequence, that of complaint/commiseration, is frequently used not only to open conversations and form temporary bonds, but sometimes even to build relationships'. While initiation/response sequences are not readily retrievable from HERMES due to the randomization of the Twitter stream collected, searching via the Twitter web interface easily locates examples of commiserating responses to fail complaints. For example, the following pair of moves was part of a larger exchange about sugar cookies that User 1 had baked for thanksgiving:

> User1: @User2 sooOoo . . . they didnt rise :(umm . . . MAJOR FAIL!!
>
> User2: aw really? Ok ima bring over some cookie dough. We can make a new batch :)

In this example the fail exclamation results in a consoling response by User2. The polarity of the emoticons :(and :) in the exchange echo the 'complain then commiserate' pattern with User2 trying to reverse the negative sentiment suggested by User1.

Another way solidarity is invoked with fail is via hashtagging. There were 5,601 instances of #fail in HERMES. The most common pattern was the hashtag as a kind of metacomment when retweeting somebody else's misfortune. While this metacommentary may often be a commiseration, it might also be teasing, as in the following example:

> And you can't cook . . . #fail RT @User: Being snowed in with no food sucks

Here, the playful use of fail seems akin to playful teasing in casual conversation. The retweet may invite response from the original user precipitating a longer exchange as a kind of ad hoc conversation. The joke in the metacommentary might be coded as aggressive and may be likened to the way 'that friends in conversation will use humour even aggressively to achieve affiliation' (Knight 2010a, p. 214), a point noted in many studies of conversational humour (Norrick 1993; Archakis and Tsakona 2005; Holmes 2000, cited in Knight 2010a, p. 214).

Various hashtags have built up around the original, #FAIL to label the everyday frustrations that plague users in a way that brings together communities of users suffering the same annoyance. The five most common fail hashtags in HERMES were

Table 8.1 The five most frequent fail-related hashtags in HERMES

N	Word	Count	Example
1	#EPICFAIL	568	watching damn House I missed the damn video! #epicfail
2	#VDAYFAIL	469	The gift u bought yo girl gone be too small #vdayfail
3	#NBCFAIL	162	Because it bears repeating as often as possible: nbc's#olympicscoverageisbeyonddysfunctional. It is as if they *hate* sports. #nbcfail
4	#MAJORFAIL	33	BEARING IN MIND that GOW is a Microsoft published game – It FAILS to run on a Microsoft OS. #majorfail #hopelesscompany #cryingshame
5	#OLYMPICFAIL	33	So embarrassing Canada! Way to break the Olympics ! #olympicfail

The most frequent hashtag, #EPICFAIL, corresponds to the term 'epic fail', a subset of the fail meme and a popular phrase which will be discussed later in this chapter. The second most frequent hashtag, #VDAYFAIL, refers to Valentine's Day. As mentioned in Chapter 3, HERMES was collected over a period of time that included February 14, thus there is an over-representation of the semantic field of Valentine's Day. Similarly #NBCFAIL and #OLYMPICSFAIL refer to the 2010 Vancouver Winter Olympics held during the corpus collection period. Both #EPICFAIL and #MAJORFAIL can be applied to a range of fail contexts, while #VDAYFAIL and #OLYMPICFAIL restrict the ideational meaning that users bond around via the fail meme. The N2 example (Table 8.1) invites users to commune around the popular cliché of a woman being unhappy with the Valentine's Day gift chosen by her partner. There are a number of potential bonds with which solidarity may be construed in the tweet:

- Shared experience of Valentine's Day disappointment in general marked by #VDAYFAIL;
- Shared experience of gender conflict about Valentine's Day construed by the invoked appraisal in the tweet.

Functions of fail in the corpus

There were 14,266 instances of 'fail' in HERMES; however, not all of these instances were 'fail' used as a slang term and contributing to a fail meme. For example the following is a non-slang use of 'fail':

> In an experiment only an art department would attempt, monkeys (incl one called Rowan) **fail to** write Shakespeare http://bit.ly/9UwgQ2

While the following invoke the fail meme:

> @User haha. That app is full of win, and makes me look **full of fail.** Yup.
>
> Dear Facebook, you **#FAIL.** That is all. Kthnxbai.

Manual disambiguation of slang and non-slang fail in this subcorpus would be time-consuming, so instead n-grams were inspected to explore the most common ways in which 'fail' is used as humorous slang. The ten most frequent 3-grams for fail are shown in Table 8.2.

Table 8.2 Examples of the ten most frequent fail 3-grams

N	Cluster	Freq.	Example
1	WAS A FAIL	118	that chatroom was a fail -____-
2	IS A FAIL	110	@User NBC coverage of this Olympics is a fail all the way around!
3	AN EPIC FAIL	102	wow french chick in the downhill, quite an epic fail there.
4	I FAIL AT	85	wow. i need to learn how to spell. i #fail at spelling today. probably the lack of oxygen in my brain from not sleeping well . . .
5	EPIC FAIL PICTURES	67	Twitter Fail – FAIL Blog: Epic Fail Pictures and Videos of Owned . . . http://bit.ly/9ngP2f #Twitter
6	FAIL ON THE	49	@User bit of a fail on the poor folks' surnames!
7	THAT WAS A	47	Well that was a fail
8	FAIL AT LIFE	46	RT @User: If you think that Wikipedia is a valid source of information, you #FAIL at life!
9	FAIL AT THE	45	hahaha canada = fail at the olympics before it even started
10	WHAT A FAIL	45	well thought i was going to see him today . . . what a fail.

At the level of lexicogrammar, the memetic fail could function as a

- process:
  @User you **fail** @ life, glasto ftw the end k bye xoxoxoxoxoxoxox <3 ;)
- nominal group :
  thinks that the cafe food is a **fail** tonight
- exclamation (minor clause)
  Wow broke my lent I guess haha I thought chicken is poultry. . . . Not meat! **Fail!** Haha
- classifier
  Around the interwebs: epic **fail** pictures – around the interwebs http://url4.eu/1Qqcl

The nominal group realization was the most common in HERMES. In this way it lends itself more directly to quantification and, as we will see in the next section, is often involved in hyperbolic play using the GRADUATION system.

Fail is an example of grammatical metaphor where grammatical (as opposed to lexical) metaphor is defined as follows:

> In all the instances that we are treating as grammatical metaphor, some aspect of the structural configuration of the clause, whether in its ideational or in its interpersonal function or in both, is in some way different from that which would be arrived at by the shortest route – it is not, or was not originally, the most straightforward coding of the meanings selected. (Halliday 1985, p. 343; 1994/1985, p. 366)

'Fail' is the nominalized form of the process 'to fail'. It may be argued that 'fail' is a shortened form of the related noun 'failure'; however, if we are to accept the popular history of the term's origin as the phrase 'you fail it', the term evolved from the verb form. The exclamation 'Fail!' is a minor clause that might be expanded to 'You fail it'. In HERMES it most often appears to be an elided form of 'this is a fail'. For example,

> Bloody hell, no matter what station I turn to, that blasted Kesha song on the radio. Fail!

The most frequent 3-gram in HERMES for fail, 'was a fail', has fail functioning as an attribute in an attributive relational clause[1]. As Table 8.2 shows, 'was a fail' was the most frequent fail 3-gram in HERMES. Examples of the most frequent kind of targets of fail include

- mode-reflexive (Twitter) – that was a fail of a tweet. I didn't even put #nowplaying or anything;

- entertainment – today was interesting. movie was a fail but we're trying again tomorrow ;] got a dress!
- technology – that chatroom was a fail -____-.

The functions discussed thus far are at the lexicogrammatical and discourse semantic level. However, in terms of affiliation, fail functions as a kind of shibboleth to indicate affinity with a particular kind of internet identity. Rather than a grammatical metaphor used to 'build knowledge and organize text' (Martin 2008a, p. 804), here we see the grammatical metaphor is used affiliatively to authenticate oneself as part of an ambient community of Twitter users who share their daily experiences and, as will we see in a later section, as an amplified value around which users commune.

Establishing a 'play frame': Epic fail, hyperbole and quantification

The tendency for upscaled graduation in social media discourse was noted in Chapter 4. The fail meme attracts upscaled prosodies of evaluation. As mentioned earlier, the nominalized form readily accommodates intensification. For example (GRADUATION highlighted):

> #RATM FTW!!!! @User *massive* fail!
>
> is it just me or is the new 'we are the world' a *huge* fail?
>
> wow *gigantic* fail i wake up to go to the gym and then have to drop my car off but instead i just doped my car off and i cant go to the gym
>
> The flannel party was a *big* fail :p
>
> 4 wheeling *epic* fail. full of mud!! lol

Fail establishes a 'play frame' (Bateson 1972), and when used in a status update it marks the co-presence of a non-serious reading of the text. In general the humorous play is around failure as a shared experience, even where the particular misadventure reported is some personal incident occurring in daily life. For example:

> so . . . I just punched myself in the face taking my shirt off . . fail on me . . .

As this example suggests, the system generating the humour is hyperbole or overstatement. In this way fail has a graduating function, intensifying the complaint via a form of verbal irony. Indeed, in other contexts such as face-to-face conversation, hyperbole is often a cue for verbal irony (Kreuz and Roberts 1995) where the irony centers on what Colston and O'Brien

(2000) refer to as a 'contrast of magnitude'. In other words, the humour arises from a contrast between the exaggerated negative appraisal and the relatively minor nature of what is appraised. So in the case of fail, the contrast is between the trivial, commonplace situation and the hyperbolic negative evaluation. The disparity creates a humorous incongruity.

Status updates, perhaps social media discourse in general, seems to make ample use of graduation. This point has also been noted by Page (2011), who found a substantial amount of intensification in Facebook status updates. Over-representation of graduation systems (though difficult to assess quantitatively without a reference corpus and a reliable way of automatically tagging a large volume of text) is perhaps due to the absence of paralanguage as a resource for supporting meanings made in verbiage. For example hyperbole in email communication 'may permit the speaker to emphasize particular words, or elements of the situation, in the absence of paralinguistic cues' (Whalen et al. 2009, p. 266). This kind of function – compensating for absent paralanguage – is also often ascribed to emoticons.

The fail meme playfully graduates the experience of the everyday, using hyperbole for humour and, in turn, solidarity with a potential audience of fellow sufferers. Within HERMES, fail often collocated with a mass quantifier, a feature that often occurs in 'hyperbolic contexts' (McCarthy and Carter 2004, p. 176). Examples of mass quantifiers of fail include

- *full of fail*:

  My #sprint phone continues to be **full of Fail**. Locked up 4 times today while texting. Texting! This is hardly a taxing activity.

- *loaded with fail*:

  @User iTunes 9 for PC is much better so far & full of #WIN. iPhone 3.1 **loaded** with **#FAIL**. 6 crashes yesterday.

- *load of fail*:

  This video is either going to be effing awesome or a **boatload of fail.**

- *bag of fail*:

  MS Virtual PC 2007 is a steaming **bag of fail.**

- *sack of fail*:

  Dolphins a huge **sack of fail** today.

- *total fail*:

  I fell asleep in my maths exam. **TOTAL FAIL** (:

As these examples suggest, fail represents a playful use of quantification, with the materiality of nominalization often emphasized. Targets are classified as being materially constituted by fail as seen in the 3-grams 'full of fail' (33 instances) and 'made of fail' (11 instances). For example:

> @User Time zones are **made of fail.** So are happy people. ;)

In addition, they contain fail:

> @User dude I'm **full of fail** . . . totally forgot to respond to your email yesterday . . .

The materiality could also be deployed for comedic effect. For example:

> What a huge, steaming, frothy bucket of FAIL I am. Hate to miss a night of frolic w/ fellow #MWC peeps but this girl is down for the count.

Here, the hyperbolic image of the 'steaming, frothy bucket of FAIL' playfully heightens the evaluation as well as marking the incongruity. 'Steaming' often occurred in descriptions of excrement used in metaphorical negative evaluation, such as 'a steaming pile of crap', 'a steaming pile of shit' and so on.

> Etymologists: We need a new word to describe a day going from simply bad, to being an insufferable **steaming pile of monkey turds.**

In addition, the rendering of fail in capitals is another intensification device adding to the humour.

A similar pattern is seen for fail's opposite, win. For example:

- *full of win*:

  god. Kanye West memes are so **full of win**
- *bag of win*:

  @user Beatles Rockband is a **bag of win.**
- *bucketload of win*:

  Video of Obama calling Kanye West a jackass. What a whole **bucketload of win.** One notion that I do support :') http://ow.ly/pLuJ
- *total win*:

  @user So true. Happy dance cannot detail the excitement. It's **total win.**

Perhaps the maximally intensified version of fail is the epic fail. There were 588 instances of the term in HERMES, with fail being the most frequent collocate of epic in the corpus (and fail's opposite, win, the second most frequent [163]). It commonly occurred as the 4-gram 'was/is an epic fail':

> Kind of glad I didn't decide to go to #van2010 esp since the opening ceremony **was an epic fail.** so embarassing.

The following are examples of epic fail:

- OMG **EPIC FAIL.** I should be like running out the door right now, but I'm not even fully ready to go out and I'm sat on Twitter. *facepalm*
- I've made the biggest mistake in my life by choosing risk management for diploma work. **epic fail**
- What's the waiting room called?' **'EPIC FAIL!'**
- puh! just remembered to save 2,5 hours of work in photoshop . . . barely escaped a massivly **epic fail** . . .
- It's no good being first in the office if you forget your keys. **Epic Fail!**
- Bahaha, I got invited to join a group called 'Ke$ha is better than Lady GaGa' WOW. **Epic fail** of a group xD

According to popular commentary these examples of epic fail should be characterized by misfortune involving hubris.

> The highest form of fail – the epic fail – involves not just catastrophic failure but hubris as well. Not just coming in second in a bike race but doing so because you fell off your bike after prematurely raising your arms in victory. Totaling your pickup not because the brakes failed but because you were trying to ride on the windshield. Not just destroying your fish tank but doing it while trying to film yourself lifting weights. (Brcam 2008)

However, the examples provided do not seem to adopt this sense of fail and instead classify a fail as epic to grade an ATTITUDE. For instance, in the first example EPIC FAIL coupled with uppercase letters and the initialism OMG (oh my God) serves to upscale the invoked negative JUDGEMENT of CAPACITY. In other words, it serves to highlight the user's humorous description of apparent ineptitude.

Fail and evaluation

Fail often collocates with INSCRIBED NEGATIVE ATTITUDE towards an event or experience. The function is generally to upscale the negative evaluation.

> I have so much work to do but i wasted the whole day being hungover argg uni FAIL!

Here, fail reinforces the INSCRIBED NEGATIVE JUDGEMENT. Indeed fail is often involved in prosodies of negative evaluation such as the following, where expletives, an emoticon representing a face with 'angry' pointed eyebrows and NEGATIVE ATTITUDE co-articulate the general meaning of dissatisfaction:

> Shit. Sony Vegas practically fucked up all of my videos. #fail. Seriously. Not even kidding. This sucks >:(

Fail can be employed as an exclamation at the end of a tweet or as a hashtag. In these cases the effect is prosodic (across the entire tweet), and the target is the sentiment or situation expressed in the body of the tweet. For example, where there was no inscribed negative appraisal in the co-text of the tweet, fail could also function to indicate negative evaluation. This most often was achieved with a hashtag.

> What would insurance companies do if they knew that #MEA shows an A332 safety video on an A321? **#FAIL**[2]

The assessment of fail in this tweet applies to the entire situation described rather than one participant, although the additional hashtag #MEA serves to sharpen focus on that entity as the target of fail.

At another order of experience, fail functions as a rallying point for affiliation. For example a frequent semantic domain of fail is the microrant against technology.

> Apple 'Experts' can't do Aperture support so back on hold. My mistake for buying $200 of extra software, Apple #apple #fail

The most common technology-related targets of evaluation were internet technologies (Table 8.3). These targets were often realized as classifiers[3] of fail. In these instances users are bonding around a kind of playful superiority regarding internet technologies, such as the aborted Google social media venture, Buzz. This is the lighter version of technology-related fail tweets, with a stronger technology rant being another emergent microgenre.

> EPIC COMPUTER FAILURE = ONE PISSED OFF #spacetweep fourtunatley all pics were exported locally this time
>
> **Dear R.I.M.** – your Facebook update for the crackberry = fail.
>
> **Dear Facebook** – the new layout = fail.

Table 8.3 Most frequent targets of evaluation in L1 in concordance line for 'fail' in HERMESIn some instances the tweet is directed, via a vocative, at a piece of software or a software company.

N	L1	Freq.	Example
1	Twitter	43	Twitter fail! let's try that again . . . @User sweet! malls are always good ^_^
2	Google	22	@User I know !!! Epic google fail or pushing innovation regardless ? I'm waiting for my identity to be stolen fun!
3	Facebook	20	yes and its posting things 2x :(RT @User FACEBOOK FAIL – it's sooo slow today.
4	Internet	14	I the powers of the internet, and i can't find a damn clip of The Time performing Jungle Love in HD from Purple Rain. Internet Fail.
5	Buzz	13	reading about all those google buzz fail stories makes me wanna say: 'I told you so'. google is evil "."

In these examples the humour of the original mimetic usage is diluted, and the tweets appear more oriented toward genuine complaint than humorous display. The pattern *Dear* + vocative was used more generally in HERMES to address a generalized entity in order to make some invoked evaluative comment about something, often something that has annoyed the microblogger. The entities addressed most often in this way in HERMES are shown in Table 8.4. The affiliative function of these examples appears to center on creating alignment with the view expressed by calling on a shared experience of the targeted entity. Where this pattern of address was used with the fail meme, humour was often employed, particularly humour conforming to the emergent microgenre of humorous complaint. For example this was often realized as a vocative addressing a form of technology or a corporate entity, concluding with 'kthnxbai' ('ok, thanks, bye'), derived from LOLspeak.

> dear computer, I'm not pressing the eject disk button, please let me watch my effing movie! kthnxbai!

Table 8.5 shows the kinds of 'micromoves' that could realize the general function of making a complaint. The type of bonding around collective frustration at technology seen here will be discussed in the section which follows.

Table 8.4 Examples of frequent instance of *Dear* + vocative

R1	Example
GOD	Dear God, please let the snow melt, its very important. Thanks.
LORD	Dear Lord I pray that you make me bigger and better on the inside than on the outside.
FRIENDS	Sorry for messing up your timelines :) i think I'm going to bed now. Goodnight, dear friends. Thank God It's Friday!
TWITTER	dear Twitter and facebook, you've made me so busy commenting about my life I don't have time for anything else
MR	Snowy day in Georgia. Dear Mr. Weather, thanks for the birthday present. you da man
NBC	Dear NBC, please stop showing footage of the Olympian who died during training. It's morbid.
FOLLOWERS	dear followers, sorry for the twitpicing ;) :L
WORLD	Dear world, I know I'm not pretty. But you didn't have to remind me constantly today. Juss Sayin'.
GOOGLE	Dear Google you may be Facebook and you may be Twitter, in the distant future. You certainly cannot be both combined. Buzz off!

Table 8.5 'Micromoves' realizing the microcomplaint genre

Function	Realized by	Example
Complaint	insult	Dear Microsoft Word . . . hate you more and more every time you abruptly close on me . . . 1,000 years of pox upon your house!
	thanks	Dear Apple, thanks for making the iPhone charger cable about 3 feet too short. #fb
	request	Agreed RT @user: Dear Apple, please put a non-shit camera in your/my next iPhone: it's the only annoying limitation of my current 3G.
		Dear excell please be generous, I wanna go home . . . please don't hang like this, I've a report to finish :(
	question	Dear Adobe, should I really have to navigate to the AIR dll and open its properties then tab to find the version info? #theanswerisfuckingno
	threat	Dear Computer, if you keep this behavior up, I will pour water on you.
	command	Dear computer, right now we are NOT friends. Stop being stupid. The end.

Fail and ambient affiliation

Using fail in a status update invokes affinity with a putative community of fellow 'failures'. Examples of fail in HERMES show users laughing collectively at the common problems of modern life. These troubles are often encountered alone and are somewhat trivial. For instance, awkward moments are common, everyday experiences that are part of the minutiae of life. Microblogging offers the opportunity for people to express frustration at such minor adversity that might otherwise be considered too inane to bother communicating face-to-face. A kind of blurring of the public and private, the individual and collective, results as we express these day-to-day happenings, affording opportunities for new kinds of social connection. In this context, as we have seen in the examples explored in this chapter, humour, typically hyperbole, is used to increase involvement. The expression of humorous misfortune gives opportunity to ambient camaraderie in the face of this adversity. Consider for example the following tweet:

> Painting my nails at 2 in the morning #fail . . . forgot I had to wait for this crap to dry :-\

The minor incident, inconvenience at waiting for nail polish to dry when wanting to go to bed, reported in this tweet takes on a more global meaning potential through the use of the fail meme. The hashtag virtually and symbolically binds this post to the stream of other possible fail experiences that might be expressed by other users. The intimate act of painting nails in the early morning becomes a public act, and the private frustration finds an ambient audience. This is characteristic of a blurring of the public and private seen in social media in general (Boyd 2010, p. 49). The personal becomes public; it also becomes amusing to an ambient audience. Just as 'Humour connects the micro-interactive, interpersonal contexts of private life with the macro-social contexts of institutionalized public life' (Eggins and Slade 1997, p. 167), it works to create community from individual, commonplace experience.

In this way we might think of fail as a kind of bonding icon (Stenglin 2004), or 'bondicon' (Martin 2008b). Bondicons arise from condensation of values through processes of iconization:

> . . . a process whereby bondicons accrue value which they in turn radiate outwards for people to align around. Among well-known bondicons are peace symbols (the dove and the peace sign) which anchor communities of protest against war. Symbols of this kind illustrate the way in which values can be materialised as images; further examples of iconisation would include ceremonies, proverbs, slogans, memorable quotations, flags, team colours, coats of arms, mascots and so on. Iconisation can

> also involve people, including well-known embodiments of peaceful protest and of liberation such as Ghandi and Mandela respectively. . . . (Martin 2008b, p. 19)

The values which fail has accrued are those shared by people experiencing the common misfortunes of daily life. As it is used on Twitter, it has become a bonding icon for humourous commiseration about collective human foibles. It may be likened to saying, 'Hey, this happens to me too! Isn't it annoying!' or alternatively, 'Look at how stupid people are!' These form two general kinds of bonds:

- self-targeted deprecation ('Hey, this happens to me too! Isn't it annoying!',):

  So I am just a complete #fail this morning. Turns out my 10am appt was at 9. O_o . . . sooo any Raleigh/Durham peeps wanna get up? Lunch?

- other-targeted mocking ('Look at how stupid people are!'):

  Just received a very expensive piece of DM with the slogan 'Marketing. Well Executed.' The letter inside is addressed to someone else #FAIL

These bond-offers invoke humorously reduce a potentially complex situation to the simple label fail. The resultant juxtaposition is inherently amusing. In addition, the content itself is often funny in a vaudevillian sense. Reducing the explanation to a single monosyllabic label such as the hashtag #Fail also renders it more shareable – particularly via Twitter, given the constraints on characters. Other more specific bonds are part of the constellation of values (Martin et al. 2010) surrounding fail and include

- corporations are incompetent/evil:

  Dear United Airlines. You suck. Goodbye. #fail

- technology doesn't work:

  Microsoft Word is not for writing. 10% of the time you write and 90% of the time is wasted for fixing problems caused by Word #fail

- a particular political party is evil:

  Tory site engages in racism and class hatred: http://tankthetories.com #toryfail #sameoldtories #ivenevervotedtory #ukpolitics

I will now consider the role of hashtagging in this kind of axiologizing.

Fail as a hashtag

The most common target of fail in the corpus was Twitter itself. Some of this discourse was automated messages indicating that 'Twitter is over capacity #fail'; mostly it was individual users complaining about outages .A common 4-gram associated with this target was IS GIVING ME TOO MUCH. This pattern consisted almost entirely of retweeting (over 300 retweets) of a celebrity gossip blogger, Perez Hilton, complaining about the service being unreliable:

> RT @PerezHilton: Twitter is giving me too much fail whale today!!!! Overcapacity bullshiz! #Fail

The 'fail whale' is an image which appears via the Twitter website when the service experiences technical difficulties such as outages due to servers being over capacity and is unable to deal with the number of requests being made at a particular point in time. The image, designed by Yiying Lu, depicts a whale held aloft by red birds holding a net and is captioned 'Too many tweets! Please wait a moment and try again.' According to popular commentary the image 'is as iconic as any corporate logo, and far more beloved' (Walker 2009). In this way it represents further interpersonal iconization of fail, solidifying multimodally its position as an ambient bonding icon. Users will directly discuss the fail whale with the kind of affection identified by Walker or with expressions of amusement:

> Heh I got the fail whale so many times yesterday that Twitter/'too many tweets' was in my drop down box as a freq visited. #fail

Twitter often falls under criticism for being a mode of communication that encourages frivolous detail and time wasting. However, what we are witnessing is the evolution of a new kind of sociality, in which collective and detailed expression of daily experiences is not necessarily inappropriate when viewed through an interpersonal lens. Personal accounts of everyday misfortune or irritation are humourously packaged by the fail meme in an exercise in ambient affiliation through communal complaint. In other words (in most instances) posting a message about some trivial quotidian irritation is not necessarily an egocentric act but is presenting a potential bond to the ambient audience. Due to its far-reaching appeal and the frequency at which daily life exasperates most of us, fail is an enduring Twitter meme that has yet to wane in popularity.

CHAPTER NINE

Political discourse online

Microblogging as a form of political expression

The 2008 US presidential elections highlighted the role social media are beginning to play in political life. Some studies argue that the 'participatory web', a term used to suggest the potential afforded by Web 2.0 for content generation and collaboration by users themselves rather than institutions, is fuelling civic involvement in the political process. Citizens use social media to express their political views and engage in discussion with others (Zhang et al. 2010). Research into the political implications of social media began with considering political blogging (Singer 2005; Lowrey 2006; Woodly 2008; Wallsten 2007; Trammell et al. 2006) and since has progressed to exploring political use of Facebook and other social networking sites (Williams and Gulati 2008; Robertson et al. 2010; Sweetser and Lariscy 2008; Kushin and Kitchener 2009). Because of the disciplinary orientation, most of these types of studies consider discourse as general social phenomenon rather than investigating particular linguistic patterns in political discourse. However, they offer useful complementary perspectives for the discourse analyst.

There have been a number of studies of social media in relation to election campaigns, with the most frequent case study being the 2008 US presidential election (e.g. Vaccari 2010). Other examples include YouTube in the 2007 Finnish national elections (Carlson and Strandberg 2008) and Twitter in the 2009 German federal election (Tumasjan et al. 2010). The last study analysed more than 100,000 posts that refer to parties or politicians prior to the German federal election in 2009. It found that '[t]he mere number of tweets reflects voters' preferences and comes close to traditional election polls, while the sentiment of political Twitter messages closely corresponds to the electorate's sentiment and evidence from the media coverage of the campaign trail' (Tumasjan et al. 2010, p. 13). This chapter will explore this type of sentiment in tweets using appraisal theory (introduced in Chapter 3).

Governments are discovering that Twitter has 'unexpected reach' (Wigand 2010, p. 66), an influence that has begun to be exploited by politicians – for example, members of the US Congress (Lassen and Brown 2010; Shogan 2010). A study of the social media use of members of the US Congress found they used Twitter primarily for self-promotion rather than for direct communication with citizens (Golbeck et al. 2010). Instead, Twitter was used to communicate the kind of information that political offices have traditionally conveyed via press release and rarely to provide novel insights into congressional activities. Unsurprisingly, busy politicians are likely to outsource their social media use to staff as a form of 'delegated listening', also used by large corporations for brand management (Crawford 2009, p. 531). Similarly, as another way of managing public relations, it is likely that public figures often employ ghost writers to author their microposts.

Obama's 2008 campaign made substantial use of social media for civic engagement (Harfoush 2009). His campaign generated a social media website of its own, My.BarackObama.com, referred to as MyBo, to leverage the community-building properties of social media for political advantage. Obama also made frequent use of Twitter, and it is claimed that the service became 'a legitimate communication channel in the political arena as a result of the 2008 campaign' (Tumasjan et al. 2010, p. 178). This chapter uses a corpus of tweets collected following Obama's election win to explore the kind of language seen on Twitter in this period, in particular the outpouring of AFFECT that occurred.

Microbloggers as citizen journalists?

The idea that social media have enabled a social movement of public journalism has popular appeal. The practice of general users reporting on the immediate events around them has led to these types of claims about the emergence of the 'citizen journalist', 'social reporting' (Schlieder and Yanenko 2010) and 'ambient journalism' (Hermida 2010). 'Citizen journalists' are average users who report on newsworthy situations that happens to be occurring in their proximity. They may make use of text-based microblogging or contribute photos and video, often taken with a mobile device that happened to be on their person at the time. Microblogging – and mobile multimedia in general – allows users to share eyewitness accounts with great immediacy. Many studies have focused on the relationship of microblogging to news media (Satyen and Latifur 2010; Owen et al. 2009; Jagan et al. 2009). For example, Armstrong and Gao (2010) used the concept of news values as a theoretical framework for exploring how Twitter is used within the news industry to disseminate content.

Eyewitness reportage of this kind is an emergent genre, one quite unlike established news genres. Comparisons with the latter are somewhat inevitable and part of the general preoccupation with comparing online and offline discourses and with comparing different genres within and across macrogenres (Martin and Rose 2008). The following exchange in the comments to a web article about the 2009 Iran election (Cashmore 2009) provides a good snapshot of two popular opposing perspectives on microblogging as a form of citizen journalism. The first perspective presents Twitter as usurping traditional news media; the second viewpoint is more moderate, suggesting that the unmediated lens of microblogging qualifies the utility of the information broadcast.

> User 1: The above data clearly shows that Twitter did a much better job at covering the Iran elections than the traditional news channels.
>
> User 2: @User1 Marketing . . . how? A huge percentage of those Tweets were RTs. A lot were unsubstantiated rumors and comments. Not to defend how the MSM initially dropped the ball on the Iranian elections, though some did recover nicely but Twitter was not coverage, not in a news sense. It was more akin to thousands of unedited Anne Frank diaries, a huge pile of telegraph cables, many out of context or relation.
>
> What this event has shown is that the information stream has gone, permanently, from one to many and the role of journalism is to not only report on an event from a journalistic POV [point of view] but also to edit, review, confirm and amalgamate all of this raw information into something useful for the news consumer to digest. And it has to be done hourly or quicker.
>
> Twitter did not cover the event, it just provided a forum for people to talk to each other and with participants about the event.

This kind of discourse is characteristic of the tendency for cross-genre comparison, a line of thinking unlikely to illuminate the complex and meaningful permutations generated by shifting between semiotic modes (e.g. news media wires, electronic newspapers, blogs, microblog feeds etc.) without adequately theorizing the kinds of social meanings that are being staged in a particular genre.

Microblogging and reaction to public events

Analysis of reactions to significant world events in real time across large populations has not been readily achievable prior to the advent of social media. Microblogging streams provide researchers with a lens on large-volume public response at particular points in time, a veritable treasure trove of linguistic data about public thought. Traditionally samples of public opinion have been gathered via opinion polling, usually using scripted questioning via phone interviews or questionnaires. These kinds of mechanisms are not able to assemble the kind of unprompted, spontaneous opinion available in microposts. However, they do have the benefit of being very targeted, without the need to find ways of automatically extracting opinion on specific issues, and the very significant natural language-processing resources required.

A social pattern has emerged whereby at times of international and local political events or crises, the general public, or the subset thereof that uses social media, will take to their platform of choice (e.g. Twitter or Facebook) to voice a political opinion or present an emotional reaction. For instance, the 2008 US presidential elections attracted widespread, large-volume response on Twitter, as this chapter will explore. Another seminal event was protest in Tehran over the announced victory of Mahmoud Ahmadinejad in the 2009 Iranian presidential election, which generated sufficient traffic on Twitter to be dubbed the Twitter Revolution. Some have questioned whether Twitter was in fact used to achieve political change or simply to communicate events to an international audience.

> Yet, there is a difference between broadcasting information and engaging in dialog or coordinating action, and it is unclear how much Twitter facilitated the latter two objectives. First, even if it was technically possible to use Twitter, Iran's censorship capabilities and repressive tendencies made posting information dangerous enough that Iranians often could not engage in robust discussion or even any discussion at all. (Solow-Niederman 2010, p. 34)

The Web Ecology Project (2009) produced the following quantitative findings about related Twitter discourse at the time:

- From 7 June 2009 until the time of publication (26 June 2009), we have recorded 2,024,166 tweets about the election in Iran.
- Approximately 480,000 users have contributed to this conversation alone.
- 59.3 per cent of users tweet just once, and these users contribute 14.1 per cent of the total number.
- The top 10 per cent of users in our study account for 65.5 per cent of total tweets.
- One in 4 tweets about Iran are retweets of another user's content.

This kind of information about the volume and distribution of tweets and the tweeting practices of users is characteristic of the quantitative data that can be used to supplement various kinds of claims about discourse made with a linguistic perspective on microposts. As I discussed in Chapter 2, wielding this kind of data means that the discourse analyst needs to have some basic skills in managing a database containing micropost metadata. In addition, visualizing hashtags alongside their collocates (see the StreamGraphs presented in this chapter) offers the discourse analyst a very broad overview of the meanings being made as the real-time discussion of events unfolds. The limitations of the purely lexical perspective that most visualization techniques adopt, due to the problem of automating detection of language, are obvious; however, they do not preclude complementary close discourse analysis of interesting hot spots of meaning. Identifying these hot spots is important even to the discourse analyst more interested in qualitative analysis, as it helps them to direct their gaze upon datasets which, in the case of social media discourse, can be vast.

Hashtagging plays an important role in tracking international events and crises. Hashtags about politically controversial topics have been shown to be relatively persistent 'with repeated exposures continuing to have large relative effects on adoption' (Romero et al. 2011, p. 1). Hashtags are often associated with politically charged events of international significance. One popular hashtag, #iranelection, became a way of following the events relating to the 2009 Iran election (Gaffney, 2010). The tag became the first prevalent political hashtag to be reported in news media. It likely contributed to further hashtagging in subsequent periods of political crisis in other contexts. Related hashtags included #cnnfail, #freeiran, #tehran, #iran, #mousavi and #gr88. Another tag, #cnnfail, referred to the outcry accompanying the Iran crisis that the US news broadcaster, CNN, had 'failed' to adequately cover events. The tag references the fail meme (Chapter 6), usually used in a humorous way to highlight some misfortune or mistake.

Another context in which hashtagging was prominent was the 2011 protests in Libya against the regime of Muammar al-Gaddafi. These protests were said to be inspired by political unrest in Egypt and Tunisia around the same time. Indeed, hashtags for the critical events in these different countries seem to be associated, as shown in the Twitter StreamGraph in Figure 9.1 (#Libya, #Bahrain, #Tunisia etc.). The hashtag #feb17 was also involved in Twitter reaction to the Libyan situation. Figure 9.2 shows this hashtag unfolding over time with related tags, such as #Gaddafi (the Libyan president at the time) and #tripoli (the capital of Libya, where protests were reported to be violently suppressed by the government). Figure 9.1 shows related lexis unfolding with this tag, such as square, gunshot, near, wounds etc. The temporal window of the StreamGraph snapshot is relatively small, visualizing approximately 13 minutes of the Twitter stream. An example of a tweet from the sample is the following retweet of an apparent eyewitness account:

> RT @User: CONFIRMED: No more gunfire heard in #Tripoli for now. Hospitals still in need of aid, death toll still unconfirmed. #Libya #Feb17

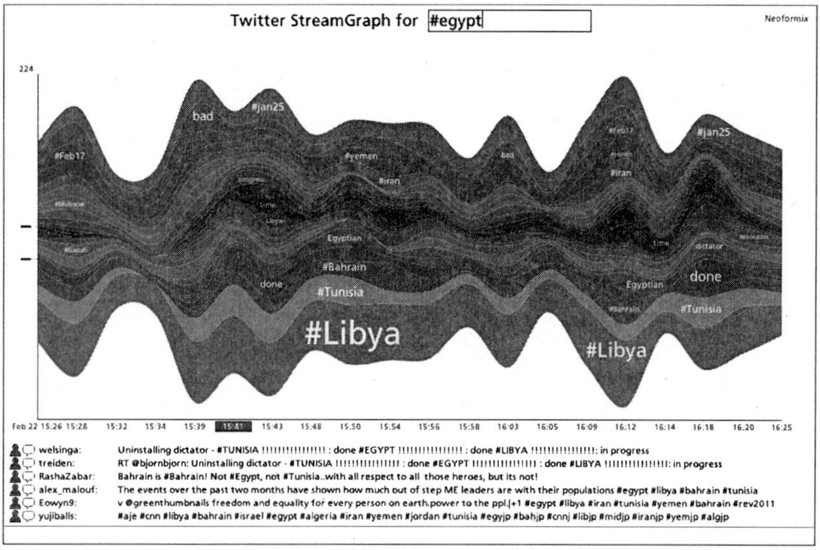

Figure 9.1 Twitter StreamGraph for #egypt created using Clark (2009)

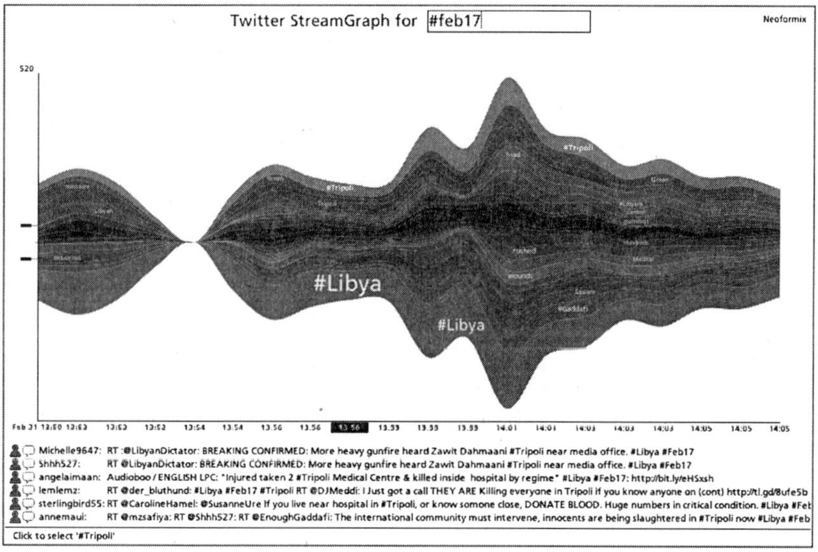

Figure 9.2 Twitter StreamGraph for #feb17 created using Clark (2009)

This tweet might be said to resemble an old-fashioned news wire, with the elided verbs and absence of inscribed evaluation. The similarity largely arises out of the similar need for linguistic economy and speed. The style of tweet is a recurrent pattern over a number of different crises. For example, the 2011 anti-government protests in Bahrain were associated with the hashtag #Bahrain, and eyewitness accounts of events were retweeted as follows:

> RT @User: Small group of protesters just reached #Bahrain Pearl Roundabout. Police firing tear gas. Nobody shot that I can see.

Whether or not we are seeing the formation of an eyewitness microgenre will become apparent as the emergent systems of meaning involved stabilize.

General social media users that may not have otherwise expressed public political comment on these issues use microposts to express sentiment and opinion and to offer support to the perceived oppressed. A frequent pattern in this kind of discourse is an expression of support, usually employing some form of AFFECT (highlighted in bold):

> RT @User: Sending **peace** and **love** to the citizens of #Bahrain

However, hashtagging is not a practice generating solely benign social engagement. For example, the notorious tweet posted by clothing designer Kenneth in 2011, 'Millions are in uproar in #Cairo. Rumor is they heard our new spring collection is now available online at http://bit.ly/KCairo-KC', precipitated a substantial negative reaction. It was largely perceived as abuse of the hashtag #Cairo via hijacking rather than clever marketing capitalizing on Twitter buzz. This hashtag had been employed to track political protest in Egypt occurring at the time. The tweet was later removed and an apology issued via Cole's account. Reaction on Twitter was scathing and often satirical; for example, the NEGATIVE JUDGEMENT invoked via irony in the following tweet:

> Starvation in Sudan! They're going to look **trim** and **sexy** in our new Spring lineup! #kennethcoletweets

Here the hashtag #kennethcoletweets functions to target the JUDGEMENT realized by irony at Kenneth Cole. The positive evaluation annotated in bold in the tweet invokes the ironic JUDGEMENT. This is also an example of a hashtag being used in the service of the interpersonal. The tag, unlikely to be used by other users, instead serves to intensify the evaluation made in the tweet.

The Obama win corpus and emotional language in political microblogging

Emotional language is often found in political contexts and indeed is central to taking a political stance. As we saw in Chapter 4, on evaluation in microblogging, there is a general interest in mining the Twitter stream for sentiment, particularly for opinion on political events and politicians. Some studies compare the traditional measures of public opinion provided via political polling with sentiment analysis. For example O'Connor and colleagues (2010, p. 128) claim 'that a relatively simple sentiment detector based on Twitter data replicates consumer confidence and presidential job approval polls'. However, as mentioned earlier, making sense of the complex, shifting patterns of evaluative language over the course of, for example, an election campaign is a difficult problem. Analysts require some kind of text-visualization support be able to cope with complex, multidimensional logogenetic patterns as they unfold (Zappavigna 2011a). An example of development in this area is exploring how visual representations and metrics can assist with comprehending unfolding sentiment in social media messages produced in reaction to televised political debates (Diakopoulos and Shamma 2010). Diakopoulos and Shamma (2010) – using a manually annotated corpus of approximately 3,000 tweets about the US presidential debate in 2008 via a crowd-sourcing[1] site (Amazon Mechanical Turk) – analyse sentiment 'to characterize the debate in terms of the overall sentiment of the tweets, whether Twitter users favoured a particular candidate, and the temporal evolution and "pulse" of the sentiment observable in the tweets'.

This chapter investigates a specialized corpus of tweets, the Obama win corpus (OWC), collected in the 24 hours after Barack Obama won the 2008 US presidential elections. The aim is to investigate the outpouring of positive emotion seen on Twitter in the period after his victory was announced by the news media. OWC was collected using a Python script and the Twitter API to scrape all tweets containing the string 'Obama' posted to Twitter in the 24 hours after the declaration of his victory. The corpus contained 45,290 tweets (813,310 words). The aim was, not to construct a representative corpus of the linguistic activity on Twitter across all topics and genres, but instead to conduct a case study in which field variables – that is, the topic of the tweets – were held relatively constant to afford a rich investigation of 'meaning making' in a single domain on Twitter.

This collection strategy is similar to the concept of Popescu and Pennacchiotti (2010, p. 1873) of a 'Twitter snapshot' – that is, 'a triple consisting of a target entity (e.g. Barack Obama), a given time period (e.g. 1 day) and a set of tweets about the entity from the target time period'. Twitter language is highly temporally bound, since the medium affords real-time updating – meaning that people will often post about events as they happen and about topics that are on their mind at a particular time, often in reaction to shared situations. Thus, the time at which the snapshot occurs impacts on the kind of language retrieved from the Twitter stream. The effect of the logogenetic window on sampling occurs even with randomized corpora such as HERMES. The collection of HERMES over the period of Valentine's Day and the 2010 Winter Olympics sees lexis related to these

Table 9.1 Comparing word lists for OWC and HERMES.

Obama Win Corpus				HERMES			
N	Word	Freq.	%	N	Word	Freq.	%
*	OBAMA	41,899	5.27				
1	THE	24,468	3.08	1	THE	3,358,659	3.15
2	TO	17,075	2.15	2	TO	2,379,223	2.23
3	HTTP	16,816	2.11	3	I	2,236,470	2.10
4	I	11,794	1.48	4	A	1,674,654	1.57
5	A	11,757	1.48	5	HTTP	1,631,187	1.53
6	OF	11,499	1.45	6	AND	1,545,943	1.45
7	IS	10,419	1.31	7	OF	1,217,398	1.14
8	AND	10,292	1.29	8	YOU	1,194,631	1.12
9	IN	9,244	1.16	9	IS	1,120,058	1.05
10	FOR	9,094	1.14	10	IN	1,118,227	1.05

fields of meaning over-represented in the corpus. Diachronic sampling would be a potential strategy for addressing this effect, but adequately representing time is not a straightforward corpus design issue (Biber et al. 1998). The rapidly changing content on Twitter is the basis of the concept of trending topics (see Chapter 3).

The most frequent words in OWC compared with HERMES are shown in Table 9.1. N1 in OWC can be ignored since the string 'Obama' was the selection criteria for tweets to be included in the corpus. At first glance, differences to note between the corpora are the higher ranking of weblinks[2] in OWC (OWC, N1; HERMES, N5) and the higher ranking of YOU in HERMES (OWC, N22; HERMES, N8). The first difference in frequency suggests an increase in weblink sharing that accords with the field orientation itself being newsworthy (i.e. an election generating many readily available news articles to be shared). The larger difference in the ranking of YOU across the two frequency lists warrants further exploration.

As the 3-grams for YOU suggest (Table 9.2), the second-person pronoun was used to foster engagement with others, most often via 'ask the crowd'-style questions such as the example for N10. These questions were often rhetorical, such as the example for N2, and were more concerned with offering a bond around positive evaluation of Obama, as this instance exemplifies. The increased frequency of YOU compared with HERMES, suggests that the language has become increasingly addressed at others, in turn suggesting that people are bonding around

Table 9.2 Most frequent 3-grams for 'you' in OWC

N	Cluster	Freq.	Example
2	DO YOU THINK	90	Obama is our President elect, do you think anyone would mind if he starts early?
3	YOU VOTED FOR	61	Congratulations all my American friends, I know almost all of you voted for Obama. Hope.
4	VOTED FOR OBAMA	47	Racist> Saying that Obama won because he is black. Not-racist> Saying you voted for Obama because he is black.
5	THANK YOU FOR	44	(@User) Dear america, I am so proud of you. Thank you for electing Obama.
6	THANK YOU OBAMA	41	It truly is a NEW day today! Thank you Obama!!!
7	PRESIDENT ELECT OBAMA	39	I don't know about any of you . . . but today just feels that much more positive. Thank you President Elect Obama.
8	WHAT DO YOU	38	@User what do you think of Obama? Young but greater than you are?
9	YOU HAVE TO	32	@User re: you have to keep saying 'President-elect Obama' to make sure it's real: 1) me, too; and 2) there are four lights.
10	YOU THINK OBAMA	30	Do you think Obama will stay on Twitter as President?
11	HOW DO YOU	28	How do you think child-related policies will change under Obama? What changes do you want?: http://tinyurl.com/5j85ty
12	IF YOU VOTED	28	If you voted for Obama because he is black, doesn't that make you a racist?
13	I LOVE YOU	27	Hi America, Thank you for voting for Obama, I love you all.
14	IN CASE YOU	26	Stay at home moms who supported Obama call themselves 'ObamaMammas', in case you haven't heard that before. :-)
15	OBAMA THANK YOU	26	@BarackObama Thank you President Elect Barack Obama. I am filled with hope and tears!

the election victory. However, close analysis is clearly needed to support this claim.

Inspecting DO YOU THINK, the most frequent 3-gram for YOU, we see that this pattern is involved in 'ask the crowd'-style questions. However, unlike genuine questions about what a user should do (e.g. purchase decisions), which as we saw earlier are frequent in HERMES, these questions seem largely rhetorical, though different to rhetorical questions in offline contexts. Here there is the potential that another user might reply; however, the main function seems to be to offer the bond to the ambient audience by making some kind of evaluative point. For example, the fourth tweet in the concordance line – about whether Obama will continue using Twitter – invokes a critique via social sanction suggesting that Obama is not the genuine author of his tweets by the quoted 'he'. Similarly, the tweets about the presidential puppy offer the bond, which will be discussed later as the hashtag #puppy, positively appreciating dog ownership.

Olsonhomes, what	**do you think**	obama will do to the housing industry
@User Palin vs Obama 2012.	**Do you think**	she'll be sweetness and light?
What kind of #puppy	**do you think**	Pres. Obama's daughters will choose? Pit bull? Dalmatian? Labrador? Chiuahua? Poodle? Basset Hound?
Now that Obama has won	**do you think**	'he' will keep using Twitter
with the election over, we can now turn our attention to the important questions: what kind of puppy	**do you think**	the obama girls will get?
If Obama is getting a puppy for his kids,	**do you think**	he'll get a pit bull and name it Sarah?
Haw many Conservatives	**do you think State?**	might have still voted for Obama if they had realized that John Kerry might become Secretary of

Looking at OWC in terms of keyness,[3] with HERMES acting as a reference corpus, we see, not surprisingly, that, in general, political terms and figures are key. More interesting is the key evaluative lexis, both inscribed and invoked: VICTORY, WON, WIN, HISTORIC, CHANGE (generally invoked positive evaluation), WINS, CONGRATULATIONS and TRANSITION. These are all involved in positive prosodies of evaluation, reflecting the general positive sentiment towards Obama's victory expressed on Twitter. This sentiment was unappealing to users who were not Obama supporters, some of whom complained about the apparent skewed representation on Twitter:

> I don't like Obama and I am not happy about his election. Almost half of the US agrees, but I guess they're not on Twitter.

Semantic prosody (Louw 1993) is generally used to refer to the positive or negative meaning with which a word may be imbued based on the kind of collocation occurring in its co-text. An individual tweet has little opportunity to build up an extended semantic prosody since posts are restricted to 140 characters. However, if we view tweets in streams over a particular time frame – either ontogenetically, as an individual user's meaning making over time or, more phylogenetically, as the unfolding of culture as it is represented via Twitter – we can note that particular terms attract particular polarities of appraisal. For example, the time period over which OWC was collected was the 24 hours after Obama's election win was announced. See Table 9.3. This chapter considers prosodies of evaluation over this time span.

CHANGE, (N21), is generally not an instance of inscribed appraisal. Instead, it invokes positive or negative evaluation depending on the co-text with which it is deployed. In general terms, it is involved in a positive evaluative prosody that preferences POSITIVE JUDGEMENT of Obama. 'Change', as part of the campaign slogan 'Change we can believe in' (alongside 'Yes we can'), was a core term in Obama's campaign. The

Table 9.3 Top 30 OWC keywords with HERMES as reference corpus

N	Keyword	N	Keyword	N	Keyword
1	OBAMA	11	PROP	21	CHANGE
2	OBAMA'S	12	ELECTED	22	WINS
3	BARACK	13	WIN	23	CAMPAIGN
4	PRESIDENT	14	PRESIDENCY	24	EMANUEL
5	ELECT	15	AMERICA	25	NADER
6	VICTORY	16	BUSH	26	CONGRATULATIONS
7	ELECTION	17	VOTED	27	VOTE
8	MCCAIN	18	SUPPORTERS	28	RAHM
9	SPEECH	19	ACCEPTANCE	29	HIS
10	WON	20	HISTORIC	30	TRANSITION

following are example concordance lines for CHANGE which demonstrate this positive skewing and which are saturated in POSITIVE ATTITUDE (marked in small caps) coupled with UPSCALED GRADUATION realized both lexically and typographically via exclamation marks, uppercase font and repetition (marked in italics underlined):

HOPE and	**Change**	kissed and America BLUSHED . . . *:)* THANK YOU, AMERICA*!! OBAMA! OBAMA! OBAMA!*
Obama for	**change!**	
YEA!!!	**CHANGE**	*HAS COME TO AMERICA!! GO PRESIDENT ELECT OBAMA!!*
well, i'm SAD because people don't undestand about EQUALITY, but i think that is gonna	**Change**	with Obama
Obama is I think the *best* election americans could make*!* uhmmm hes the	**change!**	
Waiting for 5pm to come around, *so* I can go home. EXCITED about *OBAMA winning* the election, and the	**Changes**	to come*!!!*
Though Prop 8 may have passed, I am COMFORTED knowing that with the election of Obama this country *CAN*	**Change**	in spite of BIGOTRY/HATRED.

A common pattern was 'change has come to America', often a quotation of Obama's acceptance speech:

> It's a long time coming, but because of what we did on this day, at this defining moment, change has come to America – Barack Obama

These references deploy 'change' as evaluatively loaded: the change anticipated is clearly positive rather than negative.

Another seemingly neutral term often co-opted in elections is history. Obama himself posted the following tweet on 8 November 2009 following his win:

> This is history.

Among the general Twitter population, the term had a positive evaluative resonance, as the examples in Figure 9.3 suggest. The phrase 'saw history

Congrats to Barack Obama,	**history**	maker.
Glad that Obama wins. He has great charisma. And Americans have made	**history**	Again!
From the page: 'Barack Obama's victory speech in Chicago on November 4th. It was a powerful, inspiring,	**history**	. . . re: http://ff.im/84c
OBAMA 08!!!!! THANK gOD WE MADE	**HISTORY**	!!!
Inspiring speech from Obama. Cool watching	**history**	happen. Now let's see how it translates to action.
I feel so lucky to have been witness to	**history**	last night at Hutchison Field. President Barack Obama. Soaking it in.
An inevitable victory by Obama. Now I get to watch like a mad scientist as another chapter of	**history**	unfolds.
Obama won!!!!!!!!!!!!! I can't believe I saw	**history**	Being made :-)

Figure 9.3 Concordance lines for 'history' in OWC

being made' has become a 'snowclone' (Pullum 2004), generally used in response to an event deemed of major cultural significance. This kind of formulaic language can also see history construed as part of a negative prosody; for instance, 'history will judge him harshly'.

There is a particular coupling of the mental process[4] of seeing (e.g. 'saw', 'witness', 'watch' in the concordance lines just presented) and positive evaluation with Obama and the act of seeing as targets. Users appear to be bonding around the collective act of witnessing a moment that they perceive will be important to their cultural history. This act of witness is associated with POSITIVE AFFECT ('proud', 'excited') and POSITIVE JUDGEMENT/APPRECIATION[5] ('great', 'amazing', 'cool'); for example (AFFECT shown in bold; APPRECIATION/JUDGEMENT shown in bold underlined):

> **Woo Hoo**, Obama! How **exciting** to see history made during our lives and to have **hope** for ***<u>positive change</u>***

Patterns of AFFECT in OWC

This section will explore how tweets in the Obama win corpus deploy resources for making interpersonal meaning. There appears a skew toward scaled-up positive evaluation in the corpus, though this has not yet been verified quantitatively, as it would require time-consuming manual annotation of a substantial sample of the corpus and a reference corpus annotated for evaluation to provide a meaningful baseline. Nevertheless a qualitative snapshot of the corpus suggests that positive evaluative language is highly frequent. Consider, for example, the following tweet in the corpus:

> HOLY CRAP. OBAMA WON HE WON!!!! IM SO HAPPY!!!

In this example, the expletive in initial position, the modifier 'so' and the choice of full capital letters and repeated exclamation marks realizes INCREASED GRADUATION of the interpersonal meanings expressed, as annotated below. Obama is coupled with POSITIVE JUDGEMENT about winning the election and in turn with POSITIVE AFFECT (appraisal coding in square brackets, appraisal item in bold):

> **HOLY CRAP** [increased graduation: force]. OBAMA **WON** [positive judgement] HE **WON** [positive judgement]**!!!!** [increased graduation: force] IM **SO** [increased graduation: force] HAPPY [positive affect]**!!!** [increased graduation: force]

This tweet is characteristic of an outpouring of POSITIVE AFFECT that appears to have occurred during the initial period where users were absorbing the news of Obama's victory in the election. Other AFFECT-charged tweets of this kind included the following (appraisal coding in square brackets, appraisal item in bold):

> @user It's not **crying** [POSITIVE AFFECT] over Obama so much as it's **crying** [POSITIVE AFFECT] for what that means. We moved closer to being **what we aspire to be** [POSITIVE JUDGEMENT]. #obama

> while we breathe we **hope** [POSITIVE AFFECT]**!!!!!** [INCREASED GRADUATION] **love love love** [POSITIVE AFFECT] [INCREASED FORCE] obama . . . he brought **hope** [POSITIVE AFFECT]!

> #electionwrap NGO report: McCain's coverage was **much more** [INCREASED GRADUATION] **negative** [NEGATIVE JUDGEMENT] than Obama's

Discounting 'like', since it is frequently used as, for example, a softener, 'happy' is the most frequent example of POSITIVE AFFECT in the corpus. As we will see later, it was part of the frequent 4-gram, HAPPY THAT OBAMA WON.

The most frequent evaluative items in the word list are related to Obama's election: 'victory', 'win' and' 'won'. These are instances of POSITIVE

JUDGEMENT, positively appraising the outcome of the election process. Examples for 'victory' are shown in the concordance lines presented in Figure 9.4. Instances of POSITIVE AFFECT are shown in bold. There appears, from this modest sample, a general coupling of positive affect with 'victory'. The axiology that develops around the ideation (Obama receiving the most votes in the election) assigns positive historical value to it, alongside personal affectual response.

While these concordance lines are only a random sample of the evaluation surrounding 'victory', they show a general prosody of positive affect co-occurring with this item. Some examples of related evaluative 3-grams[4] include:

Glad Obama won

Obama has won

won the presidency

So **happy** about Obama's	**victory!!!!**	So sad about Prop 8 :(
Currently suffering from election lag. Very **sad** that it seems that 8 is going to pass, but **ecstatic** over Obama's	**victory.**	
@User most certainly Obama's election was a Civil Rights	**Victory**	for people of color and women in our country.
Obama's	**Victory**	met with **tears** and traffic jams http://tinyurl.com/5lty65
must stop reading about obama	**Victory**	and go to bed. But, I **fear** nightmares involving recounts and lost ballots . . . no, really, I had them.
In **Hope** mode, after Obama	**victory.**	Let's make it viral!
is **elated** over Obama's	**victory!**	
With	**Victory**	in Hand, Obama Aides Say Task Now Is to Temper High . . . - New York Times http://tinyurl.. http://tinyurl.com/6jp23c
I'm at work **enjoying** the Obama	**Victory**	with my friends. I can't stop **smilin'**.
Pakistan, Afghanistan Greet Obama	**Victory**	With Cautious **Optimism**: http://tinyurl.com/67aqrn

Figure 9.4 Concordance lines for 'victory' in OWC with AFFECT in bold

Negative appraisal was possible but was generally used in a contrastive relation to Obama's victory. Most often it was at the passing of 'Prop 8', the California Marriage Protection Act that specified that marriage was only valid in that state if it was between a man and a woman. For example:

> @User I really hear you on feeling a bit like a wet blanket. Even though I'm elated at Obama's win, sucks to be queer today, huh?

Negative appraisal of Obama was present although much less common than positive evaluation (NEGATIVE AFFECT highlighted):

> Obama sucks and I'm **depressed**
>
> @User I am still really **sad** and **disappointed.** It would be hypocritical of me to wish Obama well when I am **not pleased** to see him win.
>
> Listening to a co-worker gloat over Obama's win. :(
>
> :(very **sad** that our country is now being led by Obama :(:(:(:(:(:(:(:(

Often the negative appraisal was qualified:

> I am not **happy** that Obama won but I will honor him! I actually **LOVE** that he is a black president, **love** that. The other issues? I pray . . . :)

Given that the news of Obama's victory was widely known, at least after the first hours post-announcement, these tweets are clearly performing a function beyond informing other users of the news. The kind of evaluative language that I have sampled above suggests that the tweets may be forming a more interpersonal social function in which users are affiliating around values relating to the election result. In the corpus these values are often construed as couplings of 'Obama' with appraisal.

There was a coupling of affect patterns with other interpersonal resources such as vocatives of solidarity. For example, 'man' and 'dude' are the most common vocatives used in OWC.[6] For example, the following tweet is characteristic of the tendency of 'man' to be coupled with positive ATTITUDE (ATTITUDE shown in bold, AFFECT specified by bold underlined):

> man im so <u>**excited**</u> obama won! seeing history first hand, and seeing our society grow and change for the **better** is **amazing!**

The coupling pattern in this example is echoed in Figure 9.5 for 'man' and 'dude':

	Man,	I am **loving** today! I have read SOOO00ooo many posts about how Obama winning will DESTROY THE WORLD . . . and look were all still here :)
@user 'Cause it's only 'God's will' when it coincides with THEIR will.	**Man**	am I **glad** to see we have President Obama! America you rock!
	Man	I watched Obama's speech and **totally got a speck of dust stuck in my eye**.
Obama? Oh	**man**	is he going to **disappoint** people . . . not because he will be a poor President but because expectations are ridiculously high.
	man,	I'd **hate** to be Obama's inbox today. yikes. I get **upset** having to clean out mine.
@User	**dude,**	I have been constantly bracing myself for the SHOCK of seeing obama shot on live tv . . . it all **feels** too **good** to last.
@User Great election show,	**dude!**	How **psyched** are you that a) it's done and b) IT'S AN OBAMA NATION!?!!?
@User: hey	**dude.**	Are u **glad** obama won? He is our next prez!
What me? No way,	**dude.**	It just got a little dusty in here during Obama's speech so I was **wiping my eyes with wet salty tissues**, duh.

Figure 9.5 Concordance lines for the vocatives 'man' and 'Dude' in OWC showing the coupling with AFFECT.

This type of coupling strengthens the kinds of interpersonal connection made with involvement systems (see Chapter 7 on slang for further details on this system). In other words, the coupling of attitude and involvement systems intensifies the affiliation, as it deploys both resources in the service of generating a constellation of values (Martin et al. 2010) around Obama. As I have mentioned throughout this chapter, prosodies of positive value are generally associated with Obama. The associated values are often related to positive evaluation of Obama's victory (e.g. positive evaluation shown in concordance lines for 'change', 'history' and 'victory' and n-grams such as 'happy that Obama won' shown earlier in this chapter). For example, in terms of involvement we see power and status instantiated as equal (e.g. realized by vocatives of solidarity), thus inviting reciprocal responses from other Twitter users.

Hashtagging in OWC

OWC contained 770 tweets employing a hashtag to refer to the topic that the user wished to ascribe to the tweet; 85 unique hashtags were used. Unsurprisingly, given that the selection criteria for tweets was that they contained 'Obama', the most common tag was #Obama (Table 9.4); 234 tweets in the corpus contained this tag. An example is the following:

> @User thats because **#Obama** is passionate and an amazing public speaker. He had grown men crying, its not girly, its moving ;)

In Chapter 5 I discussed the function of hashtags in marking the target of evaluation in a tweet. I also indicated their role in labelling a tweet as being about a particular topic when there is no explicit referent to the ideational target in the body of the tweet aside from the hashtag itself. The following tweets are examples of such instances where inscribed targets are absent. Instead the target of the evaluation is specified with a hashtag:

Its still surreal	**#Obama**
Hey I just remembered why I'm clinging to my guns and religion.	**#obama**
@User TMI. We don't need to know how you celebrated. Whee.	**#obama**
@User I'm thinking something floppy eared – a spaniel maybe.	**#obama**

Table 9.4 The ten most frequent # tags in the Obama win Twitter corpus.

ID	# tag	Explanation
1	#Obama	Barack Obama
2	#ElectionWrap	election coverage
3	#TwitVote	Twitter-based election polling
4	#election08	2008 US Presidential Election
5	#web2summit	Conference about Web2.0
6	#3News	news service
7	#election	2008 US Presidential Election
8	#haiku's	tweets conforming to haiku form
9	#puppy	US president's dog
10	#moc2008	Technology conference

The hashtag #Obama was used to label tweets about Obama during the election (and beyond; there were 554 instances of #Obama in HERMES). For example, users often expressed some stance regarding the election and appended a hashtag to indicate the target of the evaluation. For example, the following tweet specifies that Obama is the target of the INVOKED POSITIVE AFFECT realized by 'tears of joy', with the hashtag specifying the trigger of the AFFECT:

> Tears of joy! Tears of joy! #Obama

While the body of this tweet does not contain the lexical item Obama, the hashtag indicates the targets of the POSITIVE AFFECT inscribed. See Table 9.5.

A common pattern was for the hashtag to be used in as part of a projecting[7] clause, indicating the sayer;[8] for example, '#Obama said':

> Later, Mr #Obama said: 'The journey ends, but voting with my daughters, that was a big deal.' http://tinyurl.com/5rnukq

Another common hashtag was #Puppy, the incumbent presidential dog, which Obama promised his daughters in his acceptance speech:

> . . . you have earned the new puppy that is coming with us to the White House.. . . (Obama 2008)

This tag is associated with a general, widespread social bond – one that political figures often attempt to leverage – relating to dog ownership and

Table 9.5 The top ten collocates of #Obama.

N	Word
1	OBAMA
2	SAID
3	HTTP
4	CAN
5	IS
6	AND
7	THE
8	HAS
9	IN
10	JUST

@User AHH! this is counting down to the day Obama's kids get a puppy! #76days11hours17minutes	#puppy	SUPER COOL!
@User @User I would love to be the Obama's	#puppy	running around the White House and peeing on the carpets! Awesome Life!
@User Good point about the puppies! What woud be the best name for the Obama	#puppy ?	
@User @User I am certain the Disney will make a movie about the Obama	#puppy	and maybe they will even have a cat and a hamster, too!
What kind of	#puppy	do you think Pres. Obama's daughters will choose? Pit bull? Dalmatian? Labrador? Chiuahua? Poodle? Basset Hound?

Figure 9.6 Concordance lines for '#puppy' in OWC

appreciation. Political figures use this bond as a way of associating themselves with the positive cultural value that is attached to owning a dog. The bond is also allied with the popular notion of the 'American dream' – that is, being married with 2.5 kids, a dog and a white picket fence. The presidential dog is a way of aligning with the public and, seemingly at least, providing it with a more 'intimate' view of the private life of the president. Responses to this kind of bond are seen in the prosody of positive attitude coupled with the hashtag #puppy in concordance lines that follow (ATTITUDE shown in bold). The microposts in this concordance that do not directly inscribe POSITIVE ATTITUDE instead invoke it with punctuation, such as exclamation marks, and via interrogative clauses that imply substantial interest in the potential puppy. The questions given in Figure 9.6 act as a call to affiliate around the dog-owner bond by speculating on the dog breed and other details.

This chapter has suggested the role of evaluative language in political expression via microblogging. It is likely that as systems of meaning relating to this type of meaning making stabilize, we will see the emergence and development of microgenres, including the potential eyewitness report microgenre mentioned at the beginning of the chapter. We will also see political figures and government organizations begin to employ institutionalized microgenres as the methods that they use to communicate with the public in turn stabilize. The political possibilities are very interesting; there will be much room for corpus linguistics and discourse analysis to make a significant contribution in understanding how the language produced with social media realizes the complex and changing cultural processes involved.

CHAPTER TEN

Conclusion

Searchable talk and ambient affiliation

This book has explored microblogging, a form of streaming social media that allows episodic status updates, as a semiotic mode supporting interpersonal bonding. The following tweets are instances of the most common three-word pattern found in HERMES, the 100-million-word Twitter corpus that was used throughout:

> @User Thanks for the RT!!!
> @User Thanks for the #FF, love! Back at you. :)

The first tweet thanks a user for rebroadcasting one of the author's microposts. Similarly, the second tweet expresses appreciation for a mention during Follow Friday, a meme involving promoting follow-worthy Tweeters. Both posts highlight the importance of interpersonal interaction and reciprocity to the exchanges afforded by this communicative mode. They show the conversational nature of back channelling, detailed in Chapter 3, that occurs despite the non-obligation of reply. The two posts also suggest the affective nature of Twitter discourse, investigated in Chapter 4, where users draw upon appraisal (Martin and White 2005) resources to adopt stances and engage with other voices. In addition, both posts embody the general tendency toward upscaling appraisal seen in HERMES.

The tweets exemplify the properties of searchable talk that I have suggested characterize the ways people use language to affiliate via microblogging. For example, use of the @ character to track address and the hashtag to mark topic mean that the posts are aggregatable by these features and may be retrieved via search. The hashtag allows users to mark an ideational target for the post as a kind of in-line metadata in relation to the values that are co-articulated. It in turn affords potential for ambient communities of values to coalesce around particular hashtags, as was theorized in Chapter 5. This is a novel gaze on community, with the organizing principle of affiliation being an emergent bonding around searchable topics rather than direct interaction.

The general approach to analysing searchable talk in this book has been informed by two complementary traditions in linguistics: systemic functional linguistics and corpus linguistics, both of which offer useful, replicable strategies for analysing how language works in its social contexts. Throughout this book I have employed quantitative forms of analysis such as word-frequency lists and n-grams as a first step into exploring patterns of meaning in the discourse. These basic techniques can serve to guide the eye of the analyst to regions of meaning that are likely to be fruitful sites for close discourse analysis. I have worked with a 100-million-word corpus of randomized tweets to explore general linguistic tendencies and trends in evaluative language. I have also employed a number of specialized corpora to political discourse (the Obama Win corpus), internet memes (phrasal template corpora and the fail corpus) and ambient bonding around ideational targets (the hashtag corpus).

Using social media corpora to do 'internet linguistics'

Social media has become such a prominent means of communication on the internet that any genuine 'internet linguistics' (Crystal 2005, 2011) will need to consider this kind of data. In addition, to adequately explore the data, models of affiliation are needed since the main function of social media discourse is enacting relationships online. Affiliation is about more than connecting; it is about negotiating meanings within genres of language use. Corpus-based data can provide us with quantitative accounts of how the interaction occurs; for example, frequent topics and frequent grammatical patterns complement the view afforded by social network analysis. In turn, close discourse analysis allows theory-driven social-cultural interpretation of linguistic patterns, where the researcher probes further into the meanings made.

Developing social media corpora is an important part of this endeavour, providing quantitative data for corpus analysis and instance-based data for discourse analysis. As I suggested in Chapter 2, building internet corpora, even those that are purely text based and strip out metadata, is a theory-dependent process that comes with a range of challenges. Wielding the potential social insights that are captured by social media metadata requires knowledge of how to work with relational data.

In addition, given the episodic nature of social media as a form of streaming data, managing the time dimension is very important. Sampling is a challenge with streaming social media data, and the social processes involved in status updating will look different depending on the timescale (Lemke 2000) from which it is viewed. Since the corpora used in this book contained randomized tweets, they were not readily used to consider episodic structure (see Page [2011] for an example of a study that considers structure in the form of narratives in social media). In cases where linguists wish to study exchanges between microbloggers, some form of diachronic corpus will need to be generated spanning a time interval sufficient to gather strings of microposts that form exchanges or 'conglomerations of exchanges' around a topic or user. This is not a simple task. Similarly, where the analyst wishes to minimize the effect of particular context variables on the language collected (e.g. the impact of Valentine's Day discourse on the HERMES corpus), more extended diachronic sampling strategies will be needed.

Future directions

As online interaction makes increased use of multiple semiotic modes, discourse analysis that only considers verbiage will become increasingly inadequate. Most forms of social media, such as Facebook and other general social networking services, incorporate significant multimedia content, with images and video playing a significant role in meaning making. How best to generate multimodal corpora for these kind of media remains unclear and is likely to be closely tied to the particular research questions at hand. Many multimodal systems have yet to be theorized, making it difficult for the linguist to know a priori how best to generate an optimal corpus structure. Because of the complex structure of social media data and its high dimensionality – involving page layout, site layout, images, video, and links between users among other variables – the corpus will be much more complicated to manage than text-based corpora. Variables such as the layout of a micropost are dependent on the channel of publication since web syndication and mobile devices afford multiple ways of presenting and consuming media. Since users may use third-party applications to display and manipulate the content, a micropost may have multiple visual instances.

Add to this the many kinds of metadata that are collected by most social media, and you have a situation where the linguist needs more than basic database skills to wield the technology needed to interpret the relationships captured in even a text-based corpus – let alone a multimodal corpus. Factoring in the additional problem of temporally dependent data, such as microblogging streams, the issues, while fascinating, start to become intractable. It is, however, this seeming intractability that will keep discourse analysis and corpus linguistics working together, leveraging the power of paired quantitative and qualitative acumen.

Given the multimedia, multichannel nature of interaction over the internet, models of affiliation will also need to explore interpersonal bonding as a multimodal practice. This type of work is emerging as linguists begin to expand their territory into different modes of communication such as image, gesture and music, viewing these modes either as forms of semiosis that are 'parasitic' on language (Halliday and Matthiessen 1999) or as themselves having a 'grammar' that can be analysed (Kress and Van Leeuwen 2006).

Search changed the way we engaged with information resources and is now changing our social relations. In essence, I have proposed that microblogging involves a general process of offering an evaluative bond to potential bond networks. The bondability of the discourse is increased by its searchability. Searchable talk allows us to do more than retrieve information. It allows us to find common travellers who share our values. With mobile computing we can share experiences online relatively seamlessly within the activities of our offline lives. Whether we use social media to create a society where currently disenfranchised voices may yet be heard remains to be seen.

I for one welcome our new social media overlords! :P

NOTES

Chapter 1

1 Throughout this book I will refer to the messages published in microblogging feeds as microposts. A post is the general category used for time-stamped, chronologically ordered entries, including blog posts and contributions to online forums. The term *micropost* avoids this ambiguity and is somewhat less unwieldy than the longer form, *microblog post*.

2 I refer to the individuals who use social media and the internet as users, following the custom originating from discourse of software development where people using computer systems are termed end users. These discourses clearly have a range of implications, some of which are not necessarily positive, about how our relationship with technology is constructed. However, the term has wide currency and is less awkward than other ways of referring to the people who use social media. In some instances I will refer to authors of microposts as *microbloggers*, a term derived from *blogger*, the class of users authoring blogs.

3 The metaphor of a stream is commonly applied to internet data feeds that unfold in time.

4 Twitter also refers to itself as a real-time service (Twitter 2010).

5 Crowdsourcing is the act of inviting a large audience or community of people, usually over the internet, to assist with a task.

6 Supervised machine learning uses training examples to assist with the computational classification of data, in contrast to unsupervised machine learning, which attempts to automatically determine how unlabelled data is organized.

7 However, as we will see, the medium does afford new meaning potential not possible in face-to-face communication, and it is possibly not very productive to continue thinking of online communication as the poor cousin of spoken discourse.

8 For an overview of theory relating to complex adaptive systems, see Miller and Page (2007).

Chapter 2

1 Dating to 1979, USENET is one of the oldest computer-based communication networks. It is a global forum that allows people to post public messages to the internet.

2 An example of a diachronic corpus is the Helsinki Corpus of English Texts, which is a multi-genre corpus that includes texts from Old, Middle and early modern English (Rissanen et al. 1991).

3 Justin Bieber is a Canadian singer considered a teen idol with a huge following on Twitter. He had over 8 million Twitter followers at the time of writing in 2011.

4 This study likely used the original trending topic which collected frequent tweets rather than the newer version detecting emergent topics.

5 *Scraping* is the term used to describe collecting a web feed from a data source, usually using a script that automates the gathering, and using the content in some way, often not as the original author intended.

6 An example of the unescaped data problem is the Tweet 'what do u say in taking chances?:-). . . .<3<3<3'. In this example the < is an escaped version of the < character and, here, is used as part of a love-heart emoticon: formed by a less-than sign and the number three: <3 Solving this problem is simply a case of finding and replacing all escaped sequences. This can be done by using the 'find and replace' option in a text editor. Texts derived from an XML feed are likely to contain three types of escaped sequences: < , > , and &amp, which correspond to < , > , and &, respectively, and are reserved, as they have special meaning in the mark-up, such as marking the boundaries of a tag.

7 The exact size of HERMES is 100,281,967 words.

8 Mash-ups are services that combine functionality from two or more sources, such as data made available by an open API, to create a new service. For an overview of mash-ups in various domains, see Raza et al. (2008).

9 At the time of writing, Twitter was in the process of modifying the extent to which it allows third-party developers to use its data with the API and had suspended some third-party applications, such as TwapperKeeper, a site that allowed users to create archives of tweets (Yin 2011).

10 Another reason for certain levels of noise in the filtered data is that tweets are very short texts and, given that the same word can occur in multiple languages, the likelihood of being able to uniquely identify the language is reduced on this reduced-length text.

Chapter 3

1 'Ping' in networking refers to a way of detecting if there is a valid communication path between two or more computers: one computer sends out a message and the other replies with an identical copy.

2 All user names in this book have been anonymized.

3 In September 2010 Twitter began to release New Twitter, a reworked version of Twitter.com that includes a number of changes in functionality, in particular, being able to view multimedia without leaving the site and a redesign of the user interface. At the time of writing, commercial features such as sponsored 'promoted' trending topics had begun to appear on Twitter.

4 The interactive application is available at www.neoformix.com/Projects/TwitterStreamGraphs/view.php.

5 Hyper Text Transfer Protocol (HTTP) is the network protocol governing data communication on the web.

6 I have excluded n-grams generated by automated non-human services such as:

> I just took 'How will you win justin bieber`s heart ?' and got With your passionate side! Try it: http://bit.ly/9iwUcl

7 Social media memes are explored in Chapter 6. A Twitter meme is a form of internet meme that spreads virally through social media networks. Often humorous, social media memes are any form of media that self-propagates across the network from user to user. A common example is amusing YouTube videos.

Chapter 4

1 Sometimes, given the difficulty of automatically analysing evaluative language, studies will incorporate some form of crowdsourcing (Diakopoulos and Shamma 2010).

2 The cline of instantiation is the continuum between a system perspective on language as potential to an instance perspective of language as text (Halliday 1992).

3 O'Donnell and Bateman (2005) provide a useful review of SFL in computational contexts.

4 As is the convention in Corpus Linguistics, R1 refers to the position of the collocate one word to the right of the node word; similarly L1 would refer to one word to the left.

5 Moving from system to instance perspectives on language and back again is often referred to as a process of 'shunting' within systemic functional linguistics.

6 Caps lock has historically been likened to shouting in IRC (Internet Relay Chat) discourse.

7 Grammatical metaphor, according to Halliday.

8 The dominate type of emoticon is the face emoticon. However, emoticons representing bodies, animals and non-animate entities such as hearts and flowers are commonly seen. It should also be noted that Western and Asian regions manifest markedly different emoticon styles.

9 Due to the special characters used to form emoticons, they are challenging to work with using most concordance software. In order to get around this problem, the researcher working on a corpus will need to use basic text-processing skills to create regular expressions capable of detecting emoticons.

10 Non-animate, whole-body and Asian-style emoticons are not captured by this system network.

11 Tian's (2011) system network of facial articulation, used to analyse facial expressions in images in children's picture books, was helpful for developing this network.

12 This example was located using Twitter search since Unicode hearts do not occur in HERMES, as they were removed from the corpus as part of the method for filtering out non-English tweets.

Chapter 5

1 Approximately 1 in 7 tweets in the HERMES corpus of 6,740,865 tweets contained a hashtag, with some tweets containing more than one tag.

2 These are linguistic terms from SFL, used to describe the functions of a particular linguistic unit in a clause. They encode both the structure and the meaning of a particular unit. For example, in the following tweet the process, typically realized by a verb, (woke) construes an action in the world, the thing (supporter) encodes the agent that carries out the action, while the classifier (Obama) describes the type of social categories to which the thing belongs: Millions of pathetic #obama (classifier) supporters (thing) woke (process) this morning . . .

3 Adobe flash is a technology that supports streaming animation for web pages.

Chapter 6

1 Although it may be argued that the two are not mutually exclusive. Indeed, some researchers, while recognizing that work on how meanings are dynamically shared in culture is useful, have argued that memetics is a diluted version of semiotics and that a meme is, in effect, a sign (Kull 2000).

2 While it may technically be correct for 'internets' to refer to an interconnection of networks, the internet, singular and with a capital, currently refers to the worldwide connection of these networks. Users on various sites parodying George Bush suggest that he is unlikely to be aware of this technical distinction. Thus the term *internets* is a humorous intextual reference to the technologically illiterate.

3 Though disputing a meme's history is itself an act of group boundary policing.

4 Although it may have been taken from the film, *Empire of the Ants* (Internet Movie Database [date unknown]).

5 www.engadget.com/2009/11/27/roomba-saves-child-from-deadly-viper-challenges-tango-to-a-figh/.

6 (often phrasal verbs as well as relational processes).

Chapter 7

1 www.urbandictionary.com.

2 As I mentioned earlier, that status of leetspeak is not clear as it is often used as a kind of parody discourse.

Chapter 8

1 These are clauses where the main process involves an entity having some class attributed to it (Halliday and Matthiessen 2004).

2 This tweet refers to two models of airplane (A332 and A331) and to Middle East Airways (MEA).

3 A classifier 'indicates a particular subclass of the thing in question' (Halliday 1994, p. 184).

Chapter 9

1 Amazon Mechanical Turk (MTurk) is a service that coordinates humans to take on tasks, such as interpreting language, that are difficult for computers to perform.

2 Represented by HTTP in the frequency list, the Hypertext Transport Protocol occurs at the beginning of most weblinks.

3 Within corpus linguistics, a word is considered to be 'key' when it occurs more frequently than it might be expected to occur on the basis of statistical probability determined by comparing the corpus in which the word occurs with a larger reference corpus. In the present case, OWC, as a specialized corpus, is compared with HERMES, the latter acting as a reference corpus.

4 Halliday and Matthiessen (2004) define 'mental processes' as processes about perception, affection and cognition; that is, processes about thinking, feeling and knowing.

5 Whether the appraisal here should be annotated as POSITIVE JUDGEMENT or positive appreciation (since the behaviour of seeing is being appraised and APPRECIATION usually refers to the evaluations of entities and states rather than people and their behaviour) is difficult to determine. On the one hand, coding it as APPRECIATION seems to accord with the larger appraisal prosody in the Twitter stream positively evaluating the period of history. On the other hand, coding it as JUDGEMENT accords with the prosody of evaluation positively JUDGING Obama.

6 Vocatives are difficult to sample automatically from the corpus without parsing for part of speech (POS) using a POS tagger.

7 Within functional grammar, projection can be of two kinds: paratactic and hypotactic. Report of direct speech or thought is an example of paratactic projection (e.g. 'Obama said "This is history".'), whereas report of indirect speech or thought is hypotactic (e.g. 'Obama said that this is history.')

8 Halliday and Matthiessen (2004) define the sayer in relation to a verbal process (process of saying, e.g. to talk, speak etc.) as the entity that projects the verbiage (what is said) in relation to a target or receiver (the entity to whom the verbiage is directed).

REFERENCES

Adams, M. 2000. Ephemeral language. *American Speech* 75 (4): 382–4.

Agarwal, N., Liu, H., Murthy, S., Sen, A. and Wang, X. 2011. A Social Identity Approach to Identify Familiar Strangers in a Social Network, 17–20 May 2009 [accessed 24 March 2011]. www.aaai.org/ocs/index.php/ICWSM/09/paper/view/184/565.

Aharony, N. 2010. Twitter use in libraries: An exploratory analysis. *Journal of Web Librarianship* 4 (4): 333–50.

Ahn, Y.-Y., Han, S., Kwak, H., Moon, S. and Jeong, H. 2007. Analysis of topological characteristics of huge online social networking services. In *Proceedings of the 16th International Conference on World Wide Web*. Banff, AB: ACM.

Androutsopoulos, J. 2006. Introduction: Sociolinguistics and computer-mediated communication. *Journal of Sociolinguistics* 10 (4): 419–38.

Anstead, N. and O'Loughlin, B. 2010. Emerging viewertariat: Explaining twitter responses to Nick Griffin's appearance on BBC Question Time. In PSI working paper series, School of Political, Social and International Studies, University of East Anglia, Norwich, UK.

Arceneaux, N. and Weiss, A. S. 2010. Seems stupid until you try it: Press coverage of Twitter, 2006–09. *New Media and Society* 12 (8): 1262–79.

Archakis, A. and Tsakona, V. 2005. Analyzing conversational data in GTVH terms: A new approach to the issue of identity construction via humor. *Humor* 18 (1): 41–68.

Armstrong, Cory L. and Gao, F. 2010. Now tweet this. *Electronic News* 4 (4): 218–35.

Atkinson, C. 2010. *The backchannel: How audiences are using Twitter and social media and changing presentations forever.* Berkeley, CA: New Riders.

Baker, P. 2006. *Using corpora in discourse analysis.* London and New York: Continuum.

Bakhtin, M. M. 1981. *The dialogic imagination: Four essays*. ed. M. Holquist. University of Texas Press Slavic series. Austin: University of Texas Press.

— 1986. *Speech genres and other late essays*. ed. M. Holquist and C. Emerson. Austin: University of Texas Press.

Baron, N. 1998. Letters by phone or speech by other means: The linguistics of email. *Language and Communication* 18: 133–70.

— 2003. *The Stanford handbook for language engineers*. ed. A. Farghali. Stanford, CA: CSLI Publications.

— 2008. *Always on: Language in an online and mobile world.* Oxford and New York: Oxford University Press.

— 2009. The myth of impoverished signal: Dispelling the spoken language fallacy for emoticons in online communication. In *Emotion and ICTs*, ed. J. Vincent and L. Fortunati. London: Peter Lang.

Baroni, M. and Bernardini, S. (eds) 2006. *Wacky! Working papers on the web as corpus*. Bologna: GEDIT.
Bateson, G. 1972. *Steps to an ecology of mind*. Aylesbury: Intertext.
Baym, Nancy K. 1995. The performance of humor in computer-mediated communication. *Journal of Computer-Mediated Communication* 1 (2). http://onlinelibrary.wiley.com/doi/10.1111/j.1083-6101.1995.tb00327.x/full
Beam, C. 2008. Epic Win: Goodbye, schadenfreude; hello, fail [accessed 18 November 2011]. http://www.slate.com/articles/life/the_good_word/2008/10/epic_win.html
Bednarek, M. 2006. *Evaluation in media discourse: Analysis of a newspaper corpus*. London: Continuum.
— 2008. *Emotion talk across corpora*. Basingstoke: Palgrave Macmillan.
— 2009. Corpora and discourse: A three-pronged approach to analyzing linguistic data. In *Selected Proceedings of the 2008 HCSNet Workshop on Designing the Australian National Corpus*, ed. M. Haugh. Somerville, MA: Cascadilla Proceedings Project.
— 2010. Corpus linguistics and systemic functional linguistics: Interpersonal meaning, identity and bonding in popular culture. In *New Discourse on Language: Functional Perspectives on Multimodality, Identity, and Affiliation*, ed. M. Bednarek and J. R. Martin. London and New York: Continuum.
Beißwenger, M. and Storrer, A. 2008. Corpora of computer-mediated communication. In *Corpus Linguistics: An International Handbook*, ed. A. Lüdeling and M. Kytö. Berlin and New York: Mouton de Gruyter.
Benwell, B. and Stokoe, E. 2006. *Discourse and identity*. Edinburgh: Edinburgh University Press.
Bernardini, S., Baroni, M. and Evert, S. 2006. A WaCky introduction. In *Wacky! Working Papers on the Web as Corpus*, ed. M. Baroni and S. Bernardini. Bologna: GEDIT.
Bernardo, H., Romero, Daniel M. and Wu, Fang. 2008. Social networks that matter: Twitter under the microscope. *First Monday* 14 (1): 2009.
Biber, D., Conrad, S. and Reppen, R. 1998. *Issues in diachronic corpus design: Corpus linguistics*. Cambridge: Cambridge University Press.
Bisker, S., Ouilhet, H., Pomeroy, S., Chang, A. and Casalegno, F. 2008. Re-thinking fashion trade shows: Creating conversations through mobile tagging. In *CHI '08 extended abstracts on human factors in computing systems*. Florence: ACM.
Blashki, K. and Nichol, S. 2005. Game geek's goss: Linguistic creativity in young males within an online university forum. *Australian Journal of Emerging Technologies and Society* 3 (2): 77–86.
Bolinger, D. 1975. *Aspects of language*. 2nd edn. New York: Harcourt Brace Jovanovich.
Bollen, J., Mao, H. and Xiao-Jun, Z. 2011. Twitter mood predicts the stock market. *Journal of Computational Science* 2 (1): 1–8.
Bollen, J., Pepe, A. and Mao, H. 2009. Modeling public mood and emotion: Twitter sentiment and socio-economic phenomena. *arXiv*: 0911.1583.
Borau, K., Ullrich, C., Feng, J. and Shen, R. 2009. Microblogging for language learning: Using Twitter to train communicative and cultural competence. In *Advances in Web-Based Learning – ICWL 2009*, ed. M. Spaniol, Q. Li, R. Klamma and R. Lau. Berlin and Heidelberg: Springer.

Bourdieu, P. 1977. The economics of linguistic exchanges. *Social Science Information*, 16 (6): 645–68.
Boutin, P. 2009. *NowPlaying.fm adds song links to #nowplaying tweets* 2009 [accessed 26 February 2009]. http://venturebeat.com/2009/12/27/nowplaying-twitter/.
Boxer, D. 1993. Social distance and speech behavior: The case of indirect complaints. *Journal of Pragmatics* 19 (2): 103–25.
Boxer, D. and Cortés-Conde, F. 1997. From bonding to biting: Conversational joking and identity display. *Journal of Pragmatics* 27 (3): 275–94.
Boyd, B. 2004. Laughter and literature: A play theory of humor. *Philosophy and Literature* 28 (1): 1–22.
— 2009. Do You See What I See?: Visibility of Practices Through Social Media. Paper read at Supernova and Le Web, 1 and 10 December 2009, at San Francisco and Paris.
— 2009. *Spectacle at Web2.0 Expo . . . From My Perspective* 2009 [accessed 17 December 2009]. www.zephoria.org/thoughts/archives/2009/11/24/spectacle_at_we.html.
— 2010. Social network sites as networked publics: Affordances, dynamics, and implications. In *A Networked Self: Identity, Community, and Culture on Social Network Sites*, ed. Z. Papacharissi. New York: Routledge.
Boyd, D. and Heer, J. 2006. Profiles as conversation: Networked identity performance on Friendster. In *Proceedings of the Hawai'i International Conference on System Sciences (HICSS-39)*. Kauai, HI: IEEE Computer Society.
Boyd, D., Golder, S. and Lotan, G. 2011. *Tweet, Tweet, Retweet: Conversational Aspects of Retweeting on Twitter*. Computer Society Press, 2010 [accessed 24 March 2011]. www.danah.org/papers/TweetTweetRetweet.pdf.
Bradley, P. 2010. Be where the conversations are: The critical importance of social media. *Business Information Review* 27 (4): 248–52.
Bream, C. 2011. *Epic win: Goodbye, schadenfreude; hello, fail.* 2008 [accessed 23 March 2011]. www.slate.com/articles/life/the_good_word/2008/10/epic_win.html?fail
Brooks, A. L. and Churchill, E. 2010. Tune In, Tweet on, and Twit out: Information snacking on Twitter. Paper read at Workshop on Microblogging at the ACM Conference on Human Factors in Computer Systems, 10–11 April 2010, at Atlanta, Georgia.
Brown, R. and Gilman, A. 1960. The pronouns of power and solidarity. In *Style in Language*, ed. T. A. Sebeok. Cambridge, MA: MIT Press.
Brown, P. and Levinson, S. 1978. Universals in language usage: Politeness phenomena. In *Questions and Politeness*, ed. E. Goody. Cambridge: Cambridge University Press.
Bucholtz, M. 1999. Language and identity practices in a community of nerd girls. *Language in Society* 28 (2): 203–23.
Burnett, G. 2000. Information exchange in virtual communities: A typology. *Information Research* 15 (4).
Byron, L. 2011. *Last.FM listening history – What have I been listening to?* 2008 [accessed 22 February 2011]. www.leebyron.com/what/lastfm/.
Byron, L. and Wattenberg, M. 2008. *Stacked Graphs – Geometry & Aesthetics.* Lee Byron 2008 [accessed 8 July 2008]. www.leebyron.com/else/streamgraph/.

Cappelli, G. 2008. Expats' talk: Humour and irony in an expatriate's travel blog. *TEXTUS* XXI (1): 9–26.

Carlson, T. and Strandberg, K. 2008. Riding the web 2.0 wave: Candidates on YouTube in the 2007 Finnish National Elections. *Journal of Information Technology and Politics* 5 (2): 159–74.

Cashmore, P. 2011. *Staggering #IranElection Stats: 2 Million+ Total Tweets* 2009 [accessed 24 March 2011]. http://mashable.com/2009/07/01/iranelection-stats/.

Cataldi, M., Di Caro, L. and Schifanella, C. 2010. Emerging topic detection on Twitter based on temporal and social terms evaluation. In *Proceedings of the Tenth International Workshop on Multimedia Data Mining.* Washington, DC: ACM.

Cha, M., Haddadi, H., Benevenuto, F. and Gummadi, K. P. 2010. Measuring User Influence in Twitter: The Million Follower Fallacy Paper read at the Fourth International AAAI Conference on Weblogs and Social Media, 23–26 May 2010, at Washington, DC.

Chen, J., Nairn, R., Nelson, L., Bernstein, M. and Chi, E. 2010. Short and tweet: Experiments on recommending content from information streams. In *Proceedings of the 28th International Conference on Human factors in Computing Systems.* Atlanta, GA: ACM.

Cheong, M. 2010. *'What are you tweeting about?': A survey of Trending Topics within the Twitter community.* Technical report 2009/251. Clayton School of Information Technology, Monash University, 12 pp.

Chew, C. and Eysenbach, G. 2010. Pandemics in the age of Twitter: Content analysis of tweets during the 2009 H1N1 outbreak. *PLoS ONE* 5 (11): e14118.

Clark, J. 2008. *Twitter Topic Stream* 2008 [accessed 31 July 2008]. Neoformix: Discovering and illustrating patterns in data. www.neoformix.com/2008/TwitterTopicStream.html.

— 2009. *Temporal Correlation for Words in Tweets* 2009 [accessed 20 March 2011]. http://neoformix.com/2009/TemporalCorrelationForWordCountTimeSeries.html

— 2009. *Twitter SteamGraphs* 2009 [accessed 21 February 2011]. www.neoformix.com/Projects/TwitterStreamGraphs/view.php.

Colston, H. L. and O'Brien, J. 2000. Contrast of kind versus contrast of magnitude: The pragmatic accomplishments of irony and hyperbole. *Discourse Processes* 30 (2): 179–99.

Commission on Presidential Debates. 2010. *October 8, 2004 Debate Transcript: The Second Bush-Kerry Presidential Debate* [accessed 10 September 2010]. www.debates.org/index.php?page=october-8-2004-debate-transcript.

Correa, T., Hinsley, A. W. and de Zúñiga, H. G. 2010. Who interacts on the Web?: The intersection of users' personality and social media use. *Computers in Human Behavior* 26 (2): 247–53.

Cottingham, R. 2010. *Mommy, Where Do Hashtags Come From?* [accessed 1 March 2010]. www.robcottingham.ca/cartoon/2010/02/28/mommy-where-do-hashtags-come-from/comment-page-1/#comment-95.

Crawford, K. 2009. Following you: Disciplines of listening in social media. *Continuum: Journal of Media and Cultural Studies* 23 (4): 525–35.

Crystal, D. 2005. *The Scope of Internet Linguistics* 2005 [accessed 17 March 2011]. www.davidcrystal.com/DC_articles/Internet2.pdf.

— 2006. *Language and the Internet.* 2nd edn. Cambridge: Cambridge University Press.

— 2008. *Txting: The gr8 db8*. Oxford: Oxford University Press.

— 2011. *Internet Linguistics: A Student Guide*. New York: Routledge.

Cuddy, C. 2009. Twittering in health sciences libraries. *Journal of Electronic Resources in Medical Libraries* 6 (2): 169–73.

Culotta, A. 2010. Detecting influenza outbreakes by analyzing Twitter messages. [accessed 19 October 2011] http://arxiv.org/abs/1007.4748

Damaso, J. and Cotter, C. 2007. UrbanDictionary.com. *English Today* 23 (02): 19–26.

Davies, C. 1982. Ethnic jokes, moral values and social boundaries. *British Journal of Sociology* 33 (3): 383–403.

Dawkins, R. 1989. *The selfish gene*. New edn. Oxford and New York: Oxford University Press.

— 2006. *The selfish gene*. 30th anniversary edn. Oxford and New York: Oxford University Press.

De Jonge, S. and Kemp, N. 2010. Text-message abbreviations and language skills in high school and university students. *Journal of Research in Reading*: EJ 1–20.

Derks, D., Agneta, Fischer H. and Arjan, E. R. Bos. 2008. The role of emotion in computer-mediated communication: A review. *Computers in Human Behavior* 24 (3): 766–85.

Derks, D., Arjan, E. R. Bos and von Grumbkow, J. 2008. Emoticons and online message interpretation. *Social Science Computer Review* 26 (3): 379–88.

— 2008. Emoticons in computer-mediated communication: Social motives and social context. *CyberPsychology and Behavior* 11 (1): 99–101.

DeVoe, Kristina M. 2009. Bursts of information: Microblogging. *Reference Librarian* 50 (2): 212–14.

Diakopoulos, Nicholas A. and Shamma, David A. 2010. Characterizing debate performance via aggregated twitter sentiment. In *Proceedings of the 28th International Conference on Human Factors in Computing Systems*. Atlanta, GA: ACM.

Dresner, E. and Herring, Susan C. 2010. Functions of the nonverbal in CMC: Emoticons and illocutionary force. *Communication Theory* 20 (3): 249–68.

Drouin, M. and Davis, C. 2009. R u txting? Is the use of text speak hurting your literacy? *Journal of Literacy Research* 41 (1): 46–67.

Dumas, B. K. and Lighter, J. 1978. Is slang a word for linguists? *American Speech* 53 (1): 5–17.

Ebner, M. 2009. Introducing live microblogging: How single presentations can be enhanced by the mass. *Journal of Research in Innovative Teaching* 2 (1): 108–19.

Ebner, M., Muhlburger, H., Schaffert, S., Schiefner, M., Reinhardt, W. and Wheeler, S. 2010. Getting Granular on Twitter: Tweets from a Conference and their Limited Usefulness for Non-participants. Paper read at Key Competencies in the Knowledge Society, IFIP TC 3 international conference, 20–23 September 2010, at Brisbane, Australia.

Ebner, M., Lienhardt, C., Rohs, M. and Meyer, I. 2010. Microblogs in higher education – a chance to facilitate informal and process-oriented learning? *Computers and Education* 55 (1): 92–100.

Edwards, D. 2005. Moaning, whinging and laughing: The subjective side of complaints. *Discourse Studies* 7 (1): 5–29.

Eggins, S. 1994. *An introduction to systemic functional linguistics*. London: Pinter Publishers.

Eggins, S. and Slade, D. 1997. *Analysing casual conversation*. London and New York: Cassell.

Eisenstein, J., O'Connor, B., Smith, N. A. and Xing, E. P. 2010. A Latent Variable Model for Geographic Lexical Variation. Paper read at the Proceedings of the Conference on Empirical Methods in Natural Language Processing, 9–11 October 2010.

Encyclopedia Dramatica. 2010. *Sup Dawg*. 2009 [accessed 10 September 2010]. www.encyclopediadramatica.com/Pimp_my_ride

Erickson, I. 2010. Geography and community: New forms of interaction among people and places. *American Behavioral Scientist* 53 (8): 1194–207.

Evans, B. M. and Chi, E. H. 2008. Towards a Model of Understanding Social Search. Paper read at the Proceedings of the 2008 ACM Conference on Computer Supported Cooperative Work, at San Diego, California.

Facebook. 2010. *Statistics* [accessed 11 December 2010]. www.facebook.com/press/info.php?statistics.

Firth, J. R. 1957. *Papers in Linguistics 1934–1951*. London: Oxford University Press.

Fletcher, W. H. 2004. Making the Web more useful as a source for linguistic corpora. *Language and Computers* 52: 191–205.

Gaffney, D. 2010. #iranelection: quantifying online activism. In *Proceedings of the WebSci10: Extending the Frontiers of Society On-Line*, April 26–27, 2010, Raleigh, NC: US (NB: no page numbers or editors available).

Galuba, W., Aberer, K., Chakraborty, D., Despotovic, Z. and Kellerer, W. 2010. Outtweeting the twitterers – predicting information cascades in microblogs. In *Proceedings of the 3rd Conference on Online Social Networks*. Boston: USENIX Association.

Ghosh, S., Korlam, G. and Ganguly, N. 2010. The effects of restrictions on number of connections in OSNs: A case-study on Twitter. In *Proceedings of the 3rd Conference on Online Social Networks*. Boston: USENIX Association.

Goffman, E. 1963. *Behavior in public places: Notes on the social organization of gatherings*. New York: Free Press.

Golbeck, J., Grimes, Justin M. and Rogers, A. 2010. Twitter use by the US Congress. *Journal of the American Society for Information Science and Technology* 61 (8): 1612–21.

Grier, C., Thomas, K., Paxson, V. and Zhang, M. 2010. @spam: The underground on 140 characters or less. In *Proceedings of the 17th ACM Conference on Computer and Communications Security*. Chicago: ACM.

Grosseck, G. and Holotescu, C. 2009. Indicators for the analysis of learning and practice communities from the perspective of microblogging as a provocative sociolect in virtual space. In *5th International Scientific Conference eLSE – eLearning and Software for Education*. Bucharest.

— 2010. Microblogging multimedia-based teaching methods best practices with Cirip.eu. *Procedia – Social and Behavioral Sciences* 2 (2): 2151–55.

Gruzd, A. 2009. Automated discovery of social networks in text-based online communities. In *Proceedings of the ACM 2009 International Conference on Supporting Group Work*. Sanibel Island, FL: ACM.

Gruzd, A., Doiron, S and Mai, P. 2011. Is Happiness Contagious Online? A Case of Twitter and the 2010 Winter Olympics. Paper read at the Proceedings of the

44th Hawaii International Conference on System Sciences (HICSS), at Kauai, Hawaii.

Hagel, J. and Armstrong, A. 1997. *Net gain: Expanding markets through virtual communities*. Boston: Harvard Business School Press.

Halliday, M. A. K. 1961. *Categories of the theory of grammar*. Indianapolis, IN: Bobbs-Merrill.

— 1976. Antilanguages. *American Anthropologist* 78 (3): 570–84.

— 1978. *Language as social semiotic: The social interpretation of language and meaning*. London: Edward Arnold.

— 1979. Modes of meaning and modes of expression: Types of grammatical structure, and their determination by different semantic functions. In *Function and Context in Linguistic Analysis: A Festschrift for William Haas*, ed. W. Haas, D. J. Allerton, E. Carney and Holdcroft D. Cambridge and New York: Cambridge University Press.

— 1991. Towards probabilistic interpretations. In *Functional and Systemic Linguistics: Approaches and Uses*, ed. E. Ventola. Berlin and New York: Walter de Gruyter.

— 1992. How do you mean? In *Advances in Systemic Linguistics: Recent Theory and Practice*, ed. M. Davies and Ravelli L. London: Pinter.

— 1994. *An introduction to functional grammar*. 2nd edn. London: Arnold.

Halliday, M. A. K. and Hasan, R. 1976. *Cohesion in English*. London: Longman.

Halliday, M. A. K. and Martin, J. R. 1993. *Writing science: Literacy and discursive power. Critical perspectives on literacy and education*. London: Falmer Press.

Halliday, M. A. K. and Christian, M. I. M. Matthiessen. 1999. *Construing experience through meaning: A language-based approach to cognition*. Open linguistics series. London: Cassell.

— 2004. *An introduction to functional grammar*. 3rd edn. London: Arnold.

Halliday, M. A. K. and Webster, J. 2005. *Computational and quantitative studies*. London and New York: Continuum.

Harfoush, R. 2009. *Yes we did!: An inside look at how social media built the Obama brand*. Berkeley, CA: New Riders.

Harrison, S. 1998. E-mail discussions as conversation: Moves and acts in a sample from a listserv discussion. *Linguistik Online* 1 (1).

Harry, D., Green, J. and Donath, J. 2009. backchan.nl: Integrating backchannels in physical space. In *Proceedings of the 27th International Conference on Human Factors in Computing Systems*. Boston: ACM.

Havre, S., Hetzler., E, Whitney, P. and Nowell, L. 2002. ThemeRiver: Visualizing thematic changes in large document collections. *IEEE Transactions on Visualisation and Computer Graphics* 8 (1): 9–20.

Haythornthwaite, C. and Gruzd, A. 2007. A noun phrase analysis tool for mining online community conversations. In *Communities and Technologies 2007*, ed. C. Steinfield, B. T. Pentland, M. Ackerman and N. Contractor. London: Springer.

Hermida, A. 2010. Twittering the news: The emergence of ambient journalism. *Journalism Practice* 4 (3): 297–308.

Herring, S. C. 1996. Computer-mediated communication. Linguistic, social and cross-cultural perspectives. Vol. 39, *Pragmatics and Beyond*. Amsterdam and Philadelphia: Benjamins.

— 2004. Computer-mediated discourse analysis: An approach to researching online communities. In *Designing for Virtual Communities in the Service of Learning*, ed. S. A. Barab, R. Kling and J. H. Gray. Cambridge and New York: Cambridge University Press.

— 2008. Virtual community. In *Encyclopedia of Qualitative Research Methods*, ed. L. M. Given. Los Angeles: Sage.

Herring, S. C. and Zelenkauskaite, A. 2009. Symbolic capital in a virtual heterosexual market: Abbreviation and insertion in Italian iTV SMS. *Written Communication* 26 (1): 5–31.

Hill, B. M., Monroy-Hernández, A. and Olson, K. 2010. Responses to remixing on a social media sharing website. In *Fourth International AAAI Conference on Weblogs and Social Media*. Washington, DC: AAAI Press.

Hoffman, S. 2007. From Web page to mega-corpus: The CNN transcripts. In *Corpus Linguistics and the Web*, ed. M. Hundt, N. Nesselhauf and C. Biewer. Amsterdam: Rodopi.

Hogan, B. and Quan-Haase, A. 2010. Persistence and change in social media. *Bulletin of Science, Technology and Society* 30 (5): 309–15.

Holme, P., Edling, C. and Liljeros, F. 2004. Structure and time evolution of an internet dating community. *Social Networks* 26: 155–74.

Holmes, J. and Marra, M. 2002. Humour as a discursive boundary marker in social interaction. In *Us and Others: Social Identities Across Languages, Discourses and Cultures*, ed. A. Duszak. Amsterdam: Benjamins.

Honeycutt, C. and Herring, S. 2009. Beyond Microblogging: Conversation and Collaboration in Twitter. Paper read at the Proceedings of the Forty-Second Hawaii International Conference on System Sciences (HICSS-42), at Los Alamitos, California.

Horovitch, D. 2010. *#FF Follow Friday explained. Tweet Basics: Day 4* 2009 [accessed 17 February 2010]. www.teachmetotweet.com/news/ff-follow-friday-explained-tweet-basics-day-4/.

Hricko, M. 2010. Using microblogging tools for library services. *Journal of Library Administration* 50 (5): 684–92.

Huang, Albert H., Yen, David C. and Zhang, X. 2008. Exploring the potential effects of emoticons. *Information and Management* 45 (7): 466–73.

Huang, J., Thornton, K. M. and Efthimiadis, E. N. 2010. Conversational tagging in twitter. In *Proceedings of the 21st ACM Conference on Hypertext and Hypermedia*. Toronto: ACM.

Hübler, M. T. and Calhoun Bell, D. 2003. Computer-mediated humor and ethos: Exploring threads of constitutive laughter in online communities. *Computers and Composition* 20: 277–94.

Hughes, A. L., Palen, L., Sutton, J., Liu, S. B. and Vieweg, S. 2008. Site-seeing in Disaster: An Examination of On-line Social Convergence. Paper read at the Proceedings of the 5th International ISCRAM Conference, at Washington, DC.

Hundt, M., Nesselhauf, N. and Biewer, C. 2007. *Corpus linguistics and the Web*. Amsterdam: Rodopi.

Hunston, S. 2011. *Corpus approaches to evaluation: Phraseology and evaluative language*. London: Routledge.

Ian, L., Anind, D. and Jodi, F. 2009. Grafitter: Leveraging social media for self reflection. *Crossroads* 16 (2): 12–13.

Internet Movie Database. 2011. *Empire of the Ants (1977)* [accessed 5 May 2011]. www.imdb.com/title/tt0075989.

Jakobson, R. 1971. *Selected writings*. 2nd edn. The Hague: Mouton.

Jansen, Bernard J., Zhang, M., Sobel, K. and Chowdury, A. 2009. Twitter power: Tweets as electronic word of mouth. *Journal of the American Society for Information Science and Technology* 60 (11): 2169–88.

Java, A., Song, X., Finin, T. and Tseng, B. 2007. Why we twitter: Understanding microblogging usage and communities. In *Proceedings of the 9th WebKDD and 1st SNA-KDD 2007 Workshop on Web Mining and Social Network Analysis*. San Jose, CA: ACM.

Jones, Q. 1997. Virtual-communities, virtual settlements & cyber-archaeology: A theoretical outline. *Journal of Computer-Mediated Communication* 3 (3).

Kehoe, A. and Gee, M. 2011. Social tagging: A new perspective on textual 'aboutness'. In *Studies in Variation, Contacts and Change in English, Vol. 6: Methodological and Historical Dimensions of Corpus Linguistics*, ed. P. Rayson, S. Hoffmann and G. Leech. Helsinki: University of Helsinki.

Kemp, N. 2010. Texting vs txting: Reading and writing text messages and links with other linguistic skills. *Writing Systems Research* 2: 53–71.

Kilgarriff, A. and Grefenstette, G. 2003. Introduction to the special issue on the Web as corpus. *Computational Linguistics* 29 (3): 333–47.

Knight, N. 2008. 'Still cool . . . and american too!': An SFL analysis of deferred bonds in internet messaging humour. In *Systemic Functional Linguistics in Use, Odense Working Papers in Language and Communication*, ed. N. Nørgaard, Vol. 29, 481–502.

— 2010a. *Laughing our bonds off: Conversational humour in relation to affiliation*. Department of Linguistics, University of Sydney, Sydney.

— 2010b. Naming culture in convivial conversational humour. In *Directions in Applicable Linguistics*, ed. A. Mahboob and N. Knight. London: Continuum.

— 2010c. Wrinkling complexity: Concepts of identity and affiliation in humour. In *New Discourse on Language: Functional Perspectives on Multimodality, Identity, and Affiliation*, ed. M. Bednarek and J. R. Martin. London and New York: Continuum.

Knobel, M. and Lankshear, C. 2008. Remix: The art and craft of endless hybridization. *Journal of Adolescent and Adult Literacy* 52 (1): 22–33.

Knox, J. 2009. Punctuating the home page: Image as language in an online newspaper. *Discourse and Communication* 3 (2): 145–72.

Kress, G. and Hodge, R. 1979. *Language as ideology*. London: Routledge.

Kress, Gunther R. and Leeuwen, T. V. 2006. *Reading images: The grammar of visual design*. 2nd edn. London and New York: Routledge.

Kreuz, R. J. and Roberts, R. M. 1995. Two cues for verbal irony: Hyperbole and the ironic tone of voice. *Metaphor and Symbolic Activity* 10: 21–31.

Kull, K. 2000. Copy versus translate, meme versus sign: Development of biological textuality. *European Journal for Semiotic Studies* 12 (1): 101–20.

Kumar, R., Novak, J. and Tomkins, A. 2010. Structure and evolution of online social networks. In *Link Mining: Models, Algorithms, and Applications*, ed. P. S. S. Yu, J. Han and C. Faloutsos. New York: Springer.

Kushin, Matthew J. and Kitchener, K. 2009. Getting political on social network sites: Exploring online political discourse on Facebook. *First Monday* 14 (11).

Kushin, M. J. and Yamamoto, M. 2010. Did social media really matter? College students' use of online media and political decision making in the 2008 election. *Mass Communication and Society* 13 (5): 608–30.

Kwak, H., Lee, C., Park, H. and Moon, S. 2010. What is Twitter, a social network or a news media? In *Proceedings of the 19th International Conference on World Wide Web*. Raleigh, NC: ACM.

Laboreiro, G., Sarmento, L., Teixeira, J. and Oliveira, E. 2010. Tokenizing micro-blogging messages using a text classification approach. In *Proceedings of the Fourth Workshop on Analytics for Noisy Unstructured Text Data*. Toronto: ACM.

Labov, W. 1972. *Sociolinguistic patterns*. Philadelphia: University of Pennsylvania Press.

Laforest, M. 2002. Scenes of family life: Complaining in everyday conversation. *Journal of Pragmatics* 34 (10–11): 1595–620.

Lankshear, C. and Knobel, M. 2006. *New literacies: Everyday practices and classroom learning*. 2nd edn. Maidenhead, UK and New York: Open University Press.

Lassen, D. S. and Brown, A. R. 2010. Twitter: The electoral connection? *Social Science Computer Review*. http://ssc.sagepub.com/content/early/2010/09/16/0894439310382749.abstract [accessed 23 September 2010; DOI: 10.1177/0894439310382749].

Lee, R. and Sumiya, K. 2010. Measuring geographical regularities of crowd behaviors for Twitter-based geo-social event detection. In *Proceedings of the 2nd ACM SIGSPATIAL International Workshop on Location Based Social Networks*. San Jose, CA: ACM.

Leech, G. N. 1983. *Principles of pragmatics*. London: Longman.

— 2007. New resources, or just better old ones? The Holy Grail of representativeness. In *Corpus Linguistics and the Web*, ed. M. Hundt, N. Nesselhauf and Biewer C. Amsterdam: Rodopi.

Lemke, J. L. 1984. *Semiotics and education, Toronto semiotic circle monographs series*. Toronto: Victoria University.

— 1998. Multiplying meaning: Visual and verbal semiotics in scientific text. In *Reading Science: Critical and Functional Perspectives on Discourses of Science*, ed. J. R. Martin and Veel R. London and New York: Routledge.

— 2000. Across the scales of time: Artifacts, activities, and meanings in ecosocial systems. *Mind, Culture and Activity* 7 (4): 273–90.

Leskovec, J., Backstrom, L. and Kleinberg, J. 2011. *MemeTracker* 2008 [accessed 22 March 2011]. http://memetracker.org/.

Letierce, J., Passant, A., Breslin, J. G. and Decker, S. 2010. Using Twitter During an Academic Conference: The #iswc2009 Use-Case. Paper read at the Proceedings of the Fourth International AAAI Conference on Weblogs and Social Media, 23–26 May, at Washington, DC.

Lewes, G. H. 1875. *Problems of life and mind*. London: Trübner.

Li, J. and Rao, H. R. 2010. Twitter as a rapid response news service: An exploration in the context of the 2008 China earthquake. *EJISDC* 42 (4): 1–22.

Liberman, M. 2009. *In Soviet Russia, Snowclones Overuse You* 2004 [accessed 10 February 2009]. http://itre.cis.upenn.edu/~myl/languagelog/archives/000402.html.

Liberman, M. and Pullum, G. K. 2006. *Far from the madding gerund and other dispatches from language log.* Wilsonville, OR: William, James & Company.

Liere, van D. 2010. How far does a tweet travel?: Information brokers in the twitterverse. In *Proceedings of the International Workshop on Modeling Social Media.* Toronto: ACM.

Lin, Yu-Ru., Chi, Y., Zhu, S., Sundaram, H. and Tseng, B. L. 2009. Analyzing communities and their evolutions in dynamic social networks. *ACM Transactions on Knowledge Discovery from Data* 3 (2): 1–31.

Lin, Yu-Ru., Sundaram, H. and Kelliher, A. 2009. Summarization of large scale social network activity. In *Proceedings of the 2009 IEEE International Conference on Acoustics, Speech and Signal Processing.* Taipei, Taiwan: IEEE Computer Society.

Louw, B. 1993. Irony in the text or insincerity in the writer: The diagnostic potential of semantic prosody. In *Text and Technology: In Honour of John Sinclair,* ed. M. Baker, J. R., G. Francis and E. Tognini-Bonelli. Amsterdam: John Benjamins.

Lowrey, W. 2006. Mapping the journalism–blogging relationship. *Journalism* 7 (4): 477–500.

Ludeling, A., Evert, S. and Baroni, M. 2007. Using Web data for linguistic purposes. In *Corpus Linguistics and the Web,* ed. M. Hundt, N. Nesselhauf and C. Biewer. Amsterdam: Rodopi.

Makice, K. 2009. Phatics and the design of community. In *Proceedings of the 27th International Conference Extended Abstracts on Human Factors in Computing Systems.* Boston: ACM.

Malinowski, B. 1935. *Coral gardens and their magic: A study of the methods of tilling the soil and agricultural rites in the Trobiand Islands, with 3 maps, 116 illustrations and 24 figures.* London: Allen & Unwin.

— 2004. *Magic, science and religion and other essays.* Lavergne, TN: Kessinger. Original edition, 1948.

Martin, J. R. 1992. *English text: System and structure.* Philadelphia: John Benjamins.

— 1996. Types of structure: Deconstructing notions of constituency in clause and text. In *Computational and Conversational Discourse: Burning Issues-an Interdisciplinary Account,* ed. E. H. Hovy and D. R. Scott. Berlin: Springer-Verlag.

— 2000a. Beyond exchange: APPRAISAL systems in English. In *Evaluation in text: Authorial Stance and the Construction of Discourse,* ed. S. Hunston and G. Thompson. Oxford: Oxford University Press.

— 2000b. Factoring out exchange: types of structure. In *Working with Dialogue,* ed. M. Coulthard, J. Cotterill and F. Rock. Tübingen: Niemeyer.

— 2004. Mourning: How we get aligned. *Discourse and Society* 15 (2–3): 321–44.

— 2007. Construing knowledge: A functional linguistic perspective. In *Language, Knowledge and Pedagogy: Functional Linguistic and Sociological Perspectives,* ed. F. Christie and J. R. Martin. London: Continnum.

— 2008a. Incongruent and proud: De-vilifying 'nominalization'. *Discourse Society* 19 (6): 801–10.

— 2008b. Intermodal reconciliation: Mates in arms. In *New Literacies and the English Curriculum: Multimodal Perspectives,* ed. L. Unsworth. London: Continuum, 112–48.

— 2008c. Tenderness: Realisation and instantiation in a Botswanan town. In *Odense Working Papers in Language and Communication. Special Issue of* ital ok *Papers from 34th International Systemic Functional Congress*, ed. N. Nørgaard. Odense: University of Southern Denmark.
— 2010. Introduction: Semantic variation. In *New Discourse on Language: Functional Perspectives on Multimodality, Identity, and Affiliation*, ed. M. Bednarek and J. R. Martin. London and New York: Continuum.
Martin, J. R. and Rose, D. 2008. *Genre relations: Mapping culture, Equinox textbooks and surveys in linguistics*. London; Oakville, CT: Equinox.
Martin, J. R. and White, P. R. R. 2005. *The language of evaluation: Appraisal in English*. New York: Palgrave Macmillan.
Martin, J. R., Maton, K. and Matruglio, E. 2010. Historical cosmologies: Epistemology and axiology in Australian secondary school history. *Revista Signos* 43 (74): 433–63.
Marwick, A. 2010. Status Update: Celebrity, Publicity, and Self-Branding in Web 2.0. Department of Media, Culture, and Communication. New York University.
Marwick, A. and Boyd, D. 2011. To see and be seen: Celebrity practice on Twitter. *Convergence* 17 (2): 139–58.
Matthiessen, C. M. I. M. 1995. *Lexicogrammatical cartography: English systems*. Tokyo: International Language Sciences.
— 2006. Frequency profiles of some basic grammatical systems: An interim report. In *System and Corpus: Exploring Connections*, ed. S. Hunston and G. Thompson. London: Equinox.
McArthur, J. A. 2009. Digital subculture: A geek meaning of style. *Journal of Communication Inquiry* 33 (1): 58–70.
McCarthy, J. F. and Boyd, D. 2005. Digital Backchannels in Shared Physical Spaces: Experiences at an Academic Conference. Paper read at the Conference on Human Factors and Computing Systems (CHI 2005), at Portland, Oregon, 2–7 April.
McCarthy, M. and Carter, R. 2004. 'There's millions of them': Hyperbole in everyday conversation. *Journal of Pragmatics* 36 (2): 149–84.
McCracken, H. 2011. *What I Know About Twitter* 2009 [accessed 28 February 2011]. http://technologizer.com/2009/03/15/what-i-know-about-twitter/.
McFedries, P. 2008. Snowclone Is the New Cliche [technically speaking]. *IEEE Spectrum* 45 (2): 27–27.
McNely, B. 2009. Backchannel Persistence and Collaborative Meaning-making. Paper read at the Proceedings of the 27th ACM International Conference on Design of Communication, at Bloomington, Indiana.
Mertz, D. 2003. *Text processing in Python*. Boston: Addison-Wesley.
Meyerhoff, M. 2008. Communities of practice. In *The Handbook of Language Variation and Change*. Massachusetts: Blackwell.
Miller, J. H. and Page, S. E. 2007. *Complex adaptive systems: An introduction to computational models of social life*. Princeton, NJ: Princeton University Press.
Miller, V. 2008. New media, networking and phatic culture. *Convergence: The International Journal of Research into New Media Technologies* 14 (4): 387–400.
Milton, M. 1952. The case against slang. *English Journal* 41 (6): 306–09.
Mirkin, D. 1994. Deep space homer. In *The Simpsons*, ed. C. Baeza. US.

Mitchell, G. and Clarke, A. 2003. Videogame art: Remixing, reworking and other interventions. In *Level Up: Proceedings of the 1st International Digital Games Research Conference*, ed. C. Marinka and J. Raessens. Utrecht: University of Utrecht Press.

Mobius. 2010. *Bailout for Car Buyers* 2009 [accessed 10 September 2010]. http://mobiusinformer.wordpress.com/2009/04/17/bailout-for-car-buyers/.

Moh, T.-S. and Murmann, A. J. 2010. Can you judge a man by his friends? – Enhancing spammer detection on the Twitter microblogging platform using friends and followers. In *Information Systems, Technology and Management*, ed. S. K. Prasad, H. M. Vin, S. Sahni, M. P. Jaiswal and B. Thipakorn. Berlin and Heidelberg: Springer.

Montgomery, M. 1995. *An introduction to language and society*. London and New York: Routledge.

Moore, R. L. 2004. We're cool, mom and dad are swell: Basic slang and generational shifts in values. *American Speech* 79 (1): 59–86.

Morley, J. and Partington, A. 2009. A few frequently asked questions about semantic – or evaluative – prosody. *International Journal of Corpus Linguistics* 14 (2): 139–58.

Morris, M. R., Jaime, T. and Katrina, P. 2010. What do people ask their social networks, and why? A survey study of status message q\&\#38;a behavior. In *Proceedings of the 28th International Conference on Human Factors in Computing Systems*. Atlanta, GA: ACM.

Morville, P. 2006. *Ambient findability: What we find changes who we become*. Cambridge: O'Reilly.

Murphy, J. 2008. Better practices from the field: Micro-blogging for science & technology libraries. *Science and Technology Libraries* 28 (4): 375–8.

Myers, G. 2010. *Discourse of blogs and wikis*. London: Continuum.

Naaman, M., Boase, J. and Lai, C.-H. 2010. Is it really about me?: Message content in social awareness streams. In *Proceedings of the 2010 ACM Conference on Computer Supported Cooperative Work*. Savannah, GA: ACM.

Nagarajan, M., Purohit, H. and Sheth, A. 2010. A Qualitative Examination of Topical Tweet and Retweet Practices. Paper read at the Fourth International AAAI Conference on Weblogs and Social Media, at Washington, DC.

Nesbitt, Christopher N. and Guenter, P. 1988. Probabilities in a systemic grammar: the clause complex in English. Robin P. Fawcett and David Young (eds), New developments in systemic linguistics, vol. 2: theory and application. London: Frances Pinter. pp. 6–39.

Nguyen, T., Phung, D., Adams, B., Tran, T. and Venkatesh, S. 2010. Hyper-community detection in the blogosphere. In *Proceedings of Second ACM SIGMM Workshop on Social Media*. Florence: ACM.

Noob. 2006–07. www.urbandictionary.com/define.php?term=noob.

Norrick, N. R. 1994. Involvement and joking in conversation. *Journal of Pragmatics* 22 (3–4): 409–30.

Nunnally, T. E. 2001. Glossing the folk: A review of selected lexical research into American slang and Americanisms. *American Speech* 76 (2): 158–76.

Nystrand, M. 1982. *What Writers Know: The Language, Process, and Structure of Written Discourse*. New York: Academic Press.

O'Connor, B., Balasubramanyan, R., Routledge, B. R. and Smith, N. A. 2010. From Tweets to Polls: Linking Text Sentiment to Public Opinion Time Series.

Paper read at the Fourth International AAAI Conference on Weblogs and Social Media, at Washington, DC.

O'Donnell, M. 2008. UAM Corpus Tool 2.0, Computer Application, University Autonoma de Madrid, Department of English.

O'Donnell, M. and Bateman, J. 2005. SFL in computational contexts. In *Continuing Discourse on Language: A Functional Perspective*, ed. R. Hasan and C. Matthiessen. London: Equinox.

Obama, B. 2011. Full text of Obama's victory speech. BBC News 2008 [accessed 24 March 2011]. http://news.bbc.co.uk/2/hi/americas/us_elections_2008/7710038.stm.

Oring, E. 2008. *Engaging humor.* Urbana: University of Illinois Press.

Oulasvirta, A., Lehtonen, E., Kurvinen, E. and Raento, M. 2010. Making the ordinary visible in microblogs. *Personal Ubiquitous Comput.* 14 (3): 237–49.

Ovadia, S. 2009. Exploring the potential of Twitter as a research tool. *Behavioral and Social Sciences Librarian.* 28 (4): 202–5.

Owen, P., McCarthy, K. and Smyth, B. 2009. Using twitter to recommend real-time topical news. In *Proceedings of the third ACM conference on Recommender systems.* New York, New York, USA: ACM.

Page, R. 2011. *Stories and social media: Identities and interaction.* London: Routledge.

Parrish, Jr., J. L. 2010. PAPA knows best: Principles for the ethical sharing of information on social networking sites. *Ethics and Inf. Technol.* 12 (2): 187–93.

Pawley, A. 1986. Lexicalization. In: Deborah Tannen and James E. Alatis (eds). Language & Linguistics: The interdependence of theory, data & application. Georgetown University Round Table on Languages & Linguistics 1985, pp. 98–120.

Phelan, O., McCarthy, K. and Smyth, B. 2009. Using twitter to recommend real-time topical news. In *Proceedings of the Third ACM Conference on Recommender Systems.* New York: ACM.

Plester, B. and Wood, C. 2009. Exploring relationships between traditional and new media literacies: British preteen texters at school. *Journal of Computer-Mediated Communication* 14 (4): 1108–29.

Plester, B., Wood, C. and Joshi, P. 2009. Exploring the relationship between children's knowledge of text message abbreviations and school literacy outcomes. *British Journal of Developmental Psychology* 27 (1): 145–61.

Popescu, A.-M. and Pennacchiotti, M. 2010. Detecting controversial events from twitter. In *Proceedings of the 19th ACM International Conference on Information and Knowledge Management.* Toronto: ACM.

Powell, D. and Dixon, M. 2011. Does SMS text messaging help or harm adults' knowledge of standard spelling? *Journal of Computer Assisted Learning* 27 (1): 58–66.

Poynton, C. 1984. Names as vocatives: Forms and functions. *Nottingham Linguistic Circular* 13: 1–34.

— 1990. Address and the Semiotics of Social Relations: A Systemic-Functional Account of Address Forms and Practices in Australian English. PhD thesis, Department of Linguistics, University of Sydney, Sydney.

Provine, R. R., Robert, Spencer J. and Darcy, L. Mandell. 2007. Emotional expression online: Emoticons punctuate website text messages. *Journal of Language and Social Psychology* 26 (3): 299–307.

Pullum, G. K. 2004. *Snowclones: Lexicographical dating to the second. Language Log* http://itre.cis.upenn.edu/~myl/languagelog/archives/000350.html.

Puniyani, K., Eisenstein, J., Cohen, S. and Eric, P. Xing. 2010. Social links from latent topics in microblogs. In *Proceedings of the NAACL HLT 2010 Workshop on Computational Linguistics in a World of Social Media*. Los Angeles: Association for Computational Linguistics.

Ramage, D., Dumais, S. and Liebling, D. 2010. Characterizing Microblogs with Topic Models. Paper read at the Fourth International AAAI Conference on Weblogs and Social Media, at Washington, DC.

Raza, M., Hussain, F. K. and Chang, E. 2008. A methodology for quality-based mashup of data sources. In *Proceedings of the 10th International Conference on Information Integration and Web-Based Applications and Services*. Linz, Austria: ACM.

Reinhardt, W., Ebner, M., Beham, G. and Costa, C. 2009. How People Are Using Twitter During Conferences. Paper read at Creativity and Innovation Competencies on the Web, Proceedings of the 5th EduMedia Conference, at Salzburg.

Renouf, A. 2003. WebCorp: Providing a renewable data source for corpus linguists. In *Extending the scope of corpus-based research:New applications, new challenges*, ed. S. Granger and Petch-Tyson S. Amsterdam: Rodopi.

Renouf, A. and Sinclair, J. 1991. Collocational frameworks in English. In *English Corpus Linguistics: Studies in Honour of Jan Svartvik*, ed. Karin Aijmer and Bengt Altenberg, 128–43.

Rettberg, J. W. 2009. Freshly generated for you and Barack Obama. *European Journal of Communication* 24 (4): 451–66.

Rheingold, H. 1993. *The virtual community: Homesteading on the electronic frontier.* Reading, MA: Addison-Wesley.

Rissanen, M., Kytö, M., Kahlas-Tarkka, L., Kilpiö, M., Nevanlinna, S., Taavitsainen, I., Nevalainen, T. and Raumolin-Brunberg, H. 1991. *The Helsinki Corpus of English Texts.* Department of English, University of Helsinki.

Ritter, A., Cherry, C. and Dolan, B. 2010. Unsupervised modeling of Twitter conversations. In *Human Language Technologies: The 2010 Annual Conference of the North American Chapter of the Association for Computational Linguistics.* Los Angeles: Association for Computational Linguistics.

Robertson, Scott P., Vatrapu, Ravi K. and Medina, R. 2010. Off the wall political discourse: Facebook use in the 2008 US presidential election. *Information Polity* 15 (1–2): 11–31.

Rocketboom. 2009. *The Twitter Global Mind* 2009 [accessed 16 April 2009]. www.rocketboom.com/rb_09_mar_09_twitter_global_mind/.

Romero, D., Meeder, B. and Kleinberg, J. 2011. *Differences in the Mechanics of Information Diffusion Across Topics: Idioms, Political Hashtags, and Complex Contagion on Twitter* 2011 [accessed 24 March 2011]. www.cs.cornell.edu/home/kleinber/www11-hashtags.pdf.

Rosen, Larry D., Chang, J., Erwin, L. Carrier, Mark L. and Cheever, Nancy, A. 2010. The relationship between 'textisms' and formal and informal writing among young adults. *Communication Research* 37 (3): 420–40.

Russell, M. A. 2011. *Mining the social web.* Beijing and Farnham, Farnham, UK: O'Reilly.

Sacks, H., Schegloff, E. A. and Jefferson G. 1974. A simplest systematics for the organization of turn-taking for conversation. *Language* 50 (4): 696–735.

Sanderson, J. and Cheong, P. H. 2010. Tweeting prayers and communicating grief over Michael Jackson online. *Bulletin of Science, Technology and Society* 30 (5): 328–40.

Sankaranarayanan, J., Samet, H., Teitler, B. E. and Sperling, J. (2009). TwitterStand: news in tweets. In *Proceedings of the 17th ACM SIGSPATIAL International Conference on Advances in Geographic Information Systems*, Seattle, Washington (no page numbers available or editors).

Sarita, Y. 2006. The Role of the Backchannel in Collaborative Learning Environments. Paper read at the Proceedings of the 7th International Conference on Learning Sciences, at Bloomington, Indiana.

Sarita, Y., Daniel, R., Grant, S. and Danah, B. 2009. Detecting spam in a Twitter network. *First Monday* 15 (1).

Satyen, A. and Latifur, K. 2010. TWinner: Understanding news queries with geo-content using Twitter. In *Proceedings of the 6th Workshop on Geographic Information Retrieval*. Zurich: ACM.

Schifanella, R., Barrat, A., Cattuto, C., Markines, B. and Menczer, F. 2010. Folks in Folksonomies: Social link prediction from shared metadata. In *Proceedings of the Third ACM International Conference on Web Search and Data Mining*. New York: ACM.

Schlieder, C. and Yanenko, O. 2010. Spatio-temporal proximity and social distance: A confirmation framework for social reporting. In *Proceedings of the 2nd ACM SIGSPATIAL International Workshop on Location Based Social Networks*. San Jose, CA: ACM.

Schonfeld, E. 2010. Costolo: Twitter Now Has 190 Million Users Tweeting 65 Million Times a Day. http://techcrunch.com/2010/06/08/twitter-190-million-users/.

Senft, T. 2008. *Camgirls: Celebrity and community in the age of social networks*. New York: Peter Lang.

Shamma, D. A., Kennedy, L. and Churchill, E. F. 2010. Conversational Shadows: Describing Live Media Events Using Short Messages. Paper read at the Proceedings of the Fourth International AAAI Conference on Weblogs and Social Media, 23–26 May 2010, at Washington, DC.

Shaoul, C. and Westbury, C. 2011. *A USENET Corpus (2005–09)*. University of Alberta 2010 [accessed 17 March 2011]. www.psych.ualberta.ca/~westburylab/downloads/usenetcorpus.download.html.

Sharoff, S. 2006. Creating general-purpose corpora using automated search engine queries. In *WaCky! Working Papers on the Web as Corpus*, ed. M. Baroni and S. Bernardini. Bologna: Gedit.

Shifman, L. and Lemish, D. 2010. Between feminism and fun(ny)mism: Analysing gender in popular internet humour. *Information, Communication and Society* 13 (6): 870–91.

Shifman, L., Coleman, S. and Ward, S. 2007. Only joking? Online humour in the 2005 UK general election. *Information, Communication and Society* 10 (4): 465–87.

Shogan, C. J. 2010. Blackberries, tweets, and YouTube: Technology and the future of communicating with congress. *PS: Political Science and Politics* 43 (02): 231–3.

Sinclair, J. M. 1987. The nature of the evidence. In *Looking Up: An Account of the COBUILD Project in Lexical Computing and the Development of the Collins COBUILD English Language Dictionary*, ed. J. M. Sinclair. London and Glasgow: Collins ELT.

Singer, J. B. 2005. The political j-blogger. *Journalism* 6 (2): 173–98.

Smadja, F. 1994. Retrieving collocations from text: Xtract. In *Using Large Corpora*, ed. A. W. Armstrong and S. Armstrong. Cambridge, MA: MIT Press.

Solow-Niederman, A. G. 2010. The Power of 140 Characters? #IranElection and social movements in Web 2.0. *Intersect* 3 (1): 30–7.

Spolsky, J. 2010. *Don't Let Architecture Astronauts Scare You* 2001 [accessed 12 September 2010]. www.joelonsoftware.com/articles/fog0000000018.html.

Starbird, K., Palen, L., Hughes, A. L. and Vieweg, S. (2010). Chatter on the red: what hazards threat reveals about the social life of microblogged information. In *Proceedings of the 2010 ACM conference on computer-supported cooperative work*, pp. 241–50 (no editors available).

Stenglin, M. 2004. *Packaging curiosities: Towards a grammar of three-dimensional space*. Department of Linguistics, University of Sydney, Sydney.

Stenström, A.-B., Andersen, G. and Hasund, I. K. 2002. *Trends in teenage talk: Corpus compilation, analysis, and findings. Studies in corpus linguistics.* Amsterdam and Philadelphia: J. Benjamins.

Subramanian, S. and March, W. 2011. *Sharing Presence: Can and should your tweets be automated?* ACM, 10–15 April 2010 [accessed 24 March 2011]. http://cs.unc.edu/~julia/accepted-papers/chi2010_microblogging_workshop_subramanian_march.pdf.

Swales, J. M. 1990. *Genre analysis: English in academic and research settings.* Cambridge: Cambridge University Press.

Sweetser, Kaye D. and Lariscy, R. W. 2008. Candidates make good friends: An analysis of candidates' uses of facebook. *International Journal of Strategic Communication* 2 (3): 175–98.

Tagliamonte, Sali A. and Denis, D. 2008. Linguistic ruin? LOL! Instant messaging and teen language. *American Speech* 83 (1): 3–34.

Tajfel, H. 1970. Experiments in intergroup discrimination. *Scientific American* 223: 96–102.

Tang, L., Wang, X., Liu, H. and Wang, L. 2010. A Multi-Resolution Approach to Learning with Overlapping Communities. Paper read at the SOMA 2010 Workshop on Social Media Analytics in conjunction with the International Conference on Knowledge Discovery and Data Mining, 25–28 July 2010, at Washington, DC.

Teevan, J., Ramage, D. and Ringel, Morris, M. 2011. \#TwitterSearch: A comparison of microblog search and Web search. In *Proceedings of the Fourth ACM International Conference on Web Search and Data mining*. Hong Kong: ACM.

Thelwall, M. and Wilkinson, D. 2010. Public dialogs in social network sites: What is their purpose? *Journal of the American Society for Information Science and Technology* 61 (2): 392–404.

Thelwall, M., Buckley, K. and Paltoglou, G. 2011. Sentiment in Twitter events. *Journal of the American Society for Information Science and Technology* 62 (2): 406–18.

Thurlow, C. 2006. From statistical panic to moral panic: The metadiscursive construction and popular exaggeration of new media language in the print media. *Journal of Computer-Mediated Communication* 11 (3).

Thurlow, C. and Brown, A. 2003. Generation Txt? *The sociolinguistics of young people's text-messaging*. Discourse Analysis Online [accessed 18 November 2011]. http://extra.shu.ac.uk/daol/articles/v1/n1/a3/thurlow2002003-paper.html

Tian, P. 2011. *Multimodal Evaluation: Sense and Sensibility in Anthony Browne's Picture Books*. Department of Linguistics, University of Sydney, Sydney.

Tomasello, T. K., Lee, Y. and Baer, A. P. 2009. 'New media' research publication trends and outlets in communication, 1990–2006. *New Media Society* 11 (8): 1–20.

Trammell, K. D., Williams, A. P., Postelnicu, M. and Landreville, Kristen, D. 2006. Evolution of online campaigning: Increasing interactivity in candidate web sites and blogs through text and technical features. *Mass Communication and Society* 9 (1): 21–44.

Tumasjan, A., Sprenger, T. O., Sandner, P. G. and Welpe, I. M. 2010. Election forecasts with Twitter: How 140 characters reflect the political landscape. *Social Science Computer Review*. http://ssc.sagepub.com/content/early/2010/09/24/0894439310386557.abstract

— 2010. Predicting Elections with Twitter: What 140 Characters Reveal about Political Sentiment. Paper read at the Fourth International AAAI Conference on Weblogs and Social Media, at Washington, DC.

Twitter. 2001. *About Trending Topics* [accessed 22 March 2001]. http://support.twitter.com/entries/101125-about-trending-topics.

— 2010. *Streaming API Documentation* 2010 [accessed 17 February 2010]. http://apiwiki.twitter.com/Streaming-API-Documentation.

— 2010. *Twitter Is the Best Way to Discover What's New in Your World*. 2010 [accessed 11 December 2010]. http://twitter.com/about.

Ungar, S. 1984. Self-Mockery: An Alternative Form of Self-Presentation. *Symbolic Interaction* 7 (1): 121–33.

Unknown. 2011. *I am in ur dictionaries verbing ur nounz*. 2006 [accessed 5 May 2011]. www.flickr.com/photos/buro9/317157887/.

— . 2011. *im in ur fridge eatin ur foodz* 2006 [accessed 5 May 2011]. www.flickr.com/photos/buro9/299000787/.

Unknown. 2010. *I CAN HAS CHEEZBURGER?* 2007 [accessed 10 September 2010]. http://icanhascheezburger.com/2007/01/11/i-can-has-cheezburger-3/.

Unknown. 2011. *I made you a cookie* 2007 [accessed May 5 2011]. http://icanhascheezburger.com/2007/01/15/i-made-you-a-cookie/.

Unknown. 2011. *wutz ur name ill add u on facebook* 2007 [accessed May 5 2011]. http://lolcatz.net/1963/wutz-ur-name-ill-add-u-on-facebook/.

Unknown. 2011. *LOLCats: Pictures Of Cats With Funny Captions – LOLCats!* 2008 [accessed May 5 2011]. http://1.bp.blogspot.com/_b3GHoGMBNpY/STLQKnymLKI/AAAAAAAACr0/4VoHvde6rwE/s1600-h/lolcat15jpg.

— 2011. *Adaptation of Train Wreck at Montparnasse 1895* 2009 [accessed May 5 2011]. http://en.wikipedia.org/wiki/File:Train_wreck_at_Montparnasse_1895_FAIL.jpg.

Urban Dictionary. 2011. *Geek Out*. 2009 [accessed 10 February 2011]. www.urbandictionary.com/define.php?term=geek%20out.

— 2011. *Pwn* 2009 [accessed 10 February 2011]. www.urbandictionary.com/define.php?term=pwn.

Vaccari, C. 2010. 'Technology is a commodity': The internet in the 2008 United States presidential election. *Journal of Information Technology and Politics* 7 (4): 318–39.

Vander Wal, T. 2007. Folksonomy Coinage and Definition [accessed 18 November 2011]. http://vanderwal.net/folksonomy.html

van Manen, M. 2010. The pedagogy of momus technologies: Facebook, privacy, and online intimacy. *Qualitative Health Research* 20 (8): 1023–32.

Vine, B., Kell, S., Marra, M. and Janet, H. 2009. Boundary-marking humor: Institutional, gender and ethnic demarcation in the workplace. *Pragmatics and Beyond* 182: 125–39.

Volk, M. 2002. Using the Web as corpus in linguistic research. In *Tahendusepuudja. Catcher of the meaning. A festschrift for Professor Haldur Oim*. Publications of the Department of General Linguistics 3. University of Tartu. www.ifi.unizh.ch/cl/volk/papers/Oim_Festschrift_2002.pdf.*T‰hendusep„ja. Catcher of the Meaning. A Festschrift for Professor Haldur Oim.*

Walker, R. 2011. *A Successful Failure* 2009 [accessed 25 February 2011]. www.nytimes.com/2009/02/15/magazine/15wwln_consumed-t.html?_r=3.

Wallsten, K. 2007. Agenda setting and the blogosphere: An analysis of the relationship between mainstream media and political blogs. *Review of Policy Research* 24 (6): 567–87.

Wasserman, S. and Faust, K. 1994. *Social network analysis: Methods and applications*. Cambridge: Cambridge University Press.

Web Ecology Project. 2011. *The Iranian election of Twitter: The first eighteen days* 2009 [accessed 19 February 2011]. www.webecologyproject.org/wp-content/uploads/2009/08/WEP-twitterFINAL.pdf.

Weil, K. 2010. *Measuring Tweets*. http://blog.twitter.com/2010/02/measuring-tweets.html.

Wellman, B. 2001. Physical place and CyberPlace: The rise of personalized networking. *International Journal of Urban and Regional Research* 25: 227–52.

Weng, Jianshu, Ee-Peng Lim, Jing Jiang and Qi He. 2010. TwitterRank: Finding topic-sensitive influential twitterers. In *Proceedings of the Third ACM International Conference on Web Search and Data Mining*. New York: ACM.

Wenger, E. 1998. *Communities of practice: Learning, meaning, and identity*. Cambridge: Cambridge University Press.

Wesch, M. 2009. YouTube and you: Experiences of self-awareness in the context collapse of the recording webcam. *Explorations in Media Ecology* 8 (2): 19–34.

Whalen, J. M., Pexman, P. M. and Gill, A. J. 2009. Should be fun – not! *Journal of Language and Social Psychology* 28 (3): 263–80.

Whitelaw, C., Garg, N. and Argamon, S. 2005. Using appraisal groups for sentiment analysis. In *Proceedings of the 14th ACM International Conference on Information and Knowledge Management*. Bremen: ACM.

Whitman, G. 2004. *Phrases for Lazy Writers in Kit Form Are the New Clichés* http://agoraphilia.blogspot.com/2004/01/phrases-for-lazy-writers-in-kit-form.html. [accessed 19 October 2011].

Wigand, F. and Lux, D. 2010. Twitter takes wing in government: Diffusion, roles, and management. In *Proceedings of the 11th Annual International Digital Government Research Conference on Public Administration Online: Challenges and Opportunities*. Puebla, Mexico: Digital Government Society of North America.

Wikipedia: The Free Encyclopedia. *All your base are belong to us*. Wikimedia Foundation 2011. http://en.wikipedia.org/wiki/All_your_base_are_belong_to_us.

Williams, B. and Gulati, G. 2008. The political impact of Facebook: Evidence from the 2006 midterm elections and 2008 nomination contest. *Politics and Technology Review* 1: 11–21.

Wilson, M. and Nicholas, C. 2008. Topological analysis of an online social network for older adults. In *Proceeding of the 2008 ACM Workshop on Search in Social Media*. Napa Valley, CA: ACM.

Wolk, A. 2010. *What 'ThugLife' Can Teach Us about Twitter* 2010 [accessed 3 March 2010]. http://adage.com/digitalnext/article?article_id=141994.

Woodly, D. 2008. New competencies in democratic communication? Blogs, agenda setting and political participation. *Public Choice* 134 (1): 109–23.

Wu, S., Hofman, J. M., Mason, W. A. and Watts, D. J. 2011. Who Says What to Whom on Twitter. Paper read at the Proceedings of the 20th World Wide Web Conference (WWW'11), at Hyderabad, India.

Yamaguchi, Y., Takahashi, T., Amagasa, T. and Kitagawa, H. 2010. TURank: Twitter user ranking based on user-tweet graph analysis. *Web Information Systems Engineering* 6488: 240–53.

Yardi, S. 2006. The role of the backchannel in collaborative learning environments. In *Proceedings of the 7th International Conference on Learning Sciences*. Bloomington, IN: International Society of the Learning Sciences.

Yardi, S. and Boyd, D. 2010. Dynamic Debates: An analysis of group polarization over time on Twitter. *Bulletin of Science, Technology and Society* 30 (5): 316–27.

Yin, S. 2011. *Twitter Cracks Down on Another Third-Party App, TwapperKeeper* 2011 [accessed 24 March 2011]. www.pcmag.com/article2/0,2817,8149,00.asp.

Yvon, F. 2010. Rewriting the orthography of SMS messages. *Natural Language Engineering* 16 (02): 133–59.

Zappavigna, M. 2011a. Visualizing logogenesis: Preserving the dynamics of meaning. In *Semiotic Margins: Meaning in Multimodalites*, ed. S. Dreyfus, S. Hood and M. Stenglin. London: Continuum, 211–28.

— 2011b. Ambient affliation: A linguistic perspective on Twitter. *New Media Society*, 13(5), 788–806.

Zappavigna, M., Dwyer, P. and Martin, J. R. 2010. Visualising appraisal prosody. In *Appliable Linguistics: Texts, Contexts and Meanings*, ed. A. Mahboob and N. Knight. London: Continuum, 150–67.

— 2008. Syndromes of meaning: Exploring patterned coupling in a NSW Youth Justice. In *Questioning Linguistics*, ed. A. Mahboob and N. Knight. Newcastle: Cambridge Scholars Publishing.

Zhang, W., Johnson, T. J., Seltzer, T. and Bichard, S. L. 2010. The revolution will be networked. *Social Science Computer Review* 28 (1): 75–92.

Zhao, D. and Rosson, M. B. 2009. How and why people Twitter: The role that micro-blogging plays in informal communication at work. In *Proceedings of the ACM 2009 International Conference on Supporting Group Work*. Sanibel Island, FL: ACM.

Zhao, S. 2010. Intersemiotic relations as logogenetic patterns: Towards the restoration of the time dimension in hypertext description. In *New Discourse on Language: Functional Perspectives on Multimodality, Identity, and Affiliation*, ed. M. Bednarek and J. Martin. London: Continuum.

— 2011. *Learning through multimedia interaction: The construal of primary socials science knowledge in web-based digital learning materials.* Department of Linguistics, University of Sydney, Sydney.

Zimmer, B. 2009. How Fail Went from Verb to Interjection. *New York Times Magazine*, MM12.

Index

Page numbers in **bold** denote figures/tables.